The Achievement
of American Sport Literature

The Sporting Myth and the American Experience: Studies in Contemporary Fiction

Mythmakers of the American Dream: The Nostalgic Vision in Popular Culture

The Movies Go to College: Hollywood and the World of the College-Life Film

American Sport Culture: The Humanistic Dimensions (editor)

The Achievement
of American Sport
Literature
A Critical Appraisal

Edited by Wiley Lee Umphlett

Rutherford • Madison • Teaneck
Fairleigh Dickinson University Press
London and Toronto: Associated University Presses

Associated University Presses
440 Forsgate Drive
Cranbury, NJ 08512

Associated University Presses
25 Sicilian Avenue
London WC1A 2QH, England

Associated University Presses
P.O. Box 39, Clarkson Pstl. Stn.
Mississauga, Ontario,
Canada L5J 3X9

The paper used in this publication meets the requirements
of the American National Standard for Permanence of Paper
for Printed Library Materials Z39.48–1984.

Library of Congress Cataloging-in-Publication Data

The Achievement of American sport literature : a critical appraisal /
edited by Wiley Lee Umphlett.
   p. cm.
Includes bibliographical references (p.).
ISBN 0-8386-3400-1 (alk. paper)
   1. American literature—History and criticism. 2. Sports
literature—History and criticism. 3. Sports in literature.
I. Umphlett, Wiley Lee, 1931– .
PS169.S62A34 1991
810.9'355—dc20   89-46419
                                              CIP

Yes, dear reader, there really is a literature of American sport. And to all those who believed and helped build its reputation, this book is dedicated.

Contents

8   CONTENTS

Acknowledgments

For much needed support in putting this collection together, my thanks go out in many directions. But I am particularly grateful to the following "players" for their contribution to a "real team effort," to use one of sports' most overused but still apt expressions: Jack Higgs, Don Johnson, Tom Long, Chris Messenger, Lyle Olsen, Mike Oriard, and Terry Smith.

Introduction: The Genesis and Growth of Sport Literature in America

WILEY LEE UMPHLETT

All sport gives the participant a chance to compete; to pit himself against an immediate opponent and against records which have stood the test of time. In sport a person is on his own. His abilities, skills, and training are put to the test. This is only part of the story, however, for on a team the player must subordinate his personal ends to the team pattern—for it is the whole team that wins or loses. In short, the tennis court, the diamond, or the gridiron reflect the victories and defeats of life itself. Personal qualities good and bad, weak and strong, all come to the surface.

—Herbert S. Zim, editor,
*Sports Alive! Fact and
Fiction* (1960)

Since the middle of this century, American literature in which sport plays a prominent part has grown steadily as a literary force. In fact, today's bountiful evidence reveals that a rich and astonishingly varied tapestry of American life has been produced by creative writing whose major inspiration is the individual's intimate relationship with sporting experience. The essays in this collection attempt to demonstrate the worth of this literary tradition, whose inspirational origins can be traced back over one hundred years to the advent of organized team sports in America, both professional and institutional (school or college sponsored). Of course, sporting experience has always had a natural place in American life, and one can find literary evidence of Americans' special involvement with it in prototypal activities such as hunting, fishing, and contests of strength and endurance as portrayed in this country's frontier mythology and early fictional output. Indeed, the book-length critical studies of sports fiction that have appeared in recent years reveal that the sporting spirit has played a significant role in the development of American writing, particularly as it has been expressed in fiction.

With the inevitable urbanization of the United States (a key factor in the development of professional sports) and the growth of secondary and higher educational systems during the second half of the nineteenth century, the stage was set for the expansion and increased popularity of organized sports, in particular the team games of baseball and football, which since their beginnings and gradual absorption into the mainstream of American society have evolved in ways that reflect values and qualities characteristic of the American way of life. In coming under the authority of U.S. schools and colleges, organized athletics, particularly baseball, football, track and field, and rowing (the original varsity sports), were considered unique training programs designed to inculcate in American youth qualities that Americans had naturally come to admire: the value of hard work in striving to achieve a goal, the worth of competition and cooperative effort or teamwork in a game setting, as well as the sense of personal dedication to an ideal in order to become the best at whatever athletic activity one participated in. In short, involvement in school and college sports was looked upon as preparation to play the "game of life," in which a major force was the corporate world of business, whose capitalistic tenets related directly to the goal-oriented qualities that team sports promoted.

As a literary source, though, such games were at first only of interest to that vast legion of fiction writers whose output was directed at a juvenile audience. As a form of the highly popular success story pioneered by Hortatio Alger, Jr., juvenile sports novels, many of which were produced as series books structured around a central character (e.g., Frank Merriwell, Baseball Joe), had societal approval in the main in that their primary objective was didactic: to teach young readers manly virtues such as fair play and the rewards of hard work in meeting a challenge and/or achieving a goal and, most importantly, to create a healthy respect for authority. Dramatizing practical object lessons about the moral code a young man needed to cultivate if he wanted to succeed in sports and ultimately, of course, in life, many of these books turned up as birthday gifts or as Christmas presents, their flyleafs ritually inscribed with an inspirational dedication. Accordingly, from the 1890s to around the 1950s this type of fiction was quite popular with American youth, until changing mores and the temper of an increasingly liberal society began to set new social directions and radically different values regulating human behavior.

To assess the juvenile sports novel's role in the development of

the American sports-fiction tradition as well as its peripheral influence on other areas of literary endeavor, this collection leads off
with my essay on the formulaic conventions that this subgenre
depended on from its inception and their subtle contribution to the
evolution of a more mature way of writing about sports experience.
As a follow-up to the seminal research of Christian Messenger and
Michael Oriard concerning the place of the juvenile sports novel in
American literary tradition, this essay discusses some of the leading practitioners in the early juvenile sports-fiction tradition—
Ralph Henry Barbour, Everett T. Tomlinson, Gilbert Patten, and
others—who, each in his own way, set the pattern for a fictional
form that, in the words of Oriard, came to be "written against and
within" by the large number of writers who followed and reshaped
the earlier conventions to the changing sensibilities of a different
time.

After World War II and the proliferation of the television medium
in the 1950s, American youth began to be exposed to a more
realistic understanding of sports experience in contrast to juvenile
fiction's largely fantasized interpretation. Participation in sports did
not necessarily prepare one for life, they discovered through the
film portrayals of such real-life athletes as Olympian Jim Thorpe,
baseball player Jimmy Piersall, and boxer Rocky Graziano, but it
could teach the individual a lot about what might be wrong with a
system or the sports establishment and those who controlled it.
Consequently, in sport literature the system took on an adversarial
dimension, and the most significant decision the athlete hero of
later sport literature had to make, it seemed, was whether to participate within the dehumanizing constraints of the system or rebel
against it. The writer that this collection holds up as a prototypal
example of this perspective and one who bridges the gulf between
the earlier writers in the fantasy tradition and those who would
concern themselves with issues and concerns of a more adult
nature is John R. Tunis, a versatile writer whose heyday in producing juvenile fiction was the 1940s.

Leverett T. Smith's evaluation of Tunis's four novels, which contain the real-life ingredient of a Brooklyn Dodgers background,
demonstrates that even though these books were written for a
juvenile audience there can be a more serious side to the fictional
interpretation of sports than merely a fantasized approach. In ex-
pounding on a predominant theme of juvenile sports fiction—that
sports function as a mirror of the democratic process in spite of
their elitist standards—Tunis, like his contemporary William
Heyliger, probed more deeply than his predecessors to incorporate

elements of dramatic conflict in his stories. The effects of racial attitudes and commercial sellouts, the consequences of confronting the system when individual choice conflicts with team honor, and the challenge of learning how to be a leader within the system were all major concerns in Tunis's writing. Without ever realizing it, John Tunis, through his serious approach to dramatizing sport's commitment to a code of values and its impact on the athlete striving for quality performance within a team setting, was looking ahead to a more mature brand of adult fiction colored by American sports experience.

Along with the social upheavals of the 1960s as well as the continued expansion of televised sports programming, which captured and projected the realism of such events as no other medium could, American society came to accept sport as an integral part of contemporary life-style and not so much a peripheral outlet for social behavior as it had been perceived prior to now. As sociologist W. M. Leonard has assessed sport's contemporary import:

> Sport permeates virtually every social institution in the United States. The ubiquity of sport is evidenced by news coverage, sports equipment sales, financial expenditures, the number of participants and spectators, and its penetration into popular culture . . . Sports are among the most popular leisure activities in America today. . . .

Accordingly, the preeminence of sport in today's leisure-oriented society has made it a prime subject for literary interpretation in not only fiction but drama (film) and poetry. However, it is on the genre of fiction that sport has made its strongest impact, to which this collection's bibliography bountifully attests. If the serious fiction writer has always been attuned to the dominant forces of society that reveal a people for what they are, then it would be very difficult for a contemporary author to ignore sports as a conditioning factor of wide-ranging influence in this country. Consequently, since the era of the 1950s and 1960s, some of the best American fiction has been that inspired in part or whole by the sporting scene.

That the 1980s has been the most productive period for baseball fiction is forcefully brought out in Christian Messenger's overview of the plethora of novels that have appeared during this decade, and of which the end is clearly nowhere in sight. The fact that baseball is the one team sport that has inspired more writers to produce quality fiction than any other is probably due to its pervasive cultural presence in U.S. society as well as the pastoral nature of the game, which lends itself to the reflective, introspective posture so essential to the creation of mature fiction. During the 1970s the football novel made a run at critical acclaim, most notably with *North Dallas Forty* (1973), but, as Messenger points out, its productivity has since faded while the baseball novel keeps appearing in a never-ending flow of variations on a number of themes.

Another part of Messenger's survey reveals a revolutionary development in the way baseball and its offshoot, softball, have accommodated themselves to fiction that treats the complexity of women's relationships and emotional feelings. In a literature that has generally related to the concerns and issues of a predominantly all-male province, the omission of sporting experience as it reflects the feminine perspective has been glaringly evident. Because of women writers' recent discovery that sports such as baseball and softball are not only appropriate activities through which to express sport literature's characteristic ingredients of competition and heroic striving but ideal vehicles through which to express the basic feminine concerns of "nurture, family, growth," the field of sport literature should be much richer for the humanistic insights that will evolve from this breakthrough.

According to Messenger, an important reason for the continued success of baseball fiction is that it can encapsulate in its texts as can no other sport the "forms of myth, ritual, and history." Nevertheless, Robert W. Cochran's essay returns to the most primal concern of the sports-fiction tradition in his discussion of its recent emphasis on the democratic process and its corollary theme—"the worth of the common citizen." In demonstrating how sports fiction can reveal a great deal about contemporary life, Cochran draws mainly on two recent novels that have "protagonists who are not star athletes and on plots that do not follow a pennant drive or a Super Bowl week as ready-made scaffolds of organization." As John R. Tunis's juvenile novels appeared as "expressions of faith in democracy," so in their own way do the adult novels Cochran analyzes. John Hough's *The Conduct of the Game* (1986), whose central character is a baseball umpire, and Richard Ford's *The Sportswriter* (1986), whose titular hero has much to say about "the function of sport in personal relationships in America," stand out as incisive, telling statements about life in today's complex society. The fact that the nonheroic characters of these novels perform against the intrusive background of today's sports world lends more relevance and meaning to their roles' relationship to current issues and concerns of the larger world. The remarkable achievement of these two novels looks ahead to even more mature writing that expresses itself in the form of fiction inspired by the American sporting scene.

Both the legitimate stage and the Hollywood film have long been popular receptors of the dramatic and fictional interpretations of American sporting experience. In fact, in *The Movies Go to College* (1983), I have discussed at some length the impact of drama and popular fiction on the development of the Hollywood film tradition and its dependence on the mythology of American sport in both its social and heroic dimensions. Around the early part of the century, for example, college football provided a popular social backdrop for a number of New York stage productions, and the movies were just a few years away from following suit by making college football a favorite, though largely fantasized, source for both social and heroic interpretation. Actually, it has been only in recent years that drama and film have seen sport performing a more mature role in the scheme of things. Ronald K. Giles assesses this development, particularly in light of how sport in film has moved from "backdrop spectacle to full aesthetic component." Confining himself to some prime examples of recent drama and film, Giles contends that the most successful productions in this area achieve a "reflexive quality," a literary sensitivity of "returning to the sport itself, not for conventional dramatics . . . but for the metaphorical, psychological, or mythical qualities that the sport may recursively contribute to plot, character, and meaning." When it comes to sport as a suitable subject for dramatic presentation, it seems that today's playwrights and scriptwriters are exploring the tip of a gigantic iceberg.

If baseball is the favorite sport of American fiction writers, it is also the most popular with American poets. Accordingly, Don Johnson reminds the reader in his essay that just as it is in much contemporary fiction, the most popular poetic subject is not the heroic figure of the baseball diamond but rather a kind of Whitmanesque celebration of the self through direct, even nostalgic, identification with the game and its ambiance. In fact, today's poet would be hard pressed to come up with much of anything heroic about the contemporary baseball player, contending instead that the process of producing a good poem can be a heroic act, a kind of athletic achievement in itself. As poet David Evans has said, "Poets are word athletes [and] the poems they make are word performances," which is especially true of poetry inspired by athletics. Thus Evans concludes that sports poetry can "remind us that the body has its own language, its own wisdom." It is this "athletic" quality of contemporary sports poetry, Johnson intimates, that can sensitize the reader to the complexities of the human condition as can no other creative mode. Because of this propensity, the future of sports poetry as a vehicle to express insights into human nature is fraught with challenge.

This develpment is clearly borne out in recent sports poetry produced by women. In building a case for the feminine point of view in sport literature, particularly as it has been expressed in poetry, Brooke Horvath and Sharon Carson present the textual evidence for not only a whole new vision for sport literature but a unique way of dramatizing human experience. As Messenger observes in certain examples of recent sports fiction by women, so Horvath and Carson note that sports poetry written by women emphasizes the natural feminine concerns of nurturing, caring, feeling, and enhancing the creative aspects of life. At the same time, this kind of poetry tends to ignore the predominant male values generally associated with sports—antagonism, confrontation, and domination, for example—choosing rather to stress cooperation, participation, and self-actualization. As a result, Horvath and Carson contend that women's sports poetry can "carry the reader into regions of experience he or she never have visited before."

While the creative literature attempts to explore the physical and mental ramifications of the individual's involvement in athletic endeavor as complementary sides of human experience, the supplemental literature illuminates this relationship by helping one understand (criticism), appreciate (philosophy), humanize (history, autobiography, and biography), and discern (special studies) the subtle issues as well as the larger questions of sporting experience that the creative literature raises or merely suggests.

In 1983 the advent of a unique publication contributed immensely to sport literature's intent of realizing itself in all of the above areas. Of high quality in both appearance and selectivity of content, *Aethlon: The Journal of Sport Literature* (formerly *Arete*) not only helped promote this burgeoning field, it established a formal identity called the Sport Literature Association whose membership is now international in scope. However, as managing editor Lyle Olsen relates in his candidly absorbing piece, the challenge that the task of getting this fledgling journal off the group presented was a formidable one indeed. Imbued with the competitive spirit of a dedicated athlete, Olsen overcame all the odds—the prejudice against sport as an academic subject, the lack of any precedent to

steer a course by, and the cold fact that no funding was available to
support such a project—to organize an editorial staff committed to
providing sport literature not only with a voice but also with a much
needed point of identity in its inspired attempt to "encourage,
stimulate, and foster the alliance of sport with the humanities."

At one point in his essay dealing with the criticism of sport
literature, Robert J. Higgs rightly remarks: "That we can now talk
confidently about critical interpretations of sport literature is perhaps the surest sign of its success to date. A tremendous body of
quality writing is required before one can even begin to discuss it in
terms of critical schools." In attempting to establish the basis for a
critical theory to assess sport literature's "tremendous body of
quality writing," Higgs reviews the dominant critical postures extant today and concludes that "play theory . . . is everywhere on
the intellectual scene." This condition could result in the development of a valid critical framework to evaluate sport literature, Higgs
observes, and in attending to the various theories of play that relate
to his purpose, he offers meaningful insights into what he calls the
two sides of play philosophy: the "Edenic," or noncompetitive
province, and the "agonic," or strictly competitive area, which
"lies at the heart of our sport literature tradition." Thus Higgs
concludes that ". . . the literature of sport is now in an excellent
position to inform critical play theory with endless texts confirming
some aspects of play theory while casting doubts upon
others. . . ." Accordingly, he maintains that this position should
result in "a dialectic that can only advance understanding on all
fronts."

If understanding is the purpose of criticism and if the games of a
people can reveal a great deal about themselves and their true
nature, then surely sport exists as an ideal subject for the artist to
draw on to project a unique vision of life, one that has both critical
import and aesthetic appeal. So if sport can aspire to the realm of
art, as some philosophers would contend, then understanding sport
as a proper literary subject could lead to a fuller appreciation of the
achievement of sport literature in an aesthetic sense.

For this reason, I have included Daniel J. Herman's essay, which
deals with some of the most recent philosophical theories about
sport from an aesthetic viewpoint. As Herman points out, a vig-
orous debate has been going on over the past decade as to whether
or not sport can be considered an art form in itself. At the heart of
this argument are the theories of British philosopher David Best,
whose controversial thought has stimulated American philosophers
to come up with a series of rebuttals. While the primary concern of

the debaters whom Herman singles out has to do with whether sport itself can be viewed or experienced in the same way in which one views or experiences a work of art, the implications of these antithetical perspectives are sufficiently wide ranging to afford some challenging insights into the aesthetic worth of sport as a literary subject. That sport is a subject not only worthy of literary interpretation but aesthetic appreciation there can be no doubt; for as Marshall McLuhan once observed, games are akin to art in that they are "a translator of experience," and as such, of course, they are a major source of artistic expression. While criticism's function to aid in understanding a work of art may be considerably enhanced by the artist who works in an area of experience that his audience can personally identify with—as, for example, sport—aesthetic appreciation is largely a matter of individual taste. In this respect, one may wonder if there can be a more discriminating observer than a sports spectator.

In recent years the increasing popularity of the sports autobiography has offered today's media-made athlete a viable mode with which to tell a curious public about what has made him or her into a special kind of image, whether such an athlete's motive be "to chronicle, to confess, to expound, or to rebut one's public character," as Mary McElroy points out in her essay on the prominence of this genre. Paradoxically, the fact that most sports autobiographers are moved to tell everything—whether their off-field problems be related to alcoholism, drug addiction, or even homosexuality—has contributed a great deal to the athlete's loss of a heroic image in the eyes of the public. Through such revelations, today's athlete is seen as all too human, since readers of these works seem more obsessed with a player's weaknesses or problems as a human being than with his or her strengths as an athlete. In this light the sports autobiography has provided a powerful sounding board for the minority athlete, particularly for the female to speak her mind about the barriers against participating in what has heretofore been considered an all-male world. There will undoubtedly be many more works of this type flooding the market. Actually, the popularity of the sports autobiography in America is practically guaranteed, for as long as sports retain their mass appeal the sports fan will continue to generate a curiosity about the athlete and his or her relationship not only to the game but to life itself.

That a productive field such as sports history can point the way toward future endeavors in the general area of sports literature is attested to by Michael Oriard in his review essay of Elliott Gorn's brilliant 1986 historical study of nineteenth-century prize fighting in

America. As social history, Oriard awards *The Manly Art* superior marks, and on Gorn as a historian who forcefully demonstrates how his "literary" sources—mainly newspapers and popular pamphlets—can lend substantive support in developing his premise, Oriard bestows even more praise. Those active in sport literature have for too long ignored the wealth of source material that exists in the province of mass literature, Oriard contends, particularly that of sporting journalism, which in its own way has contributed a great deal to the development and ultimate richness of the language. Thus he maintains that a closer attention to this neglected area by sport literature scholars would result in "a fuller understanding of the relations among gender, class, audience, and 'literature' itself."

While sport literature, both creative and supplemental, has made great strides with respect to critical achievement and acceptance, its supplemental side is confronted by myriad challenges today, many of which await the research methods of the social historian. Accordingly, Oriard enumerates some of the projects he feels are ripe for interpretation using mass literature as a resource—in particular, a history of the language of sport, a study of the culture's positive and negative images of the athlete, and even studies of the popular iconography of sport. What is now needed, of course, are contenders willing to take on the challenges. If in practicing the social historian's methodology they are able to accomplish these ends in the manner of Elliott Gorn's pioneering treatise, then the real achievement of sport literature is yet to be.

The Achievement
of American Sport Literature

I
The Creative Literature—Fiction, Drama (Film), and Poetry

. . . American writers are notoriously unphilosophic, their imaginative energies intuitively heading for where the action is, where life is most intense, where human possibility—in all its splendor and folly—is most open. No wonder, then, that so many language players are drawn to the stadium. It's a natural. Maybe this is what Norman Mailer meant when he said that American writers see themselves as athletes.

—David L. Vanderwerken,
"Knowing Sport—Analysis
or Experience?" in
*Coroebus Triumphs: The Alliance
of Sport and the Arts* (1988)

Formulaic Sources of the American Sports-Fiction Tradition: The Code of Quality Performance in Juvenile Sports Fiction

WILEY LEE UMPHLETT

Good sports novels do not simply avoid the formulaic: to do so entirely is probably impossible. In fact, the existence of such persistent formulas in the sports world can be as much an advantage to the good novelist as a limitation for the bad. The novelist can assume readers' familiarity with the stock characters and situations of the sports world, and can thus easily work contrapuntally against the readers' expectations. The norm exists in any sports novel simply by the fact that the book is about sports: the novelist is freed to work his or her variations off the standard themes without even having to establish the standard. Thus, Malamud structures his novel on the simple tale of the unknown rookie from the country who appears suddenly in the Big Leagues to lead his previously unsuccessful team to contention for the pennant. But *The Natural* constantly works against that formulaic plot, complicating it with Roy Hobbs' age, with preternatural happenings that break through the placid surface of the story, with a constant struggle between the simple tale and a prose style that keeps the reader off balance, unable to accept dialogue and events at face value. The result is the kind of tension one feels in jazz music: the familiar melody is there in the background; the artist's ability to surprise is dependent on the audience's recognizing a melody that is never quite stated. All good sports novels share this quality of appropriating the formulas while working against them either technically or thematically. . . .

—Michael Oriard,
"On the Current Status of
Sports Fiction" (1983)

The American 1890s was an athletically aggressive and physically expressive age, a time of bold optimism, supreme confidence, and boundless energy—all prominent characteristics of the heroes and heroines portrayed in the popular literature of the time, but qualities especially representative of the young athletic heroes who emerged in the inspirational sports fiction written primarily for adolescent boys. This was a type of success story that came into its own during this era, and, as this essay points out, exists very much as a reflection of the values of the time that produced it. It also started the tradition in American literature of the novel inspired by organized sports—a literary form that may be categorized as a subgenre but one whose cultural impact was dominant enough to influence the youthful reading habits of countless American business/political leaders as well as some notable fiction writers and their later attitudes toward certain aspects of American experience.[1] This early influence in itself should be reason enough to assess the juvenile sports novel's place in the mainstream of American fiction, but the continuing output of this tradition's serious adult fiction inspired by contemporary sports experience is even more reason.

Although millions of boys had read and undoubtedly been much impressed by the "strive-and-succeed" stories of Horatio Alger, Jr. (1834–99), with their peculiarly American message of economic success through integrity, diligence, and hard work, Alger's books, as a rule, ignored sports experience and consequently were not really as meaningful or as compelling as they could have been for their youthful audience. By the 1880s and 1890s the American boy was beginning to take an avid and enthusiastic interest in the proliferating team sports of baseball and football, especially as they were being played in the schools and colleges of that day. Seeking both the freedom of self-expression and an outlet for the pent-up energies that the monastic atmosphere and rigid disciplinary controls of nineteenth-century college life had suppressed, students themselves conceived and implemented the brand of team sports that would evolve into institutionally controlled varsity programs by the close of the century. In fact, by that time, interscholastic and intercollegiate sports had become generally popular not only with students but also with alumni and the general public.

One of the era's most popular, prolific, and perceptive writers of school-life fiction, Ralph Henry Barbour (1870–1944), caught the fraternal spirit inspired by his day's growing allegiance to school and college sports in his novel *The Half-back* (1899), when alumni and students join in the school song following a football game:

Off came the silk hats of the frock-coated graduate and the plaided golf caps of the students, and side by side there in the sun-swept street they lifted their voices in the sweet, measured strains of the dear familiar hymn. And stout, placid-faced men of fifty, with comfortable bank accounts and incipient twinges of gout, felt the unaccustomed dimming of the sight that presages tears, and boyish, carefree students, to whom the song was as much an everyday affair as D marks and unpaid bills, felt strange stirrings in their breasts, and with voices that stumbled strangely over the top notes sang louder and louder. . . . (226–27)

While participation in sports, either as player or spectator, may have periodically freed the real-life student from the ascetic demands and dull routine of scholarly pursuit, it ultimately bound him in a lifelong relationship with his school and classmates. Accordingly, writers of juvenile sports novels were quick to expand upon the implications of this intimate relationship between school, sports, and loyal son, especially when that son was an athlete. It is through this interrelationship that most of these writers expressed their understanding of a standard of quality performance, a striving for excellence that is best captured in the Greek concept *arete* but that supposedly predicted success in life according to the American way. They felt, too, that this formulaic standard of behavior was most symbolically expressed in the dedicated athletic performance that occurred on the playing field. As a football coach in *The Halfback* charges his team during halftime of the big game:

"There isn't time for any fine phrases, fellows, and if there was I couldn't say them so that they'd do any good. You know what you've got to do. Go ahead and do it. . . . The college expects a great deal from you. Don't disappoint it. Play hard and play together. Don't give an inch; die first. . . ." (247)

These spare words pointedly reflect the basic inspiration for the code of the athlete in action that pervades the tradition of the juvenile sports novel in America: it isn't through platitudes or talk that one gets something done; rather, one achieves a goal through meaningful action or quality performance. Such a code was derivative of the "self-reliance" philosophy of Ralph Waldo Emerson whose basic thought grew out of his uniquely American vision of nineteenth-century romantic idealism. Because to the writers of boys' fiction a school or college stood for an ideal, then dedication to this ideal could supposedly bring out the best in exemplary action, particularly in the athletic contests that extended this ideal. In *The Sporting Myth and the American Experience* (1975), I have contended that this standard of physical expression pervades the development of organized sports, both collegiate and professional, in late nineteenth-century America and that "the maxims of Emerson asserting this attitude were put to work as the coaching philosophy of these sports" (37). This outlook also contributed to a way of life or code of behavior that not only inspired our original writers of sports fiction but by the early twentieth century found a dynamic proponent of the code in no less a person than the president of the United States.

As an exemplary athletic individual himself, whose life spanned the demise of the American frontier and the developing urbanized lifestyle of the late nineteenth and early twentieth centuries, Theodore Roosevelt (1858–1919) was the apostle of the "strenuous life" of strife and hard work, which underscored quality of performance and action in deed as the hallmarks of the manly individual as well as the keys to success in life. In his speeches and writings, Roosevelt often drew metaphors from the world of sports experience to make a point; as, for example, his popular advice that "in life, as in a football game, the principle to follow is: Hit the line hard; don't foul and don't shirk, but hit the line hard."[2] Essentially, Teddy Roosevelt's manly code derived from his belief that older people could best realize their personal capabilities through direct, active participtaion in the traditional outdoor sports like fishing and hunting; and youth through the organized intercollegiate sports that had come into their own in the latter half of the nineteenth century, mainly rowing, track and field, baseball, and football.

Respecting direct participation in intercollegiate athletics during Teddy Roosevelt's day, a personal code of conduct—a badge of honor, as it were—began to express and assert itself among that select group of prep school and college students known as varsity athletes. Because not everyone was skilled enough to participate in varsity athletics, those who did were looked up to as models of the dedicated play and honest, disciplined life-style that others might emulate through observation. Through its brand of muscular Christianity, the code of the varsity athlete was peculiar to American athletics, and since its inception America's changing social values may have altered it considerably, but it has always been most widely and influentially expressed in the vast outpouring of juvenile sports novels from the 1890s to around the 1950s. Notwithstanding the radical changes in the behavioral patterns and social values of adolescent boys since the 1890s, these books continued to adapt to the times that produced them while expressing the constant ideal of quality performance, which supposedly contributes to character development through sports involvement.

In 1899, the year of Horatio Alger's death, Ralph Henry Barbour may have unwittingly announced the official birth of the code when he dedicated the first of his many novels, *The Half-back,* to "Every American boy who loves honest, manly sport," since this dedication reflected and established the spirit and tone of a writing style and posture that were to inspire an astronomical number of books with similar themes over the next half century—a type of literature descended from the code of quality performance and mode of dynamic action that young readers thought team sports of late nineteenth-century America demanded. In spite of these books' pervasive presence and steady popularity during these years, their overall impact as a literary force was all but totally ignored. Not until the book-length sports-fiction studies of Michael Oriard and Christian Messenger appeared in the early 1980s was there a serious attempt to evaluate the worth of this literary form (see n. 1). Obviously, the popular audience for which it was designed as well as its overdependence on formulaic themes and situations kept juvenile sports fiction from being taken seriously by the taste-makers of society during its heyday.

Most writers of juvenile fiction during the 1890–1920s era were quick to recognize and capitalize on the fact that American schools and colleges provided the ideal environment and expressive mode for dramatically rendering the influence of athletic experience on character development. Probably no writer of juvenile sports fiction ever expressed his understanding of this condition more aptly than Everett T. Tomlinson (1859–1953) in his preface to *Ward Hill, the Senior* (1897):

> A school has been termed correctly a little world in itself. Within it the temptations and struggles and triumphs are as real as those in the larger world outside. They differ in form, not in character, and become for many a man the foundation upon which later success or failure has been built. (Preface)

Even though most writers of schoolboy fiction readily subscribed to such opinion, they placed their characters in the kind of setting that focused not so much on their conflicts in the classroom as on their struggles on the playing field, feeling that what transpired there, no matter how fantasized, was eminently more significant and meaningful to the young reader in his preparation for life in the real world.

Ralph Henry Barbour, more so than any of his competitors, though, was obsessed with the atmosphere of the entire campus and went to greater descriptive length to stress the contrast between the idyllic world of the school and that of the "larger world outside." In *The Half-back,* Hillton Academy is affectionately described as a tradition-bound place comprising numerous red-brick buildings,

> many of them a hundred years old. . . . Ivy has almost entirely hidden the walls of the academy building and of Masters Hall. The grounds are given over to well-kept sod, and the massive elms throw a tapestry of grateful shade in the summer, and in winter hold the snow upon their great limbs and transform the Green into a fairyland of white. From the cluster of buildings the land slopes away southward, and along the river bluff a footpath winds past the Society House, past the boathouse steps, down to the campus. The path is bordered by firs, and here and there a stunted maple bends and nods to the passing skiffs. . . . (17)

This passage from chapter 2, which Barbour devotes entirely to not only a description of Hillton's picturesque locale but a summary of its history and mission, provides some idea of his fictional intent of creating a real place for his readers to identify with.[3] Yet within the society of the school itself, Barbour is akin to all other writers of juvenile sports fiction in establishing a contrast between the classroom and the playing field, that hallowed place which holds more real meaning for the youthful reader than any other because it is the one place where the quest for personal identity through quality performance can be put to its ultimate test.

As suggested above, this custom persists even in fiction written on a more mature level as, for example, John Knowles's *A Separate Peace* (1966), whose prep school setting derives much of its dramatic conflict from the antithesis of classroom and playing field or the conflict between authority and self-expression. Although traditional schoolboy fiction makes a valiant attempt to reconcile the world of the schoolmaster—the monastic retreat to ponder Greek roots and philosophical arguments—and that of the athlete and the natural expression the playing field encourages, the conflict persists and contributes a great deal to overall dramatic development.

For example, the basic problem of Tomlinson's hero, Ward Hill, is one that stems from his poor classroom performance. Having fallen in with bad companions, Ward fails the examinations that would qualify him for his senior year at Weston School, but he returns after summer vacation determined to make up his grades and keep up with his class. Typically, though, Ward discovers that he must prove himself not so much through classroom achievement as through his relations with his classmates, especially on the baseball diamond where he has been relegated to the second team because of a personal conflict with the varsity captain, who, as usual, is molded after the stereotyped bully of schoolboy fiction. Nevertheless, when opportunity presents itself, Ward turns in the obligatory quality performance on the field, teaches the bully a lesson in human relationships, and establishes himself in the school community. As a result, Ward's community image is complemented by his successful athletic image, and the implication is that he will go on to even greater success in college and, later, in life.

By comparison, Barbour's hero in *The Half-back* is a studious young man dedicated to quality performance in the classroom as well as on the playing field. Nevertheless, as the conventional country boy of sports fiction, whose hayseed image is the butt of his classmates' jokes, Joel March is compelled to prove himself on the football field to gain social acceptance. When he is falsely accused of instigating an injury to a staff member, Joel is put on probation by the school officials and not allowed to play in the big game with Hillton's arch rival. However, the real perpetrator confesses, and Joel is reinstated just in time to enter the game and kick the winning field goal. Accordingly, the quality performance code of the successful schoolboy athlete is projected through a pervasive social symbol the reader could readily understand and identify with—the big game.

That there is something larger than a game at stake in these stories, though, is always their central focus, which is expressed through their equation of the game with life itself. In *Stover at Yale* (1912), Owen Johnson interprets college athletic experience as reflective of the American competitive sense and drive for material success. His hero, Dink Stover, is advised on his arrival at college to "play the game as others are playing it. It's a big game, and it'll follow you all through life" (29).

At this time, a number of Dink Stover types were extant, but the one character who contributed the most to the conceptual understanding of the athletic contest as a microcosm of life and to the myth of the super athlete as the epitome of quality performance was the impeccable Frank Merriwell, created by Gilbert Patten (1866–1945). Patten, who wrote a veritable deluge of his hero's stories from 1896 to 1913 under the pen name Burt L. Standish, unwittingly originated a character of momentous mythical significance.

Much has already been said and written of Frank: how his sensational heroics and last-minute comebacks on the Yale athletic field inspired what sports commentators refer to commonly as the "Merriwell finish"; how his stilted, artificial behavior, his genteel manner of speech, and his dedicated code of responsible action come across today with the opposite effect from that which these qualities were originally intended to convey. Yet in spite of what one may think of his puppetlike function as a literary character, Frank Merriwell persists as the stuff of legend simply because he was dreamed up in response to his day's ideal of symbolic action or quality performance to which his creator knew most American boys wanted to aspire—a larger-than-life heroic type whose actions spoke louder than words, and consequently someone that both the isolated farm boy and the street-wise city boy could identify with. Writing on the occasion of Patten's death in 1945, Wendell Hazen was speaking in behalf of "that great legion of boys who for nearly twenty years read with eagerness each successive weekly issue" of Pattern's prolific output in the Merriwell saga. According to Hazen, Patten was the

> man who took me through prep school, who took me through college, who taught me the wonders of baseball, football, basketball, hockey, and track athletics . . . who taught me good sportsmanship and fine manly habits of courage, honesty and perseverance. . . .[4]

"Habits" of quality performance, I might add, that may still seem honorable but that by today's more cynical and sophisticated standards of social behavior do not hold up, mainly because such character traits belong to an innocent age lost somewhere in the irrecoverable past.

No matter how unreal Frank and his fantasy world actually were, though, the fact remains that his dynamic role of quality performance did cast a pervasive spell over a great number of young boys like Hazen, who grew up reading and relishing his exploits. The compelling fictional image that Frank Merriwell commanded is also what prompted journalist-historian Stewart H. Holbrook to write from the perspective of his own boyhood:

> I could not quite disbelieve that somewhere there *must* be a Frank Merriwell, complete with keen grey eyes, strong cleft chin, muscles of steel, and heart of gold. Frank became the nearest to "real" of any fictional character in all my reading, youthful or adult. (24)

And when one realizes the extent of influence that a character in the Merriwell mold could have on the literary education of a writer like F. Scott Fitzgerald, for example, a clearer understanding of the American writer's preoccupation with the great distance between illusion and reality in American life is realized, particularly as this distance might be measured by the athlete's achievements on the field and his failures off. *The Great Gatsby*'s Tom Buchanan, a former Yale All-American, is really a disenchanted Frank Merriwell, whose later life can never measure up to the lost glory of his athletic days. The theme of disenchantment resulting from the loss of Edenic innocence is pervasive in American literature, and sporting experience has provided the contemporary writer a significant way to dramatize this predicament, as other essays in this collection bear out.

Obviously, it would be impossible to measure the extent of influence of both Frank's fantasy and "real" sides on the multitude of boys who fell under his spell, but I would venture to say that the underlying inspiration for Frank Merriwell's fictional stature stems from his creator's intuitive awareness of and sensitivity to this country's dynamic transformation in the late nineteenth century: from the challenges of its natural heritage of frontier and rural experience to those of a more competitive nature generated by a rapidly developing urbanized and industrialized society.

Gilbert Patten, whose life spanned the era of American expansion from a predominantly rural country into a nation controlled mainly by the intensely competitive capitalistic concerns of business and industry, experienced both areas of influence on his life, having departed the pastoral setting of his Maine youth in 1891 to seek his fortune in the American writer's mecca—the fast-growing metropolis of New York City. Accordingly, in many of Patten's stories the reader feels something of the clash between small-town rural life and that of the big city, between individualism and conformity, and between natural innocence and the loss of it to something bigger, more impersonal and uncontrolled. In his autobiography, Patten devotes a fair amount of space to his special feelings about the differences between his smalltown roots and his big-city experiences and observations, especially as they influenced his understanding of this growing-up period in American history.

It is in Patten's novel *The College Rebel* (1914), however, that one obtains a clearer, though more dramatic, perception of his attitudes toward the polarities of individual expression and societal restrictions in American life. In this contrast, we are afforded considerable insight into the underlying nature of American sports experience and what it can tell us about ourselves, particularly as it has been dramatized in the vast number of juvenile novels inspired by school and college sports. And, of course, as it has been presented since the 1950s by the mature novel written for an adult audience and generally inspired by organized athletic experience, both collegiate and professional. In fact, a novel such as *The College Rebel* can be looked upon as an archetypal model for the basic formulas that the contemporary sports novel works both within and against.

At heart, Gilbert Patten harbored serious writing ambitions, and the fact that he signed his actual name to *The College Rebel* reveals his desire to escape the stereotyped reputation of the Frank Merriwell stories and produce a more mature level of writing. Even though the hero of this novel, Roger Boltwood, is drawn in the traditional image of the Ivy League athlete whose code of behavior is based on the ideals of discipline, duty, and service, he comes off more fully developed than most boys'-book heroes of the time in that he readily asks questions of the system that has made him what he is.

As a varsity player on the Yale football team, Roger is a prime candidate for all the social honors that attend such an achievement, but because of past questionable associations, he is deliberately passed over by his classmates. Roger then begins to shun the conventional behavior expected of him, choosing to operate independently in order to test a theory he has about Yale student society. As he tells his wealthy father upon refusing his offer of financial aid:

> For a real man—a young man, anyhow—there's a heap more enjoyment in bucking the tide, in pulling hard for some purpose, in being a doer independent and alone against all the world, if necessary. (25)

His outlook is similar to that of the sporting hero of contemporary fiction, whose societal conflict I have analyzed in *The Sporting Myth,* someone, for example, like the socially disoriented football player Phil Elliott in *North Dallas Forty,* although in Elliott's case his sense of quality performance is both aided and distorted by booze and drugs.[5]

Thus Roger Boltwood feels compelled "to show his independence . . . to snap his fingers in the set face of convention" by setting his own standards of behavior and paying little attention to anyone else's wishes. He even goes so far as to turn down the baseball captain's invitation to come out for the team on the pretext that he is being loyal to Yale by being loyal to himself, and asserting that even those who represent the school in so highly honorable and respected an endeavor as sports are selfishly working for themselves.

The paradox of Roger Boltwood's position and one that extends to today's serious literature inspired by sports experience is that to belong to any societal system—an organization, a school, or an athletic team—one must conform to its demands to realize individuality within the system.[6] Even though the natural heritage of American literary sports heroes conflicts with the social conformity that a system demands, the system forces such a hero to choose an acceptable pattern of identity or else be forever alienated. In sports fiction written for a youthful audience, however, formulaic convention demanded that there be a resolution to the hero's conflict; thus Roger's rebellious nature is eventually subdued through his acknowledgment of college life's important role and effect on the development of personal character and individual success. As one of his associates admonishes him early in the novel:

"Do you think you're bigger'n the college? Got an idea you're bigger'n the unwritten social law that prevails here? Well, you're not. Buck against it and it'll break you. . . . If you don't conform to that unwritten law of Yale you'll never realize the best and dearest of [your] ambitions. You've got to do certain prescribed things; you've got to conform in every particular." (88–89)

By the story's climax, the day of the Yale-Harvard baseball game, Roger's return to the society of students is expressed in Patten's usual melodramatic fashion for the windup of his tales. Having finally relented and joined the baseball team, Roger is scheduled as the starting pitcher against Harvard, but on the morning of the game he learns (in true juvenile-fiction fashion) that his father has been injured in an automobile wreck. After rushing to his side, Roger discovers that his father's injuries, fortunately, are not serious; that, in fact, his father wants him to return and play in the game. With most of the plot's complications resolved by now, Roger shows up just in time to strike out the final batter—who just happens to be the best hitter in the league—win the game, gain acceptance among his peers, and reemphasize what I have observed about the tradition of juvenile sports fiction in America: quality performance on the playing field equates with success in life. That Roger's social acceptance into Yale student life assures his ultimate success in life is brought out near the close of the novel when one of his friends tells him, "You're the sort of man who is bound, because of his own bigness and broadness, some day to do big things" (277).

While all competitive sports are projected in juvenile novels as appropriate laboratories to test the experience of quality performance, the team sports of baseball and football are clearly the most popular, with the more establishment-oriented game of football coming through as the most meaningful for demonstrating the degree of personal courage and moral fortitude that a player must possess in the face of adversity and seemingly insurmountable odds. Whereas baseball generally relied on the highly individualized skills of pitcher or batter to express its dramatic high points to a reading audience (e.g., the "Baseball Joe" series), football, through its corporate sense of the value of teamwork, had more to say to young readers looking to make their way in the highly competitive world of industry and business. The basic ingredients of the game—its specific emphasis on direct bodily contact to carry out a plan of attack, its concentration on individual achievement and determination within a team situation, and its reliance on periodic craft and deception to achieve a designated goal—contribute to the game of football in juvenile fiction as a graphic metaphor for the corporate world and the test of quality performance.

For example, the highly popular Rover Boys series by Arthur H. Winfield (a house name of the most productive source of juvenile series books—the Stratemeyer Syndicate) contains two books that deal primarily with school life, *The Rover Boys at School* (1899) and *The Rover Boys at College* (1910), and both of them have climactic chapters with the same title: "The Great Football Game," in which a bitter foe is dealt with on the gridiron. The earlier book saw Dick, Tom, and Sam Rover as cadets at Putnam Hall where, in addition to the usual schoolboy problems with bullies, they must reckon with the devious plans of the scheming stepfather of Dick's girlfriend. However, when the big game with Pornell comes up and the honor of the school is at stake, all these matters are conveniently relegated to the background. In fact, the significance of this game overshadows all other events in the story in its attempt to emphasize and demonstrate the level of standards a player must adhere to to bring off the quality performance.

Not until the fourteenth book in the series did the boys make it to college, a delay, it was explained, that was due to the extensive search for their lost explorer father, whose predicament was the basis for many of the books' plots. As to be expected, the boys' college tenure is colored by tiffs with bullies and the pranks and hijinks of dormitory life, but once again such foolishness is cast aside when the football team faces Roxley College. Against their much heavier opponents, the Rovers' team is forced to come up with a quick, deceptive style of play, and it is finally Dick himself who turns in the requisite quality performance that saves the day for his team:

> How he got the ball from the burly Roxley right guard nobody could exactly tell afterward, but get the ball he did, and rounded two rival players before they knew what was up. Then down the field he sped, with hie enemies yelling like demons behind him, and his friends on the benches encouraging him to go on. He saw nothing and heard nothing until in the grandstand he perceived a slender girlish form arise, wave a banner and fairly scream:
> "Dick! Dick! Run! run! run!" "It's Dora," he thought. "Dora sees me! She wants me to win!" (188–89)

In the traditional boy's sports novel, girls, as a rule, have little or no function, as, for example, in Ellery H. Clark's *Dick Randall, the Young Athlete* (1910) and Lester Chadwick's *Baseball Joe on the School Nine* (1912), which depict the campus community as an all-male world. Written primarily for boys approaching young manhood during an age of suppressed emotional feeling for the fair sex, juvenile fiction, in most cases, obviously preferred to keep the innocent world of the schoolboy free from the complexities and temptations that the opposite gender represented. Girls who do appear in these stories are portrayed in platonic relationships and as paragons of virtue whose roles, other than to complicate the plot, are to inspire young athletes like Dick Rover to improve their athletic performance on the field and their social role off.

Graham B. Forbes (another Stratemeyer house name), in the *Boys of Columbia High* series (1911–1920), apparently capitalized on the popular success of Dora's role in the Rover Boy books and added a number of roles for girls in this series. Certainly to do so was sound salesmanship, for who knows how many feminine readers this practice might have attracted? Then, again, boys in their mid-teens no doubt found these books more appealing because of their references to girls who, by this time in their lives, must have become real enough concerns in spite of what genteel standards dictated. In the initial book of the series, *The Boys of Columbia High* (1911), the suggestion of one of the lead characters "that the ride to and from . . . a dance, with a dandy little girl tucked under the bearskin robe with you, is about half the shooting match" is a clear indication of changing mores in the wind (128–29). Even the hero of this series, Frank Allen, is allowed a girlfriend, but his affection for Minnie Cuthbert never gets beyond the blushing, hand-holding, and eye-contact stage. While the athletic hero—or anti-hero, if you will—of contemporary adult fiction might womanize to his ego's content, he rarely ever strives to know his women in any way other than the sexual. Because woman represents socialization and its attendant constraints on male individuality, the athletic hero of adult fiction shuns serious involvement with women to indulge himself in that special experience which serves to enhance his ego—quality performance in the bedroom.

Actually, Frank Allen is such an all-round fellow that he does not have much time for romancing. Not only is he a super athlete in all sports, he is also president of his class, editor of the school newspaper, and the leader in all social events. (Concentrating on the social side of school life in addition to athletics made this series unique among most boys' books.) Nevertheless, the main interest in Frank Allen's life is obviously the honor of his school for which he is prepared to do about anything to keep it undefiled. As he tells a freshman candidate for the baseball team, "Columbia High is calling to you, Ralph. You are supposed to have the good name of your school placed above everything else" (93). The pious tone of Frank's words informs the reader that if any experience ever approaches religious significance in these books, then joining the select fraternity of varsity athletes does and helps contribute to the meaningful ritual of quality performance on the playing field. Although the school may have come before self in these books, winning for one's school was tantamount to winning for one's self. It is a feeling akin to that of Phil Elliott's in *North Dallas Forty* when he contends: "There is a basic reality where it is just me and the job to be done, the game and all its skills . . ." (265).

Published as a series of eight books during 1911–20, the Columbia High stories were reissued in 1926 as the Frank Allen series with some new titles added. Apparently, the publishers felt that these books' more mature approach to boy-girl relationships would carry over to a new generation of readers, but what is appealing to the taste of one generation may be interesting only in a nostalgic sense for another, and the Frank Allen books soon faded in popularity.

Another revealing indication that the times were changing was the growing interest in series books dealing with military-school life, particularly during the years just before World War I, when unsettled European conditions were beginning to anticipate the mlitary conflict that would result in a major step toward this country's loss of innocence, and pursuant to the impact of Ernest Hemingway's athletic writing style in the 1920s, a new wave of fictional realism.

During this time, two popular military-school series were produced by H. Irving Hancock (1868–1922), one of the most prolific of series book writers. Dick Prescott was his title character who went to West Point, and Dave Darrin was Dick's counterpart at Annapolis, but both series purported to dramatize what it was like when "average bright American boys" attended military school. *Dick Prescott's Second Year at West Point* (1911) is exemplary of this series' sports focus, which builds toward a big-game climax when the Cadets play Lehigh in baseball.[6] To add to the game's dramatic intensity, much is made over the competitive disadvantages of military schools, with their stricter physical standards and disciplinary controls, in playing civilian schools who have much larger players and more relaxed rules. However, a major point of these books is to address the advantages of the disciplined life, and as if to exemplify this end, Dick, who is the pitcher for his team, turns in the standard quality performance, striking out the final batter with the bases loaded to preserve a 2–1 win. Obviously, Hancock had little problem in plotting and coming up with appropriate titles for these series, and the Naval Academy's equal-time recognition came in books like *Dave Darrin's Third Year at Annapolis* (1911), in which the big football game with West Point is won on Dave's dramatic field-goal kick.

The Hancock books, true to the tradition of the boys' sports novel, always held to the formulaic situation dictating that regardless of the extent of adversity confronting a key player, or a team, or even a school, winning the big game was an obligatory part of the plot since it was a foregone conclusion that no reader would believe that the hero of a boys' sports novel could ultimately lose. This was a standard situation that would be approached and interpreted in a variety of ways in the next significant era of juvenile sports fiction, 1920–50. But in spite of the revolutionary social and cultural developments and influences that would affect a writer's outlook during this period, the essential quality-performance ingredient of the juvenile sports novel remained as it always had.

Reflective of an expanding industrialized society and an attendant acceptance of sports as spectacle, the 1920s represents that decade when the concept of sports as pure entertainment was first introduced. The result was a big parade of heroic sports personalities, both amateur and professional—legendary figures such as Jack Dempsey, Babe Ruth, Red Grange, and even a football coach,

Knute Rockne of Notre Dame. The fact that a midwestern college coach cracked this lineup was indicative of the inevitable nationalization of American sports, especially college football, which finally rid itself of the dominance of the eastern Ivy League schools. The increasing popularity of professional sports, particularly baseball, was attributable in large part to the abundance of publicity they received in growing urban centers through the mass media forms of journalism (newspapers and magazines), radio, and the movies, all modes of popular expression that found receptive audiences during this time.

A number of juvenile-fiction writers of this era were inspired by these influences as well as by the Hemingway manner of writing to develop a more realistic style and attitude toward their subject matter, and among the best and most popular of these writers was Harold M. Sherman (1898–1966). In his *Touchdown!* (1927), for example, young readers were exposed to the effects of a variety of contemporary developments brought to bear on narrative content. In fact, the plot revolves around three high school football stars popularly known through their newspaper publicity as Milford High's "Big Three." At one point in the story, Sherman interpolates a newspaper account of a recent resounding victory in which the trio (nicknamed Stuffy, Pepper, and Brick, in the popular manner of the time) and the fourth member of the Milford backfield have prominently figured, so prominently, in fact, that the sportswriter dubs them, after the Notre Dame backfield of the day, "The Four Horsemen of Milford High." Responding to increased public interest, newspapers of the Twenties had already begun their policy of extended coverage of sports events ranging from the local high school contest to a college game of national import. The popular athlete had to learn to adapt to and accept this kind of publicity lest he catch what was referred to as the athlete's social disease—"the big head." Such, unfortunately, happens to be the case with Milford's "Big Three," who subsequently become alienated from the rest of the team, with the result that the team's record begins to suffer.

Furthermore, when Stuffy, Pepper, and Brick consent to the use of their names in a commercial scheme, they come under the charge of "capitalization of athletic fame" and are barred from playing in the state championship game against their biggest rivals. On the day of the game however, evidence is located that clears the boys, and they appear in the fourth quarter in time to spark a come-from-behind win for the championship. The lesson of the necessity for team cohesiveness produces the obligatory quality performance, which also helps cure the star players' "big-head" problems. In stories like *Touchdown!*, it was obvious that writers of boys' sports novels had become sensitive to the larger issues and dominant influences of their time—in this case, the growing problem of successful athletes having to cope with scandal while trying to keep a sane perspective in the midst of the adulation and hero worship that the expanding publicity of sports events promulgated. Accordingly, the Roy Hobbses, Rabbit Angstroms, and Phil Elliotts of later adult fiction would exemplify in their special ways how this sort of thing could affect the athlete's psyche.

The psychological concerns of the fictional athlete carried over into the 1930s, but largely because of the escapism-oriented Depression years, fantasized sports fiction found additional popularity through its dissemination in the cheap pulp-magazine format. Popular pulps like *Argosy* and *Top-Notch* had already explored the receptibility of a growing sports-minded public in the 1920s, but the troubled times of the Thirties invited even more forms of escapist fiction, and the result was a variety of pulp magazines that specialized in a particular sport, some seasonal, some year round. Although they were directed primarily at an adult male audience, many boys, who were attracted to the pulps' colorful, action-packed covers, undoubtedly found themselves reading them, too. Concurrently, the slick magazines, *Boys' Life* and *The Open Road for Boys,* which featured a significant amount of sports fiction, achieved a popularity during the Thirties that has never been equaled. One of the main reasons for this popularity was the frequent appearance in their pages of the stories of William Heyliger (1884–1955), who has to rate with John R. Tunis as the most stylistically polished and psychologically perceptive writers of earlier juvenile sports fiction.

In his novel *The Big Leaguer* (1936), Heyliger combines a realistic feel for his setting with humanistic insight to produce an appealing story respecting both writing style and narrative development. Marty Gage, the son of a major league manager, lives a boy's dream: he spends his summers traveling with his father's team. As a result, he develops some high-minded notions about the game of baseball and how it should be played. He is especially impressed by the team's catcher, the loquacious and highly opinionated Buck Olsen from whom Marty learns much about the manner in which a catcher should control a pitcher's performance. Since Marty is a catcher himself on his school's team, he takes his major league knowledge back to school with him and attempts to impose it on his team, even going so far as to upstage the coach. The outcome is disastrous as Marty's dictatorial tactics backfire and erode the confidence of the team's star pitcher. Luckily, through a combination of factors, Marty finally recognizes the error of his ways in time to get his pitcher back on the quality-performance track.

Heyliger's stylistic technique in his story is highlighted by his sure ear for dialogue, probably influenced by fiction's new realism and the popular movies of the Thirties. In marked contrast to the artificial manner of speech earlier schoolboy characters engaged in, Heyliger's people talk to each other in the way that a reader would expect. This talent allowed him not only to develop believable relationships but to get inside his characters' thoughts in a psychological sense. The fact that he would dare to buck a basic convention of juvenile sports fiction by permitting a player to challenge the authority of a coach in *The Big Leaguer* (a common enough occurrence in later adult fiction) also reveals Heyliger's original approach to dramatizing human relationships through his characters' intimate involvement in a game. His insight into the power of a game over human concerns is demonstrated in his justification for Marty Gage's actions:

> You had to take into account the fact that Marty had been thrown into contact with a world that was far beyond his years. It wasn't a world that made baseball a sport. It was a world that took its bread and butter from baseball and made baseball an intensive business, a science and a profession. A world of men who, if they didn't play baseball successfully, didn't eat. (180)

Marty Gage's growing realization of the difference between the world of those who play baseball for money and the world of those who play it for fun exemplifies not only William Heyliger's perceptiveness in dramatizing this difference but also his ability to suggest the moral implied by Marty's recognition of this difference.

During the 1940s and 1950s—the waning years of juvenile sports fiction that leaned toward fantasy—realistic trends continued in the work of John R. Tunis (see following essay) and Clair Bee, talented writers who both expressed a deep empathy with the on- and off-field experiences of the young athlete. This feeling is particularly evident in the fiction of Bee (b.1900) who, with his own athletic background as both all-round player and successful coach, created one of the most popular heroes of the sports-novel genre in Chip Hilton, the all-star athlete and model student of Valley Falls High School. Bee's skill in relating to all the components and concerns of the typical American high school and not just what happens on the athletic field is especially evident in *Pitcher's Duel* (1950), a story containing many of the traditional elements of juvenile sports fiction but colored by the fresh human approach of a writer who undoubtedly enjoyed his subject matter.

Actually, *Pitcher's Duel* is the story of Henry Rockwell's last coaching stint at Valley Falls. Past the age of mandatory retirement, Coach Rockwell refuses to give in to those who would like to see him gone. Even though Chip Hilton and his teammates, who have never known any other coach at Valley Falls, are on Rockwell's side, the press and local politics, it appears, are not, and an unrelenting campaign to remove Rockwell is underway. This movement is played out against the basic story line of Chip's final days of his senior year and the baseball team's run for the state championship. Mixing local politics and school life, Bee tells a story that has the wide-ranging human interest of a popular television series, building, after a number of complications, toward the climax of the game for the state championship. In ironic terms the game itself proves to be the ultimate variation on the quality-performance code of juvenile sports fiction: a nineteen-inning contest in which Chip pitches the last nine, only to lose in what has to be among the most surprising twists in the genre.

But as I have indicated, the story is really Rockwell's, and typically it does end on a winning note when, at the sports banquet honoring the retiring coach, it is announced that Henry Rockwell will become the freshman coach at State University. So in the tradition of the juvenile series book, the promise of Chip Hilton continuing his relationship with his beloved coach at college hints at more stories to follow.

It is a tribute to the fertile imagination of Clair Bee that in the large number of books he wrote he could come up with such a variety of plots within the restrictive demands and confines of the quality-performance convention of juvenile sports fiction. As it turned out, though, Chip Hilton is one of the last larger-than-life characters molded in the manner of the fantasized sports hero of juvenile fiction. Since the 1950s, there have been ". . . radical changes in the general characteristics of the adolescent sports hero and in the people who make up his environment, such as parents, coaches, and girl-friends" (Sherrill, 112). Because of today's more liberal attitudes toward what fiction may say and do as well as the influence of the adult sports novel that began to proliferate in the 1960s, the young athletes [of today's juvenile fiction] speak a harsher language; the language of the locker room is not off limits. They have more active sex lives and are not threatened by aggressive girls who are successful in their own right. They explore the concept of winning and definition of self in more depth than did most of their counterparts of earlier sport fiction. . . . (Sherrill, 129)

Even though our times have grown hardened to the abstractions of duty, service, and discipline that constitute the code that the novels of writers such as Tomlinson and Barbour seemed so concerned with, the lesson of the traditional juvenile sports novel still reveals that sports experience, whether in real life or in fiction, is grounded in the dedication to an ideal of excellence that will never change. Perhaps William Heyliger was speaking on behalf of all writers in the juvenile sports-fiction tradition from Barbour to Bee when he responded to a query about his writing philosophy: "I began as an idealist. I am still an idealist. For that I offer no apology. This world of ours, often glorious, often sordid and stupid, can do with a few ideals" (Kunitz and Haycraft, 161). In writing for a well-defined audience, though, Heyliger and his predecessors had no way of knowing that the literary genre they had set in motion would ultimately examine sport's ideal of quality performance and the success ethic it promoted in an entirely new light, one that would question and criticize the very sources of its origin as well as the institutions that helped spread it.

Notes

1. See Christian K. Messenger, *Sport and the Spirit of Play in American Fiction: Hawthorne to Faulkner* (New York: Columbia University Press, 1981), in particular the chapter dealing with the "School Sports Hero." Also see Michael Oriard, *Dreaming of Heroes: American Sports Fiction 1868–1980* (Chicago: Nelson-Hall, 1982), in particular the chapter entitled "Frank Merriwell's Sons: The American Athlete-Hero." An extensive bibliography of juvenile sports fiction is also included in this volume.

2. Quoted in *This Fabulous Century, 1900–1910* (New York: Time-Life Books, 1969), p. 194. Although the game of football was catching criticism from all sides during the 1890s due to the game's extreme brutal aspects, Roosevelt would play an instrumental role in saving the game from itself in the early years of the twentieth century.

3. Hillton Academy must have been real enough to some impressionable readers since Barbour was known to have received numerous queries for further information about his "school."

4. Source of this quote is Wendell Hazen's column in the *Boston Sunday Post* (22 April 1945).

5. See Peter Gent, *North Dallas Forty* (New York: New American Library, 1974), p. 265. For an analysis of this novel and its relationship to the concerns of contemporary sport, see my essay *"North Dallas Forty* and the Tradition of the American Sporting Myth,"* in *American Sport Culture: The Humanistic Dimensions,* ed. W. L. Umphlett (Lewisburg, Pa.: Bucknell University Press, 1985).

6. Note that contemporary American literature has produced numerous examples of nonconforming athletes: James Jones's boxer who won't fight *(From Here to Eternity);* Jeremy Larner's basketball player who won't play *(Drive, He Said);* John Updike's ex-basketball player who won't play the game of life *(Rabbit, Run);* and Peter Gent's football player who won't perform according to the system *(North Dallas Forty),* to cite some of the more prominent.

7. This book's subtitle, *Finding the Glory of the Soldier's Life,* reveals in itself a great deal concerning changes in youthful attitudes toward the military experience since the time of Hancock's books.

Works Cited

Barbour, Ralph Henry. *The Half-back.* New York: D. Appleton, 1899.

Forbes, Graham B. *The Boys of Columbia High.* New York: Grosset and Dunlap, 1911.

Gent, Peter. *North Dallas Forty.* New York: New American Library, 1974.

Heyliger, William. *The Big Leaguer.* Chicago: Goldsmith, 1936.

Holbrook, Stewart H. "Frank Merriwell at Yale Again—and Again and Again." *American Heriage,* June 1961, 24–28, 78–81.

Johnson, Owen. *Stover at Yale.* New York: Frederick A. Stokes, 1912.

Kunitz, Stanley J., and Howard Haycraft, eds. *The Junior Book of Authors.* New York: H. W. Wilson, 1951.

Patten, Gilbert. *The College Rebel.* New York: Barse and Hopkins, 1914.

Sherrill, Anne. "The Male Athlete in Young Adult Fiction." *Arete: The Journal of Sport Literature,* Fall 1984, 111–30. See also Michael Oriard, "On the Current Status of Sports Fiction," *Arete: The Journal of Sport Literature,* Fall 1983, 7–20.

Tomlinson, Everett T. *Ward Hill, the Senior.* Cleveland: Goldsmith, 1897.

Umphlett, Wiley Lee. *The Sporting Myth and the American Experience.* Lewisburg, Pa.: Bucknell University Press, 1975.

Winfield, Arthur H. *The Rover Boys at College.* New York: Grossett and Dunlap, 1910.

John R. Tunis's American Epic; or, Bridging the Gap between Juvenile and Adult Sports Fiction

LEVERETT T. SMITH, JR.

In a 1962 *Sports Illustrated* article Robert Cantwell celebrates the fantasy element in early juvenile baseball fiction and laments its abandonment in later works of this century.* "These new, realistic books," he writes, referring primarily to the works of Jackson Scholtz, Duane Decker, and John R. Tunis, "didn't take up where the old ones left off; they tended to become a different sort of work altogether, a boy's version of an adult story" (76). It is hard to imagine what adult sports books they might be boys' versions of, preceding, as they do, the extraordinary outburst of serious sports fiction of the last thirty years. It is more likely that their influence has been largely the other way around: the serious sports novels produced today are adult versions of boys' stories in the sports-fiction tradition.

The sections of Christian Messenger's *Sport and the Spirit of Play in American Fiction* and Michael Oriard's *Dreaming of Heroes* that deal with juvenile sports fiction suggest this development. Messenger, for instance, says, "The School Sports Hero . . . affords a classic study of how a formulaic pattern in a culture grew into an established popular literary formula: that of the boys' school sports story, and how that convention would be subsumed by the ironic and satiric statements of authors such as Fitzgerald, Hemingway, and Faulkner" (10–11). Oriard treats all contemporary adult sports fiction as dealing with heroes (or anti-heroes) whom he calls "Frank Merriwell's Sons," and he asserts that "the purest embodiment" of the American athlete-hero "is the hero of juvenile sports

---

*Editor's note: For examples of the "fantasy element," see the first essay in this collection.

fiction, who became the norm for all subsequent sports heroes" (27). Nonetheless, the special interest of both Messenger and Oriard lies primarily in fiction written for an adult audience, and both largely refrain from discussing juvenile works when adult fiction is available for their purposes. Oriard concludes that "the juvenile novel is . . . a valuable indication of the polar issues in the individual's role in society, but mature sports fiction explores this theme with more sophistication and complexity" ("The Athlete-Hero," 510). Ironically, though, Oriard's treatment of juvenile sports fiction in *Dreaming of Heroes*—particularly, Owen Johnson's *Stover at Yale* (1912) and John R. Tunis's *Iron Duke* (1939)—contradicts this notion in his very assertion of these works' "sophistication and complexity" (40–41).

I would contend here that Tunis's baseball stories for boys are sophisticated and mature enough that four of his books about the Brooklyn Dodgers written from 1940 to 1944—*The Kid from Tomkinsville* (1940), *World Series* (1941), *Keystone Kids* (1943), and *Rookie of the Year* (1944)—constitute something of an American epic that helped establish a serious role for sports as a literary source. Figuratively playing out the conflicts and triumphs Americans experienced during World War II, these four books together have captured the spirit and feel of the epic form in that they make up a literary work that is fundamentally celebratory of the culture it grows out of. Though the epic form is perfectly capable of being critical—indeed, criticism seems an essential ingredient—its ultimate purpose is to embody and celebrate the values of a particualr civilization. Its two other chief qualities are those of length and the delineation of a hero who embodies the culture's values. Although modern conditions of the literary market place dictate against any work approaching the extended length of an epic, I contend that Tunis's version of the epic form is actually contained within these four books and, moreover, is achieved without conscious literary intent. These works' embodiment of a heroic ideal, whose intent was to unite the United States in time of crisis, also turns out as more complex than it seems; for it is really the team, and no specific individual, that is the hero of Tunis's epical canon.

John R. Tunis (1889–1975), who was recognized by the 1940s as a reputable writer of boys' sports stories, actually came rather late to this occupation, having published his first boys' sports story in 1934 when he was 45. Before that, he made his living as a free-lance magazine writer, publishing over 2,000 articles in such disparate trade publications as *Good Hardware* and *The Railway Man's Monthly*. For a number of years, he also wrote a weekly sports column for *The New Yorker*. It wasn't until he was nearly fifty years old, however, that he found himself earning his living writing books—mostly sports stories—for, surprisingly enough, an audience of children (Donelson, 321–26).

Tunis's image of himself as a literary figure and his relation to sport is somewhat ambivalent. His autobiography, *A Measure of Independence* (1964), finds its central focus in the freedom he achieved through being a free-lance writer. He begins the book by announcing its subject as "the struggle of one writer in the United States" (3) and concludes it by saying, that "mine was an ordinary American story, but a happy one, chiefly because I was able to do what I wanted to do in life, and make a living so doing" (287). Although he professes that sport has been a significant factor in his life, there is reluctance in this admission. "Sport in general and tennis in particular," he writes, "must be the contrapuntal theme of this book" (4). And later, in describing his intent of learning to play tennis, he extends this assertion, explaining that "sport must be the theme of this book because it was my great passion as a boy, and a means of earning a living as a young man" (80). Nevertheless, Tunis's thinking reveals a degree of uncertainty about the relative importance of sport in society. Assessing the quality of his writing output during World War II, he says, "I was writing, writing, but who wanted drivel about sports?" (251). Later he seems grateful to be writing about subject matter of more significance than sports: "Once in a great while, some piece of mine shed a little light upon a vital subject" (253). In his autobiography, then, sport for Tunis seems a relatively unimportant subject, yet one he cannot ignore.

In spite of his ambivalent attitude, I think Tunis discovered a deeper understanding of the importance of writing about sport when he began to write for a juvenile audience and that writing about it in the context of World War II was essential to this discovery. Thus I am convinced that these three factors—World War II, his lifelong interest in sport, and his discovery of himself as a writer for juveniles—helped him produce his best work. He came to believe, as he says in his autobiography, that "a book written for [children] doesn't have to be merely as good as a book for adults, it must be—or should be—better" (259). Accordingly, he felt that a sports book for juveniles must show what sport does to people, which probably explains why he identifies himself at the beginning of his autobiography as a man who in his books was "forever trying to reform or to educate" (3). Essentially, he was writing "about the values, good or bad, of our leisure-time activities in the United States" (4). In fact, he constantly raised the question of whether sport was a constructive social force or not (80), concluding that although sport was one of the "sacred cows" of American civilization, "our games and sports are the essence of our civilization" (280).

In light of this conclusion, Tunis chose the Brooklyn Dodgers organization to provide a symbolic setting for all but one of his novels about baseball. Having previously convinced his editor that a boys' book with a professional baseball background would sell, he set out in the late 1930s for spring training in Florida. "The only way to get material for a baseball story," he had decided,

was to spend time in Florida at the training camps where, supposedly, the players were more relaxed and also more approachable. I decided to go with the Brooklyn Dodgers. . . . This turned out to be a lucky break, first because the squad at the start was full of lively and interesting characters, starting with Leo Durocher, the manager, and also because they were obvious pennant contenders that season. (244)

Tunis was probably drawn to the Dodgers for at least two other reasons—the style of play advocated by manager Durocher and the borough of Brooklyn itself. Tunis was not your usual dyed-in-the-wool baseball fan, but he does recall in his autobiography being taken to games during his youth: around "1900 or 1901 when I was ten or eleven" (46), an experience that aroused his interest in a time when he could still remember the fielding feats of players like Fred Tenney and Billy Hamilton (46–47). When Tunis came to write about baseball forty years later, he chose to honor this earlier dead-ball style of play with its focus on defense, speed, and intelligence rather than on power hitting, a preference Durocher would most dramatically underline in rebuilding the New York Giants at the end of the Forties.

Brooklyn and its Dodgers also appealed to Tunis because together they served as an image of American society as a whole. Frederick Roberts's "A Myth Grows in Brooklyn: Urban Death, Resurrection, and the Brooklyn Dodgers" shows how Brooklyn's mythical significance transcends "a negative image of urban anonymity and coldness and, instead, convey[s] an All-American sense of community and home to the rest of the country" (13). Though Roberts doesn't mention them, Tunis's books relate to this particular myth in a highly meaningful way.

In approaching epic stature, Tunis's four books come across to the reader as one complex but unified and continuously developed action. Actually, they are two pairs of books rather than four separate books. The first two, *The Kid From Tomkinsville* and *World Series*, focus on Roy Tucker's intent to establish himself as a major leaguer. This process takes two years, the action of which in *The Kid* takes the reader through the successful pennant race of the second year. *World Series* then describes the subsequent events of the championship games. The narrative action of these novels reveals what is expected of a player to perform as a team member and raises many questions about leadership, particularly in its depiction of two managers with contrasting styles as well as that of the owner of the Dodgers.

The last two books attempt to answer these questions in their portrait of Spike Russell, at first a rookie infielder, then, in his second year, a rookie manager. The two novels closely resemble the first pair in structure: *Keystone Kids* covers a year and a half and ends in mid-season with the question of Russell's ability to lead finally settled; *Rookie of the Year* concludes that same season successfully (the Dodgers win the pennant) and examines in some detail the nature of Russell's leadership. By the last of the four books, the reader has been thoroughly instructed in the nature of the community (as represented by the team) and how it is supposed to work, as well as how to belong to it and how to lead within it.

In *The Kid from Tomkinsville,* Roy Tucker spends the entire story achieving a place in the Brooklyn Dodgers lineup. What he learns ultimately is a lesson of character. What he achieves initially is a place on the team, a sense of belonging. Thus he thinks, "He was one of them, one of the gang, not an outsider anymore"; at last, he was "part of that secret fraternity, a baseball club." The story slowly divulges to the reader through its protagonist the inner nature of the world of major league baseball, some of whose characteristics are dealt with at length in the later books.

To Tunis the most important physical quality for a player to possess in professional baseball is speed, and he emphasizes its importance from the beginning of this novel to its end. Roy Tucker himself is impressed with the quality of speed from the advent of his first spring training camp, but when Roy's manager, Dave Leonard, is released by the Dodgers, his thoughts give rise to another ironic meaning of the word "speed":

> Speed, he reflected . . . , speed was what counted in baseball. Well, here was a speed they didn't often mention: the speed with which a player rises—and goes down. Speed? Yep, there was speed for you. (110)

Essential to Tunis's underlying intent, then, is his effort to make the word resonate metaphorically, as in the following:

Once again, and not for the last time, Roy felt the speed of baseball.
Speed, speed, speed. It was Clearwater. It was spring. Then all at once it
was late August; it was almost fall. Time passed, . . . a jumbled mass of
plays in games won and lost. (239)

Speed, for Tunis, is "the essence of our civilization" because it
refers literally to the pace of the game and metaphorically to the
accelerated pace of modern urban industrial life and the shortness
of human life itself.

The basic fact of speed as the "essence" of existence is underscored in the book through the various bizarre and catastrophic
events that occur away from the field, involving subject matter
normally alien to juvenile fiction; for example, madness and even
death. Razzle Nugent, star pitcher of the team, described by Tunis
as "a tall fellow with shoulders like a taxi" (36), goes berserk one
evening and tries to throw Roy out of a 10th-floor hotel window.
Ironically, the Dodgers' dynamic little manager, Gabby Gus
Spencer, trying to relax from the stress of the pennant race, is killed
in an automobile accident.

The problem these events seem to underscore is one of survival
in an unpredictable, stressful world (more symbolically, the world
of World War II). It is what Roy Tucker has to learn to cope with,
and his education comes in two parts. First his mentor, Dave
Leonard, convinces him that he cannot allow himself to become
discouraged. Leonard even gives him a slogan for dealing with
adversity: "Only the game fish swim upstream" (191). This makes
Roy resolute enough to keep his level of play up to major league
standards. The second lesson Leonard emphasizes is that baseball
is a team game. In an effort to get Tucker out of a hitting slump, he
tells him, "You forgot that you were playing for Brooklyn and
started playing for Tucker" (241). He concludes by admonishing
Roy that "baseball's a team game and don't forget it" (242). Thus,
Leonard implies that individual effort needs to be thoroughly sub-
ordinated to the group's goals for the success of either.

Other themes that will become more important later in the series
are simply touched on in this book, as, for example, the question of
the commercial nature of professional baseball. Roy, in finding he
can get his job back at the Tomkinsville drugstore during the off-
season, ironically recalls

Old Mr. McKenzie telling him in a sharp voice that he "wasn't keeping
the place open for no ballplayers." There had been scorn in his tone as
he mentioned the last word. Yet when the Kid returned it appeared Mr.

McKenzie had said nothing of the sort. . . . the Kid was now famous, and being in the drugstore again didn't hurt business (193).

The issue of the relation of commerce and sport is to become a central one for Tunis beginning in *World Series*. Tunis also comments on the relation of players to sportswriters, managers, and club owners. Casey, the sportswriter, is tolerated when he is positive but is easily dismissed when he is critical (see p. 136). In general, the good people of Tunis's world are all associated with playing the game. Even Jack MacManus, owner of the Dodgers, is given a background as a major-league player. Tunis's first description of MacManus is of special interst, even in part:

> Jack MacManus, [was] the man who broke into the big leagues straight from Minnesota, the guy who enlisted as a private in the war and came out a colonel, who went back to college and played on a Big Ten championship football team, who started off in the big leagues by spiking Ty Cobb when Ty tried to run him down as a fresh young busher. Man who'd made a million dollars in oil, lost it in the market, re-made it in radio, bought a minor league club, and finally picked up the Dodgers the year before. (20)

Here in a nice mix of sports, war, and speculative business success is presented a man who clearly represents to Roy Tucker the ideal of success.

World Series, sequel to *The Kid from Tomkinsville,* is concerned with the Series immediately following the regular season games that conclude *The Kid*. In the course of the action, the Dodgers come back to win the last three of a seven-game series and become world champions. The central concerns of this novel are three: the implications of the World Series being a commercial spectacle, Roy's own battle to achieve self-control as a player and a man, and the whole question of the proper role of management. At the center of the action are Roy's perception of his manager, Dave Leonard, and of the club-owner, Jack MacManus.

During the team meeting before the Series gets underway, Roy daydreams as the coaches go over the opposing lineup: "Gosh! Just think of it. Two . . . maybe four thousand bucks at stake. Four thousand dollars!" He continues thinking in this vein until the manager demands him to wake up and get his mind on the game. But thoughts of the Series money compete for Roy's attention throughout the book. A second way money intrudes in his life is through the persistent demand for commercial endorsements. Roy is asked to endorse a particular brand of cigarettes before the first game (16). After he is beaned in the first game, requests for endorsements pour into his hospital room (36). More fees are guaranteed him if his team wins the Series (160). That the Series is essentially a commercial spectacle that can detract a player's true course of action is continually asserted by Tunis.

Because of this new focus on the commercial dimension of the game, Roy Tucker first learns to practice self-control and finally to admire his leaders. Before the first game, Tucker feels "all tight inside" (23). Then he is hit on the head by a pitch from Cleveland fastballer Gene Miller. In the locker room after the game, he attacks Miller verbally. "For several minutes he went on, unable to stop, pouring out abuse on the distressed man" (32). The next day, however, he apologizes to Miller. Later, though, he physically attacks the reporter Casey and gets himself into a more complex situation, one that involves both his own self-control and the business of baseball. After Casey insults Tucker, Tucker slugs him twice. Dave Leonard then convinces him that he must apologize to Casey because "without publicity baseball would be dead" (119).

Roy Tucker learns even more about self-control and leadership from watching the relationship between Dave Leonard and Jack MacManus. One of Roy's essential motivations for winning the Series is to preserve Leonard's job, rumored to be on the line. After all, as Roy realizes, there is "no room for sentiment in baseball. Baseball is a business" (197). This is certainly the dimension of baseball that *World Series* serves to clarify. The emotional intensity Roy Tucker feels in winning the Series is underscored by the rumor that Jack MacManus will fire manager Dave Leonard if Brooklyn does not win. Because Roy admires both men so thoroughly, this situation sets up a conflict within himself he cannot openly acknowledge.

So the reader receives Roy's open approval of MacManus throughout the book. In one place he's "one of the smartest men in baseball" (45). In another, Roy is "dazzled into silence by MacManus and his eloquence" (168), who is even compared to movie star Clark Gable (168, 174). But MacManus is also subject to humiliation at the hands of some of his players at a civic banquet given for the team. In a gashouse gang sort of trick, players drop paint over him, and for a moment he loses his composure.

At this same banquet Dave Leonard is accorded a standing ovation (175), and from this time on, he is the heroic figure of the book, both as player and manager. Because of an injury to the starting catcher, Leonard assumes the catching duties himself, and both his play and managing help bring the team victory. Perhaps the first indication of Leonard's heroic nature is his handling of Roy's fight with Casey, the reporter. Leonard leaves Tucker thinking that "Dave was right all along about Casey. Dave was always right. Dave was his friend, the best in the business. Now they'd have to go out and win for Dave. They would, too" (131).

Dave's first game is an unqualified success:

> The Dodgers had won. True, but old man Leonard was the story. Old man Leonard who pulled a shaky pitcher through to triumph, who caught a grand game of ball, who started the rally that won, and who at forty actually stole second under the eyes of the best catcher in the American League. (153)

His age and comparative debility are further emphasized when Roy passes the trainer's room before the last game and notices that "Dave was being strapped in a corset of tape over his back and thighs, with more tape around his legs. It was not a pretty sight" (198–99). But it is Leonard's leadership ability that transcends his physical problems, and Tunis catches this quality in a brilliant image:

> At the plate, Dave held up one clenched fist, turning slowly from left to right, waving it at Jerry and Karl, then at Harry and Swanson in deep center, then at Ed and Red and himself, pulling them up, onward, knitting them together as a team. (241)

Tunis provides a resolution to Tucker's conflict by revealing at the end of the book that MacManus (crafty soul) had signed Leonard to a new contract before the Series began. The story then concludes with images of Leonard, MacManus, and, then, the ultimate major-league authority figure, Judge Kenesaw Mountain Landis, who appears in order to congratulate the Series winners.

The second pair of books, *Keystone Kids* (1943) and *Rookie of the Year* (1944), seem written at a higher level of intensity and deal with more complex issues than the first two. Part of the reason for this, I suspect, stems from their being written during America's entry into World War II. For the first third of *Keystone Kids*, Tunis introduces Spike and Bob Russell, country boys having arrived in the city; he also presents several different images of leadership (Spike and Bob's minor league manager Grouchy Devine and Dodger manager Ginger Crane are two); and he deals with issues of baseball as a business enterprise in which he describes Dodger owner Jack MacManus in a more complex and human light. All these elements function as a long introduction to Tunis's treatment of the nature of leadership, which expands into a depiction of how racial prejudice in America operates and concludes with an expression of how such prejudice can be overcome and a harmoniously functioning community achieved.

The Keystone Kids—Spike and Bob Russell—are from North Carolina, and at the beginning of the novel, Tunis uses their confusion at becoming a part of big-city, major league life as a device for humor. For instance, when the reader first meets Ginger Crane (who like Gabby Gus Spencer seems modeled after Leo Durocher), he is said to be "at home in this luxury" of big-city life (31). When he mistakes Bob Russell for the hotel electrician after Bob has fixed his lamp for him, the reader learns several things. First, Bob is a country boy who is too intimidated to tell his manager who he really is. Also, however, he is a capable workman in action, and he is more admirable than Ginger Crane, who seems a negative image of a manager; in fact, he is markedly contrasted in Spike and Bob's minds with Grouchy Devine, their manager in Nashville who will soon become manager of the rival St. Louis Cardinals. Devine is laconic but deeply religious, sensitive, and affectionate; Crane is loquaciously loud, nervous, excitable, and belligerent (see pp. 90–92). The Russells, who are orphans, are first presented through Grouchy Devine's eyes, suggesting his parental relationship to them. (In fact, the Dodgers' eventual triumph over the Cardinals in those two books amount symbolically to a son's triumph over his father.)

In *World Series* Tunis had confronted the essentially commercial nature of professional baseball; in *Keystone Kids* he acknowledges commercialism as an inevitable part of the game and the quality of business sense as an important dimension of leadership. This acceptance makes Spike Russell, who becomes the Dodgers' manager in his second year, a more complex and interesting character than Roy Tucker; and it also makes Dodgers' owner Jack MacManus, who was idealized in the first books by Tucker but realistically dealt with by Spike, a more human character. Spike doesn't drop buckets of paint on MacManus; instead he engages successfully in business negotiations with him. Early in the novel one learns that Spike "acts as business manager for" himself and his brother (13). Later, after brother Bob is almost sent down to the minors, Spike contrasts Bob's play in his mind with that of the veterans, and he thinks of Bob's chatter: "Those yells, so natural to his ears, sounded almost schoolboyish on this team of veterans . . . to whom baseball was not excitement and romance but business and nothing else" (58). So Spike realizes that he is a businessman, too.

During the winter following their first season, he negotiates contracts for the two brothers in such a way that owner MacManus, realizing that a new manager is needed the next season, picks Spike. Tunis presents this sequence of events to dramatize the extreme disadvantage that a player had in contract negotiations in those days. But he also reveals Spike's acumen in their desire to stay together. An angry MacManus finally gives in to their contract demands, and when Spike prepares to manage the team the next season, MacManus says, "You're the only player who ever got the better of me in a business deal, . . . You got an old head on those shoulders, and I believe you can handle this job" (139).

The job, specifically, is to produce a competitive team, for the Dodgers are disorganized and have fallen to sixth place. Prophetically, Fat Stuff Foster warns Spike that "there's too darned many factions on this club" (98). Consequently, the team plays so poorly that MacManus hires a psychiatrist to travel with them (104). Then when a young catcher named Klein joins the team, the fact that he is immediately perceived to be Jewish creates another faction. Swanson, an outfielder, tells Spike, "He won't last here, the bench jockeys will get him, these Jewish boys can't take it. Haven't any guts" (117–18). Spike finds that even his brother Bob agrees with this estimate.

With racial prejudice now the focus of the team's disorganization, Spike's problem in trying to unify his players is how to deal with this attitude. Although Klein's character is fully presented, Spike is himself bewildered by it. Klein plays well, but then, as any rookie might, he gets into the wrong card game and by winning, offends his veteran teammates. As a consequence, when rival bench jockeys insult him and opposing pitchers throw at his head, the team doesn't give him any support. Spike and Bob's disagreement about Klein's value adversely affects their play, too. According to Bob, Klein "ain't an American," but for Spike "a Jew's like anyone else" (167–68).

So Spike is moved to have a talk with Klein, insisting that he must defend himself and "fight back." Klein observes that his Jewishness makes such a response difficult, that it's easy for Spike to talk. Spike replies, "I know. But I'm the manager of the team. I gotta tell you these things. I hafta smooth out these troubles, that's what managers are for" (183). He eventually convinces Klein that he must fight for himself, and that in doing so, he can be a successful major leaguer.

The team starts to play so poorly, however, that Spike convenes a team meeting without Klein to deal with the problem. He begins by

pointing out what a team should be, an organization "pulling together." Reminding the players that they haven't been pulling for
Klein, he defines Klein as "a scrapper," one who's "fighting what
all of us who aren't Jews have done to all those who are" (193). And
what the rest of the team is doing to Klein he defines first as
"ruining him" and then actually as "murder" (194). When Spike
uses this word, even the dullest of all possible readers begins to
equate the fictional Dodgers' situation with the real-life global situation. And as far as the Dodgers are concerned from now on, as
Spike succinctly puts it, "this Jew-boy stuff is out" (195).

To help Klein get "this Jew-boy stuff" out of his head, Spike tells
him that being a member of the Dodgers gives him a new identity
that transcends his ethnic background. He is no longer to think of
himself as a Jew but as "the catcher of the Dodgers" (200).

This suggestion works for Klein, but a great deal of team dissen-
sion ensues, which dominates the rest of the story. First, Klein
faces down his chief antagonist on the team, an outfielder with the
symbolically Germanic name of Karl Case. But then after Klein's
collision at home plate with a Giant baserunner, the Dodgers rise
up as a team to fight with the Giants. Finally, in a game later in the
week in Philadelphia, the entire team even goes into the stands to
take on abusive fans. After all this, "Spike felt the whole team begin
to move at last, to move at last as a team" (219).

Although Klein hits the game-winning home run in this game, it is
really the entire team that hits it, as Tunis implies when he describes the situation from both the point of view of the opposing
pitcher and Klein himself:

> The Philadelphia pitcher saw them [Klein's teammates] shouting. . . .
> He felt the team backing the man at the plate, felt he was not only trying
> to outguess one batter but facing the whole club, determined and
> united. [Klein] felt it, too, felt the rise of team spirit. . . . they're with
> me. I'm the catcher of the Dodgers now! (219–20)

In the next chapter, Spike Russell meditates on the nature of
teamwork and on the particular kind of team the Dodgers are:

> And what was a team? It was everything in sport and in life, . . . A team
> was like an individual, a character, fashioned by work and suffering and
> disappointment and sympathy and understanding, perhaps not least of
> all by defeat. (222–23)

Accordingly, Tunis proceeds to tell the reader, in perhaps this
story's most significant passage, what "Spike Russell did not know

and could never know" about his players, that is, the details of their ethnic backgrounds. He describes the Dodgers as

> the team that was lost and found itself. For now they were a team, all of them. Thin and not so thin, tall and short, strong and not so strong, solemn and excitable, Calvinist and Covenanter, Catholic and Lutheran, Puritan and Jew, These were the elements that, fighting, clashing and jarring at first, then slowly mixing, blending, refining made up a team. Made up America. (227)

Here Tunis arrives at his own vision of a team as a melting pot for America. Not only does a team function as a melting pot designed to transform Old World discord into New World harmony, but it functions as an image of America. Naturally, the underlying significance of this image had a particular importance for Americans during World War II: to win, America must be a team. In the Dodgers' newfound team spirit, there is even a sense of religious conversion in Tunis's phrase, "was lost and found itself." In fact, the last chapter of the book finds the Dodgers celebrating "the rebirth of their team," which "like an individual" stands forth as the real hero of Tunis's "epic."

Of the four books, the last, *Rookie of the Year*, is probably the least effective. The adventures of Bones Hathaway, the rookie of the title, during the remainder of Spike Russell's first year as manager, are either dull or improbable. What gives the book strength, and knits it to the other three, is Tunis's continuing concern with the nature of leadership in his developing portrait of Spike Russell. In *Keystone Kids* Russell brought the team to life. In *Rookie of the Year* the dramatic interest lies in how he leads it to victory. Once a team is created, how can it best be led?

Basically, *Rookie of the Year* is not about the game on the field at all but about how the managerial hierarchy operates. Throughout the book considerable attention is devoted to the best way to manage players. It is talk that essentially sums up and pulls together threads that have existed in the preceding three books, culminating in a meeting between Spike and Dodger owner Jack MacManus. By now, it is safe to conclude that Spike is a player-oriented manager. After all, like Dave Leonard, he's a player himself, who knows how to generate extra effort, how to make each

> player come through with his best all the time, which man to drive, which to coax along, which to holler at, that's the job of the manager. That's my job, thought Spike. (34)

In addition to treating "his players the way he wants to be treated" (141), Spike makes a point of learning from his players: "Whenever possible the young manager sat beside his old hurler, never failing to learn something valuable" (26). In return, the players are grateful to him. Pitcher Rats Doyle says, "Spike Russell stays with you to the limit, he likes to give a man a chance to win his own game. Over the long haul it teaches you to rely on yourself" (105).

Maintaining his faith in speed and hustle, Spike tells the players: "If we aren't a speed club, we're nothing" (14), and a New York sportswriter attributes the Dodgers' rise to second place to Russell's having "got them playing together, [and having] injected speed until at present it's the fastest club in baseball" (107). The team is also a unit in which there are no stars: "Their rise was easy to explain. They were a unit, a team playing together" (125). Spike contends that "There isn't a single man on my club who considers himself a star. That's why we play well together, why we've been able to come from so far back to fight for the lead" (143).

However, this philosophy is challenged when Spike has to release Bones Hathaway for an alleged rules infraction. This decision results in a meeting with club owner Jack MacManus, now by no means the Olympian he used to be in Roy Tucker's eyes. MacManus has been offstage for practically the whole novel until this scene, in which the reader is told why he questions Spike's decision to suspend Hathaway:

> Jack MacManus loved baseball. But first of all he was a businessman; he was not in there solely for the love of the game but to make money. Sport was one thing, and he was sincerely interested in sport; yet money was something else. And anything that interfered with a profit was apt to rouse his ire. (167)

Spike's basic defense is that "baseball is built on discipline" (170), but MacManus argues that if Hathaway is reinstated, the financial rewards and consequent improvement in the quality of the team will be enormous (171–72). Spike replies, "No one man is indispensible to a ballclub. It's a lesson these kids all have to learn" (172), which prompts MacManus to conclude that it's also a lesson Spike needs to take to heart himself, and Spike departs, shaken.

The conflict between commercial interests and team discipline is by no means the fundamental one of the book. Rather it is that which occurs between Spike and Bill Hanson, the Dodgers' traveling secretary. Occasionally appearing in the first three volumes in the series, Hanson is a major figure in this fourth in that he represents the bureaucratic dimension of a baseball club. Although Brooklyn beats St. Louis for the National League pennant in this story, the real triumph occurs when Bill Hanson's plans are defeated.

Tunis takes special care to develop Hanson's character fully, to make him human even though he eventually becomes the villain in the eyes of all the other characters. Hanson is a veteran baseball man, fond of citing examples from times no one else can remember (32), and along with the coaches and manager, he is presented as a key member of the Dodgers' administrative team. Spike, the two coaches, and Hanson routinely share a taxi, and during their conversation Tunis depicts Hanson as a workhorse who labors long hours at his job and is proud of the job he does. Taking his leave of two players at one point he says, "I have a report to make out and some work to do. The boys play ball, . . . and they're all finished but the secretary never finishes" (69, 150).

Although Bob Russell sees Hanson as genial and agreeable, the thing that makes Bill Hanson disagreeable to the reader is his conviction that Spike Russell is not a good manager. Initially, this attitude seems like resentment toward the younger generation on the part of an older man (see p. 40). After he informs Bones Hathaway that "Spike's a darn good ballplayer, but good players don't always make good managers" (67), he tells Chiselbeak, the clubhouse man, that Spike doesn't handle his players properly. But later in the same conversation, he reveals that it is Spike's youth that upsets him, referring to him as "this kid" and "this johnny-come-lately" (89).

Spike doesn't like Bill Hanson either, feeling that he "had no business snooping round at meetings for the team" (19). In an especially significant passage, his attitude toward Hanson is characterized as "the soldier's half-expressed contempt for the non-combatant" (25), and Spike correctly suspects him of being a busybody who reports back to Jack MacManus.

Actually, Hanson does more than this. He works actively to destroy the team, trying hard to get rookies Baldwin and Hathaway in trouble with Spike. Spike's brother discovers this scheme and tells MacManus, who apologizes to Spike and attacks Hanson, calling him "the biggest double-crosser in baseball" (188). And so Hanson retires in disgrace, Hathaway is restored in time to win the final game, and the Dodgers win the pennant. The organization is now running smoothly again.

In conclusion, one can now realize that John R. Tunis's four novels—*The Kid from Tomkinsville, World Series, Keystone Kids,* and *Rookie of the Year*—promise and deliver more than just exciting baseball stories focused on youth and action. My contention is that in light of Tunis's inspirational source (World War II), they constitute a single complex action, epic in scope, one that dramatizes what it means to be a member of a team and what it takes to lead that team. Accordingly, because these novels have no hero, unless it is the Dodger team, the villains are not so much the opposition as they are those who prevent the smooth functioning of the team. That this philosophy might most naturally emerge during a national crisis like World War II is clear. Though Tunis mistrusts the profit motive and opposes authoritarian bureaucracy, he embraces many other values associated with the American business community, above all the primary value ascribed to teamwork.

Concerning his writing technique, Tunis's modest self-description in his autobiography seems both just and significant: "I was merely a reporter who cared about his country, [and] described what I saw" (260). Nevertheless, these four novels reveal him as a keen observer of what it takes to hold a nation together in time of crisis. From this larger perspective, they can be viewed as a bridge between the earlier fantasy element of the sport-fiction tradition and the more realistic or humanistic concerns of later adult fiction that began to proliferate in the 1950s and 1960s.

Works Cited

Cantwell, Robert. "A Sneering Laugh With the Bases Loaded." *Sports Illustrated* 16 (23 April 1962): 67–76.
Donelson, Ken. "John R. Tunis." In *American Writers for Children 1900–1960, Dictionary of Literary Biography* 22: 321–26. Detroit: Gale Research, 1983.
Messenger, Christian K. *Sport and the Spirit of Play in American Fiction: Hawthorne to Faulkner.* New York: Columbia University Press, 1981.
Oriard, Michael. "The Athlete-Hero and Democratic Ideals." *Journal of American Culture* 1, no. 3 (Fall 1978): 507–19.
———. *Dreaming of Heroes: American Sport Fiction, 1868–1980.* Chicago: Nelson-Hall, 1982.
Roberts, Frederick. "A Myth Grows in Brooklyn: Urban Death, Resurrection, and the Brooklyn Dodgers." *Baseball History* 2, no. 2 (Summer 1987): 4–24.
Tunis, John R. *Keystone Kids.* San Diego: Gulliver, 1987.
———. *The Kid From Tomkinsville.* San Diego: Gulliver, 1987.
———. *A Measure of Independence.* New York: Atheneum, 1964.
———. *Rookie of the Year.* San Diego: Gulliver, 1987.
———. *World Series.* San Diego: Gulliver, 1987.

Expansion Draft: Baseball Fiction of the 1980s

CHRISTIAN K. MESSENGER

More than thirty adult baseball novels have been published since 1980. Such a prolific output comes after the transitional baseball novels of Jay Neugeboren, Jerome Charyn, and others with their links to the flowering of serious baseball fiction since the 1950s in the work of Mark Harris, Bernard Malamud, Philip Roth, and Robert Coover.[1] Here is an unprecedented sports-fiction expansion that brings with it the problems, perhaps only metaphorical, of any sports expansion—a thinning of talent, some ragged games, retread veterans, callow rookies, careers open to talent, a few major surprises, and realignment of the competition.[2] All this expanded activity is more tentatively played out against and in the shadow of the influence of past heroes (novelists) and teams (their works).

The baseball fiction of Harris, Malamud, Roth, and Coover had been informed by these authors' sense of baseball's aesthetic properties and by baseball's resultant bonding with literature. Each of their novels had been very different in intention and style. The fact that baseball could serve so many varied authorial purposes—comic realism, myth, satire, self-reflexive fiction—suggests that the game as a cultural form with referential and aesthetic properties is solidly historical as well as endlessly allusive.

Baseball's deep historical structures relate strongly to its sense of cultural differences. The preoccupation with journeying, returning home, and plumbing national origins is written into baseball's master narrative, one assimilated by players, fans, and readers in endless repetition. The specific historical contextualizations of this narrative are diverse but may be summarized in two large patterns. They are baseball's "Legend of the Fall," as particularized in the Black Sox scandal of 1919 and its resultant banishments and exile, and the exclusion of blacks from major league baseball before 1947.

These exiles and exclusions have fostered an entire counterhistory of baseball that has limned America's hypocrisies and prejudices.

Neugeboren's *Sam's Legacy* and Charyn's *The Seventh Babe* contain by far the most imaginative studies of blacks, exiles, and baseball history. The novels do not treat the baseball subject in chronicle or sentiment but rather construct a dialectic in which whiteness and blackness are both damnation and salvation. Both novels have imagined Negro League histories at their center that define their protagonists' dilemma. *The Seventh Babe* ends, as does *Sam's Legacy,* with a baseball reconciliation, bridging decades and recalling teammates to life. Like Neugeboren, Charyn also has taken the suggestive pose of outlawry and exile and made it meaningful in individual historical terms. The history of black exclusion in baseball taps veins of psychodrama (Neugeboren) and inventive mythologizing (Charyn) to provide two of the most satisfying endings in baseball fiction.

The Black Sox remain the primal cautionary tale of American sports' ensnarement by money and greed. Here all the abuses of the economics of sport are in evidence. Baseball since 1919 has regarded itself as an innocent game above all compromising scandal. Yet its fiction writers know how to work its dialectical opposite of experience and rueful knowledge. If innocence is the official baseball myth, then experience is the bitter legacy in baseball fiction. Homelessness (the baseball equivalent is being left on base) is extended to permanent banishment, wandering, and severance, so clearly present in Malamud, Roth, Charyn, and W. P. Kinsella. From being footnotes to history, players slip beneath baseball's official history. Or they wander in shadow leagues so far below the major leagues as to be invisible. This slippage below baseball history frees authors to create mirror baseball worlds that may be parodic, grotesque, or lyrical.

The Black Sox scandal was early utilized by F. Scott Fitzgerald in a famous scene in *The Great Gatsby* where Gatsby proudly points out Meyer Wolfsheim to Nick Carraway as "the man who fixed the World Series in 1919." Though potentially a symbolic center to fictional baseball representation, the Black Sox scandal itself was not addressed in its specific historical moment again until quite recently. Three novels—Harry Stein's *Hoopla* (1983), Kinsella's *Shoeless Joe* (1982), and Eric Rolfe Greenberg's *The Celebrant* (1983)—pick up the subject in different ways. Stein is a Lardnerian, Kinsella, a magician after Malamud, while Greenberg writes a legitimate historical baseball novel. *Hoopla* is alternately narrated by a fictional sportswriter, Luther Pond, and by Buck Weaver, the Black Sox third baseman banned for life in 1920. Although Pond is a potential Lardner and Buck Weaver reads *You Know Me Al* and even sounds like a tepid echo of Jack Keefe, Stein's prose never really comes alive. There are set scenes where Pond interacts with historical icons such as John L. Sullivan, Ty Cobb, and William Randolph Hearst, but the novel, while earnest and historically correct, is more of a history designed to flesh out dramatically the life and times of an early twentieth-century sports culture. It is potentially a novel such as E. L. Doctorow's *Ragtime* (1975) in its conception but not in metaphor or execution.

Stein's Shoeless Joe Jackson is illiterate, cantankerous, and dull. In *Shoeless Joe,* Kinsella's Jackson is a dignified shade, as are his teammates, the men for whom Ray Kinsella builds a diamond on his Iowa farm to redeem them from their wandering and give them a place to play. Kinsella does not judge or question the ghostly crew and is satisfied merely to have them there. Neither *Hoopla* nor *Shoeless Joe* is ideologically aware, Stein being more a transmitter of history than a transformer and Kinsella, a baseball mystic of high sentiment. Thus two of the specific addresses to the Black Sox in recent fiction are somewhat thin.

Greenberg's *The Celebrant* is a historical novel that re-creates baseball's first two decades of this century, climaxing with the 1919 World Series and Black Sox scandal. *The Celebrant* is narrated by Jackie Kapp, third son of a Jewish family of jewelers in New York City, whose life and work cross the path of New York Giant pitcher Christy Mathewson from 1901 to 1919. Until the scandal in 1919, each section of the book is built around a pivotal big-game moment in Mathewson's career (1901, 1905, 1908, 1912) that defines his greatness for Kapp and that allows Greenberg, like Stein, to describe early modern sports culture, its mores and habitues. The structure of baseball history punctuates Jackie Kapp's narrative and moves it along. In designing jewelry to commemorate events and ceremony, Kapp practices an art that provides Mathewson with keepsake gems while he himself idolizes the pitcher in reserved appreciation. Potentially about a vital, growing immigrant culture and the Giants under the brawling John McGraw, *The Celebrant* nonetheless takes its tone from Greenberg's vision of the refined, college-educated Mathewson and Jackie Kapp's appropriately dignified response. Almost against its will, *The Celebrant* becomes a sort of school sports novel about an "amateur" hero of great reserve and stature and his worshipful witness. Mathewson quotes Alexander Pope in describing McGraw to Kapp, and speaks in a mannered fashion as in, "You have an aversion to the man, don't you? I sensed it at my apartment" (Greenberg, 90).

Through the Black Sox debacle in 1919, Greenberg is determined to expand Mathewson into a full-fledged Christ figure, but Mathewson comes unhinged at his realization of Black Sox perfidy and shifts from his reserve into a manic keening for his sport. He curses its defilers:

> "I do damn them," he said. "With a mark I damn them. I damn Cicotte. I damn Jackson. I damn Risberg and Gandil and Williams. And if there be others I will damn them as well, I will root them out and damn them for eternity. And I damn the filth that corrupted them, the dicers and the high rollers. They will pay. They will pay in time. I shall not rouse them now, for I will allow them their full portion of loss, and when the corrupters are counting their gains I shall spring upon them and drive them from the temple!" (262)

Here is an Old Testament prophecy wedded to baseball's Fall. Some middle style of energy and wit between the intensity of Mathewson's final mad scene and the genteel representation of Jackie Kapp and his classical pitcher-hero might have allowed Greenberg to succeed more fully in establishing Mathewson as the wounded historical body of American baseball. Nonetheless, for sheer theatrics, *The Celebrant*'s climax will be hard for future baseball fiction to beat.

Along with ballplayers banned or excluded because of crimes, other players in baseball fiction choose to dehistoricize themselves in willed exile. Donald Hays's narrator, Hog Durham, in *The Dixie Association* (1984) drops back in. He is an ex-convict released to play for the Arkansas Reds, a lively but disaffiliated minor league team of stoic Indians, exiled Cubans, and young blacks. Their manager is a one-armed, ex-major leaguer of Communist sympathies who runs a food co-op for the poor and who between innings leaflets the stands with manifestos. The Reds battle a regressive, racist team from Selma, Alabama, display great solidarity, and give positive meaning to the concept "collective." *The Dixie Association* is baseball fiction's ideological counterpart to James Whitehead's *Joiner* (1971) in football fiction.

The majority of baseball novels still take place in the mode of "baseball as education," one solidly established by Mark Harris in his Henry Wiggen novels. Here is where a series of mostly orderly transactions between the individual sports hero and the collective takes place, one in which the protagonist "adjusts to" or "rebels against" this or that social or economic power that the team may represent. Such traditional novels are extant in all periods up to the present.

A very orderly passage is contained in John Hough, Jr.'s *The Conduct of the Game* (1986), which has an umpire as the improbable protagonist. Young Lee Malcolm works his way up to a major league assignment and along the way learns judgment and tolerance, the tools of his trade, as well as the human foibles and weaknesses that skew "conduct." He loses a bad old girlfriend, wins a loyal new one, confronts a black superstar, and defends a gay umpire, Roy Van Arsdale, against prejudice and exposure. When Van Arsdale commits suicide, Lee Malcolm calls his own game on account of the hypocrisy of the baseball establishment and walks away from sports. A quiet maturation novel of personal baseball history is Don J. Snyder's *Veteran's Park* (1987), in which promising pitcher Brad Schaffer spends a minor league summer in Maine learning his craft and deepening his emotional range. All the verities of baseball's geography and history are present: small towns, farms, a good woman, children, staunch old timers. *Veteran's Park* is Kinsella without the hocus-pocus and a good generic example of current neorealistic fictional expression. Actually, the best recent narrative of baseball is Ron Shelton's film *Bull Durham* (1988), a sensual, knowing account of a Lardnerian bumpkin-pitcher, "Nuke" Laloosh (Tim Robbins), and the proud veteran minor league catcher, Crash Davis (Kevin Costner), who teaches him the game. They in turn compete for and are sustained by the captivating "baseball Annie" (Susan Sarandon), who loves them toward their respective triumphs ("Nuke's" call to the major leagues, Crash's resignation to his own accomplishments and baseball future, perhaps with his Annie). *Bull Durham* is ahistorical, with a benign view of organized baseball, and is antithetical to both myth and fantasy.

In the postmodern era, baseball novels still partake deeply from the sense of baseball as education, and extend the legacy of fantasy and myth that Malamud and Roth provided. Veteran literati step up to the plate with wit and style. Roger Kahn turns his considerable sportswriting talents to fiction in the sentimental *The Seventh Game* (1982). George Plimpton's *The Curious Case of Sidd Finch* (1987) is about a New York Met rookie pitcher with a 160-mph fastball, who also is an Eastern mystic. Wilfred Sheed's *The Boys of Winter* (1987) is a wicked comedy of manners about a group of very competitive writers and artists whose summer softball team on Long Island affords them all sorts of plots, both literary and otherwise. Also, current authors on the baseball fiction beat have looked to Coover's baseball treatise *(The Universal Baseball Association)* as ultimate (universal) guide and influence in the sense that he stipulated the making of universes as a proper inquiry and subject matter for fictions of baseball. Be that as it may, with such expert players in the baseball fiction hall of fame, current authors, instilled with the same diamond religion of restoration and search for origins, appear somewhat derivative at this juncture. Steve Kluger's *Changing Pitches* (1984) is a shallow tale of a veteran left-handed pitcher's infatuation with his catcher that strives to be utterly contemporary. The novel's resolution comes when the pitcher learns that the catcher is really in love with a pro football quarterback. Harris's Henry Wiggen and Bruce Pearson would blush—and then be bored. David Carkeet's *The Greatest Slump of All Time* (1984) has solid baseball action and strives for Coover's metaphysics but has too many interchangeably depressed characters who are articulate without a Damonsday to vivify them.

The baseball history of the Yankees and Dodgers in the 1940s and 1950s has provided the nostalgic material for three recent novels. Two of these novels, Gary Morgenstein's *The Man Who Wanted to Play Centerfield for the Yankees* (1983) and David Ritz's *The Man Who Brought the Dodgers Back to Brooklyn* (1981), are fictional extensions of the current baseball "fantasy camps" where adult males live out their childhood baseball dreams. Morgenstein's Danny Neuman, in early mid-life crisis, chases his goal of playing centerfield for the Yankees to the dismay of his wife and others. When the current Yankees call him up from the low minors at the climax of an improbable promotional campaign, he hits a home run in his only at bat and then abruptly and rather pompously walks right out of Yankee Stadium and baseball. The reader is not so fortunate in Ritz's novel, in which a Brooklyn kid from the 1940s, now a Los Angeles tycoon in the 1980s, buys the Dodgers and installs his boyhood pal as manager. They build an exact replica of Ebbets Field and move the team back to Brooklyn. It is a delightful idea (to this lifelong Dodger fan), but Ritz's characters are wooden, his nostalgia unfocused and poorly evoked.

Robert Mayer's *The Grace of Shortstops* (1984) is, however, quite successful in entwining baseball history with the education of his fourth-grade protagonist, Pee Wee Brunig, a Bronx boy who idolizes the 1947 Dodgers and grows in different ways during the season. Mayer utilizes real baseball events—Jackie Robinson's first game, the first regularly televised baseball games, the heart-stopping Dodger-Yankee World Series of 1947—to punctuate Pee Wee's growing consciousness of winning, losing, and adult weaknesses as well as adult responsibilities. Pee Wee's idol is Pee Wee Reese, and the boy wants to learn "the way a shortstop becomes what he was" (85). Mayer's adults lead lives of compromise and complexity. Pee Wee's father, a rabbi, worries about his position and debates whether to become involved in running guns to the Hagannah in Palestine. At novel's end, Pee Wee has helped save a tiny neighborhood girl through considerable courage, but as the Dodgers lose the World Series, he must try to summon the "grace" to understand and forgive his mother, whom he has accidentally found out to have been deeply in love with his best friend's father. Such a knowledge of error and loss (the Dodgers', his own) weighs heavily on the young boy at the novel's open-ended conclusion. Where Morgenstein and Ritz use a baseball childhood as stagnant nostalgia, Mayer depicts baseball's seasonal history to be dynamic as it moves ahead with personal history. *The Grace of Shortstops* is about growth, feeling different toward baseball and self, and playing toward the future rather than recovering the past.

In James McManus's *Chin Music* (1985), the narrative journey is a literal coming home of father and son under the grimmest and most moving of circumstances. Ray Zajak, an ace lefthander for the Chicago White Sox, awakens from a coma after being beaned in a World Series game. It is the last morning of earth: nuclear missiles have been launched and Chicago's death sentence can be measured in minutes. Zajak is an amnesiac, but "he assumes without question that he's got some sort of family out there, waiting for him to come home" (McManus, 15). Zajak himself, without memory but with good intentions, has become the awful buzz of apocalypse. He weaves home through a nightmare city, while his son plays a pick-up baseball game at school, falls in love with a girl on the other team, and then moves toward home himself. McManus acknowledges the beanball ("an enormous white blur, eclipsing your view of all else," 143) as baseball's individual analogy to nuclear explosion. However, he is equally interested in baseball's structural rhythms of coming home and fathers and sons who counter death and destruction. Working from the starkest of fictional premises, McManus uses baseball's deep thematics with sentiment and grace.

Two of the most prominent recent baseball novels, Kinsella's *Shoeless Joe* (1982) and *The Iowa Baseball Confederacy* (1986), suffer from what Fredric Jameson has discerned in postmodernism, "a new depthlessness," "a whole new culture of the image or simulacrum."[3] As an heir of Mark Harris, Kinsella weaves tales that are sincere and educative with no complicated plot or thematic devices. He is reverent toward baseball itself: there is no higher ground or authority, no questioning of history, no shaking of fists at the cosmos, no formal subversion into fragments. His novels are static and vivid at the same time. Joe Jackson and his Black Sox mates will patrol Kinsella's farm diamond in *Shoeless Joe* for as long as he can summon them in mind and spirit. Kinsella is all affect and attempts to speak of what endures in baseball, and ends with thin images of players as ghostly copies of historical figures, shades of shades, who fittingly take J. D. Salinger off with them into a sort of baseball twilight zone.

The *Iowa Baseball Confederacy* strives toward even greater magic and fantastic effects than *Shoeless Joe*. The *IBC* seems both extensively copied and overly magical. The Confederacy is a regional league that might have existed from 1902 to 1908 and is lodged initially only in the minds of father and son, Matthew and Gideon Clarke, who want to keep its memory alive. The IBC itself thus becomes a cross between Roth's Patriot League (*The Great American Novel*) and Coover's UBA. In addition, there are magical events—young lovers at carnivals struck by lightning (Hobbs and Wonderboy, Harriet Bird of *The Natural*), "back to the future" time travel, a fifteen-foot Indian named Drifting Away who is in touch with tribal ancestors who may or may not be in control of all temporality. A movable Black Angel stone monument from an Iowa City cemetery ends up playing right field. Leonardo Da Vinci arrives in a balloon to announce he invented baseball in 1506. There is even a biblical flood. Kinsella tries hard to unfold all events through his baseball frame. A desperate man blows himself up on a baseball field; an isolated old pitcher builds a fence exactly 60' 6" around himself; Matthew Clarke is killed by a line drive. Many characters are notable baseball aestheticians, including the cosmic Indian. There are "cracks in time"; opinions that "life is full of evil jokes" (95); powers that float "suspended in the silk and satin of the darkness" (103).

The center of the novel is a 2,648-inning game that begins on July 4, 1908, between the Chicago Cubs and the IBC All-Stars and that goes on too long in every sense. Kinsella is unsure of what he wants to do with this creation, and the reader sees little of the field action. In about the 1,000th inning, when Gideon Clarke says "I want to see more of this special magic" (220), he may be the only one. Kinsella has run out of magic by this juncture. He is confident that baseball has wondrous associations for the reader, but his own conceptualizations are not tied to larger myth patterns or to any ideology in his baseball historicizing or to substantive issues in the creation of fiction. With the richness of the 1908 season at hand (versus Greenberg's *The Celebrant,* for instance), Kinsella chooses to trick up a history of his own that pays remarkably little attention to the real ballplayers. Nor does Kinsella take a significant interest in creating fictional baseball players, preferring to control the narrative from the standpoint of a magic spectator-historian. It is no mistake, however, that two imagined baseball players are exceptions: Johnny Baron, a boy in the IBC in 1908 and an old man in 1978 in the novel's present, and Stan Rogalski, a 1970s career minor leaguer hurled back into sudden stardom in the IBC-Cubs marathon in 1908, are Kinsella's most winning pair of baseball characters. Kinsella is at his best when he gives his fictional game over to his players, as in *Shoeless Joe,* where Moonlight Graham, Kid Scissons, and Ray Kinsella's father are more interesting than the Black Sox shades and Kinsella's presumptions with "Jerry" Salinger. All the sweetness and solemnity of Matthew and Gideon Clarke's (and Kinsella's) love of baseball cannot compensate for the randomness of the special effects and the absence of much coherence to the general baseball metaphysics in *The IBC.*

Tony Ardizzone's *Heart of the Order* (1986) is a baseball novel of education clothed in magic raiment but glib and preachy in and around its fantasizing. The unpleasantly self-possessed first-person narrator, Daniel Bacigalupo, is a third baseman of considerable promise who as a youngster kills a playmate with a line drive and from then on must deal with enormous guilt that determines his relations with family, peers, and girls. He imagines that the dead boy, Mickey Meenan, comes back to life inside him and becomes an alternate source of control. This ventriloquist act makes the reader a bit queasy, though actually Mickey is a somewhat harmless cut-up. Ardizzone plays for reader sympathy, but his hero is such an egotist that little in his passage appears moving or sincere. Danny's first major league at bat results in a near re-creation of Mickey's death, Mickey perhaps travels to another body, a magical son is found in the bullrushes for Danny, Mickey's father becomes an improbable avenger, and Danny is almost killed. The last page redresses much of the overbearing narrator's line, but Ardizzone has waited too long.

Baseball novels by women have become a flourishing subgenre in recent sports fiction. Women's baseball fiction centers on the mode of cooperation, of interaction and support among teammates. Baseball appears to be the team sport most congenial to women athletes, with its lack of aggressive physical contact and premium on attributes other than size and strength. Competition and heroic striving are present in the fiction but are integrated with the team's other potentials: nurture, family, growth.

The histories involved in this fiction are personal histories. Barbara Gregorich's *She's on First* (1987) takes female participation in baseball to its extreme: "the first woman to play in the major leagues." Gregorich writes very seriously of her heroine, Linda Sunshine, a talented shortstop who is shocked to learn that she is the daughter of her major league team owner and of a great female player from the Women's All-American League of the 1940s. Gregorich isolates her heroine in competition with men against men and thus creates the most excessive male reactions. The "first woman to . . ." paradigm prevents Linda from the affiliative team experience. One suspects that Gregorich's real imaginative task would be to re-create the historical fact of the Women's All-American League in all its relations, but that team history makes only a cameo appearance to help explain the blood lines for her pioneer who is still in thrall to Daddy—progenitor and "owner."

Softball is a thriving team sport for women and the sport of choice in Sara Vogan's *In Shelly's Leg* (1981) and Ellen Cooney's *All the Way Home* (1984). Vogan's team plays fast-pitch softball, and Cooney's team plays slow-pitch. The choices say much about the novels' repsective viewpoints. Vogan writes a more intense romantic narrative about a pitcher and catcher on a state championship team who are vying for the same man. The novel is set against a Montana backdrop of open vistas, sentiment, and personal nostalgia. Cooney's women are suburban housewives and mothers who have never played organized ball or competed for anything until they are brought together in a common effort where they slowly learn to exercise their muscles and capabilities. In both *In Shelly's Leg* and *All the Way Home* the female players come to know each other through their sport and its lessons. Baseball as an education is invoked yet again in a new context.

Shelly's Leg is the name of the bar that sponsors the women's softball team. Vogan's heroines Margaret (pitcher) and Rita (catcher) are very different personalities. Margaret is a transplanted easterner; she is all pattern and definition, desiring stability and control after a failed first marriage and two children. Rita is more of a free spirit from a bad childhood on an Indian reservation; she has little plan to her instinctive affiliations, except to keep struggling. Woody, the object of their affections, is a classic western dreamer who wants to go on the road and try for a country-and-western singing career. Woody wants Margaret to go with him; she hesitates and Rita presents herself as an alternative. The softball season for the Shelly's Leg team proceeds along with this central drama.

Vogan does an excellent job of adapting baseball's field aesthetics to the lives and reactions of her central characters without ever forcing the comparisons. Margaret is the star pitcher: she always wants the ball and will never come out of the game. In effect, by her temperament and choices, she "pitches" Woody to Rita, who "catches" him. Yet Vogan gives the women a complex relation to each other with regard to their feelings of cooperation (on the field) and competition (for Woody). Vogan's baseball voices are authentic. She writes a fine scene of Margaret and Rita alone on a ball field at dusk after another Shelly's Leg victory. Margaret's children are off playing in the distance. The pitcher and catcher have it out. Rita takes the initiative and walks with Margaret off the mound toward the plate:

> "Get down here," Rita said. She crouched behind the plate, her knees splayed as if waiting for the pitch. "Things look different from down here."
> Margaret knelt next to Rita, looking out at her children on the pitcher's mound and across the still field. From this angle the field looked more rolling, not as flat as Margaret had always assumed. She saw hollows accentuated by the dusk light, rises that looked as if they would lead off into the trees. (200)

Vogan has used the subjective perspectives formed by positions on the diamond to present her characters in relation to each other. To Margaret, choices are flat and either-or; to Rita, from where "things look different," there are "hollows" and "rises," open-ended choices. Vogan does not take sides: both women argue their field of vision. Rita says, "It's being in the prime of life that's so hard for a woman. You don't know whether to lead or be led" (200). They begin to walk the diamond in the dark. To Margaret, "it seemed . . . that women never had anywhere to go and men surely and always did" (203). She resents Woody and Rita as well, who tells her, "You're just starting to make a home here, in a town that *is* my home. We'll know each other long after Woody's made his first million or gone belly-up for the fiftieth time" (203–4). The familiar tension in baseball fiction of leaving home and returning is invoked in a female context. Their heated dialogue flares and subsides as they explain selves and each other. Finally, Margaret "felt the pressure of Rita's hands holding her own" (207); they acknowledge that they are both afraid, that they are both doing what they must. Nurture holds an equal place with competition.

Cooney's *All the Way Home* is less evocative. It is really an anatomy of a team whose women of various ages and circumstances hardly have time for romantic flight, are indeed barely coping with children, spouses, and parents. Cooney's book has its dark touches—a battered wife and child, the trauma of a double parental death that follows a woman into adulthood and mothering of her own. Yet there are warmer moments as well—the pride of a husband in a wife's new sports interest and competence; a family's encouragement of a middle-aged mom's attempt to lose weight and acquire softball skills and confidence. The Spurs' team is coached by the intense Gussie Cabrini, a star athlete now home in Currys Crossing, Massachusetts, after failing to stick with a traveling women's softball team in the Southwest. She has been in a horrible motorcycle accident that has left her scarred and with an all-but-useless leg. Yet her power and authority, almost that of the male ritualist, inspires her team to take shape and each woman to do her best; they, in turn, bring Gussie back to life.

Nancy Willard's *Things Invisible to See* (1984) is a fine example of how to wed the lyrical to the prosaic in baseball fiction. Willard's strategy is to invoke God-play from the outset that is nonetheless absolutely historical:

> In Paradise, on the banks of the River of Time, the Lord of the Universe is playing ball with His archangels. Hundreds of spheres rest like white stones on the bottom of the river, and hundreds rise like bubbles from the water and fly to His hand that alone brings things to pass and gives them their true colors. What a show! He tosses a white ball which breaks into a yellow ball which breaks into a red ball, and in the northeast corner of the Sahara Desert the sand shifts and buries eight camels. The two herdsmen escape, and in a small town in southern Michigan Wanda Harkissian goes into labor with twins. She will name them Ben and Willie, but it's Esau and Jacob all over again. (3)

Everything and everyone, not just baseball, is determined by the same cosmic play; no privileges are reserved for narrators such as those of Kinsella and Ardizzone. Baseball resides within Willard's magic power and is part of the novel's original vision. No rhetorical claims about the sport's special magic need be made. Ben and Willie cut deals with God and Death, Ben paralyzes a girl with a battered ball (a variant of the new favored plot device in recent baseball fiction), and the girl, Clare, receives instruction in her powers from a guardian "ancestress."

Woven in and around this magic is an engagingly American Gothic story of families on the homefront in Ann Arbor, Michigan, during early World War II, the grounding from which Willard repeatedly returns to cosmic play (36, 147, 218, 263). Her subject is the battle between love and death. The cosmic choice-making occurs when a decision of some grave import is made about a character who nonetheless must carry it forward in courage and love within his or her own history. Clare takes the form of a bird to be shot down for food by the sailors as Ben's raft drifts helplessly in the South Pacific (191); later, she steals into Ben's hospital room in Ann Arbor to metaphorically light the lamps of his body anew (251).

The novel's gravest encounter is the final baseball match proposed by Ben to Death (to stave off Ben's own); it is the most portentous "big game" in baseball fiction since that on Coover's Damonsday. Death sets the terms: Ben's boys' team from Ann Arbor, the South Side Rovers, will play the "Dead Knights," Death's squad of baseball immortals, for three innings. If the Rovers win, they will survive the war; if not, Death takes them. If any of the Rovers now scattered all over the world cannot play, they must be replaced by their next of kin. Death and his client, Willie Harkissian, contrive a bus crash that injures the Rovers. They are replaced by their mothers who "look like they all work in a defense plant" (253), perhaps comparable to Cooney's women from *All the Way Home* now entering the lists with their sons' lives in the balance. This inexperienced "team" faces Mathewson, Gehrig, and other great stars and ultimately wins. Death moans, "Do you think Matty had to walk Mrs. Bacco? They want the living to win. Even the umpire wants the living to win. They remember how it was. All the pain, all the trouble—they'd choose it again—they'd go extra innings into infinity for the chance to be alive again" (261). Clare pitches heroically, her ancestress telling her to put "the stuff of being alive" (258) on the ball.

Willard lets the fantasy go on just long enough (3 innings and 10 pages as opposed to Kinsella's 2,648 innings and 249 pages in *The Iowa Baseball Confederacy*). She reunites Clare and Ben after the final ball toss by the Lord of the Universe: "Clare starts running and Ben runs after her as they round the bases, past the living and the dead, heading at top speed for home" (263). Baseball's finest diamond rhythm is invoked yet again. Willard has charmingly enlisted baseball to play through her magic and mothers to play for their sons in a history coextensive with time itself.

Baseball fiction in the 1980s carries forward all the baseball thematics heretofore mentioned. Stein's *Hoopla* has Kinsella's Black Sox, but only as historical replicas with their historical "image" intact. Kinsella, Willard, and Ardizzone believe in magic, whereas Vogan, Cooney, Herrin, Hays, Hough, Snyder, and Shelton write solidly of baseball as education, in the wake of many baseball novelists and narratives. Jameson writes that "we are condemned to seek History by way of our own pop images and simulacra of that history, which itself remains forever out of reach."[4] The mix of characters in some of the most recent baseball fiction suggests just such a recycling of baseball history and popular culture[5]: *Hoopla* (Cobb, Buck Weaver, John L. Sullivan, Jackson); *The Seventh Babe* (Ruth, Landis, Dizzy Dean); *Sam's Legacy* (Ruth); *Suder* (pianist Bud Powell); *Shoeless Joe* (Black Sox, Salinger); *Things Invisible to See* (the "Dead Knights"); *The Celebrant* (Mathewson, McGraw, Hal Chase, Black Sox); *The Iowa Baseball Confederacy* (the 1908 Cubs, Frank Luther Mott); and *Ragtime* (McGraw, Charlie Faust). Such "copying" is not necessarily enervating if delivered in inventive form, with *Ragtime* the primary example of a postmodern treatise on replication and copying.[6] Nonetheless, baseball fiction at present needs a less complacent use of magic and history, a stiffening against the national romance with baseball, without losing its memory and pleasure. A cinematic triumph such as *Bull Durham,* bawdy, wise, and sentimental, while respectful of baseball's passages and rhythms, may signal a narrative return to comic realism, the most enduring baseball fictional mode through Lardner and Harris.

Furthermore, some hard edges need to be beveled around the diamond. They are installed in the baseball frame of William Kennedy's *Ironweed* (1983), which squarely addresses the issues of fantasy and sentimentality in a dialogue with personal history. Kennedy creates this dialogue within the action of the novel itself in the responses of its protagonist, the blasted ex-Washington Senators third baseman, Francis Phelan. For heart-stopping grief, *Ironweed*'s fictional presentation of the father-son relation in baseball is unmatched. Francis Phelan had been a wondrous fielder with great hands, but in 1916, as he is diapering his infant son Gerald, he unaccountably drops him on the floor and the baby suffers a broken neck and dies. Francis flees his family in mortal devastation, condemning himself to a guilty flight of wandering and vagrancy. The novel opens in late 1938 with Francis back in Albany on Halloween night where ghosts are rising.

Kennedy balances Francis's reveries, his visions of his past and his victims, with his unsparing and violent presentation of self. Francis has killed two men as well as Gerald. The first was a strike-breaking trolley-car conductor "with a smooth round stone the weight of a baseball" (Kennedy, 25) in 1901, making him a labor hero and precipitating his first flight from Albany and into organized baseball, for which he left every year. His second murder victim is a bum, "Rowdy Dick" Doolan, who challenges him on the road. After this incident, he runs again as he "reconstituted a condition that was as pleasurable to his being as it was natural: the running of bases after the crack of the bat, the running from accusation . . . the running from family, from bondage, from destitution of the spirit . . ." (75). Francis has colloquy with all his dead spirits in *Ironweed,* including a lovely early summoning of the dead Gerald who redeems Francis through prophesying Francis's "final acts of expiation": "then when these final acts are complete, you will stop trying to die because of me" (19). Francis attempts stewardship of his own meager flock of friends, Albany's male and female vagrants.

For Francis Phelan, his shades are haunting, not summoned as in Kinsella or Ardizzone to magic up baseball art. Kennedy finally has it out with fantasy and the pull of the past when Francis, having returned to his home and to wife Annie, tentatively opens an old trunk of baseball memorabilia and imagines the people of his past: "the bleachers were all up, and men were filing silently into them" and "they kept coming: forty-three men, four boys, and two mutts . . ." (176), when suddenly Kennedy shifts from the mode of "summoning" that had informed *Ironweed* since Gerald's stunning appearance. Francis closes his eyes "to retch the vision out of his head" (176–77), and as the light brightens, "with it grew Francis's hatred of all fantasy, all insubstantiality"; "I am sick of your melancholy histories, your sentimental pieties, your goddamned unchanging faces." He exclaims, "You're all dead, and if you ain't, you oughta be," and concludes, "So get your ass gone," for "I'm the one is livin'. I'm the one who puts you on the map" (177).

Within Francis, Kennedy has fought the battle between the pull of the past, the summoning of shades, the grief-filled magic, and the need for the living man to continue out of his paralysis. Kennedy has the power to "put [Francis] on the map" and the power to draw the map. The "livin'" writer chooses as well, in this case a positive agency in Francis Phelan (what other baseball fantasists lack in their dreaminess), to embrace the patterns his own history makes beyond the fantasies and myths he constructs to keep himself imprisoned in the past. Francis Phelan's internal debate between fantasy and history in representation, his private agony and public torment, are everywhere related through the baseball frame both real and imagined. Such antagonists in debate define the two major modes in the creation of baseball fiction at present. Francis learns that he has more left than just his guilt. He lays to rest his friend Rudy and his beloved Helen, takes a few good bat swings at a gang that comes to break up a hobo encampment, then flees to his own home at last. He forages in the old trunk for his warm-up jacket, not for pictures of ghosts, and thinks perhaps of moving his bed into his grandson Danny's room; a hope of a future bond born of Gerald's memory is held out at last. Kennedy ends with "sure hands" himself, in the rhythms of coming home, an exile ended. As son Gerald had hoped in the graveyard, his father Francis has "stop[ped] trying to die," his "fugitive dance" (215) at least in abeyance.

Further reaction against the control of myth and fantasy in baseball fiction is David Small's *Almost Famous* (1982), a decidedly antisentimental novel in which minor league stand-out Ward Sullivan loses his career and lover in an automobile accident at age twenty-one. Though possessed of a Roy Hobbsian urgency and natural talent, he will not have a mythic rebirth. Instead, half-crippled at age thirty-three, he lives past baseball in his personal history with his pride and sense of order, attempting to shut out a reconnection to his family and an emotional life. He buries his father, becomes a father, breaks a young woman's heart, grudgingly learns to admire an artist brother, and deals unsparingly with a mad and inspired mother. Ward Sullivan painfully comes home, not through victory or revelation but through a slow imperfect education of his own failings. He is still learning at novel's end, one in which his extended family plays a pick-up game in the fields on family property in Maine. Ward yells to his brother, "Get back, kid! I'm going to hit this one a country mile," whereupon "the kid turned and bounded like a gazelle toward the dark trees at the edge of the clearing" (Small, 416). Small's final image (similar to Vogan's diamond at dusk in *In Shelly's Leg*) is of Ward's exultation as well as of the inner diamond (clearing) glossed with the "dark trees," the space beyond where life is always unbeknown, to which he must "turn." Small provides a fitting encapsulation of baseball's geometry and outer possibility.

Recent novelists, alert to forms of myth, ritual, and history, are alive to their rich embodiment in baseball. Coover's metaphor of universe-making in *The Universal Baseball Association* casts the widest net for baseball tropes in fiction. The creation of his Association and the playing of its games are seen to be part of the same function, that of the tension among the familiarization of baseball, the aesthetic roughening of the sport by Coover, and the reader's refamiliarization with baseball and fiction. The reader "comes home." Baseball encapsulates such voyages and returns, yet is still firmly represented in the present as material for a living history. As Coover's Hettie Irden says in a different but wholly complimentary sense after a night in bed with Henry Waugh playing the role of

Damon Rutherford, "Oh, that's a game, Henry! That's really a *great old game*" (Coover, 31).

Notes

1. The seminal novels in baseball fiction are Bernard Malamud's *The Natural* (1952); Mark Harris's *The Southpaw* (1953) and *Bang the Drum Slowly* (1956); Robert Coover's *The Universal Baseball Association* (1968); Philip Roth's *The Great American Novel* (1973); Jay Neugeboren's *Sam's Legacy* (1974); and Jerome Charyn's *The Seventh Babe* (1979).

2. In contrast, during 1971–78, in what might be called the discovery of football as fictional subject, there were about half as many football novels published as there were baseball novels published during 1980–88. Football fiction has slowed to a very few titles in the 1980s.

3. Fredric Jameson, "Postmodernism, or the Cultural Logic of Late Capitalism," *New Left Review* 147 (July–August 1984): 58.

4. Ibid., 71.

5. Mixed-genre baseball novels have begun to appear. In detective and crime fiction, there is Robert B. Parker, *Mortal Stakes* (1975); James Magnuson, *The Rundown* (1977); Gary Pomeranz, *Out at Home* (1985); and R. D. Rosen, *Strike Three, You're Dead* (1985). The thriller is represented by Charles Brady, *Seven Games in October* (1979); and Daniel Keith Cohler, *Gamemaker* (1980).

6. Jameson, "Postmodernism," 71.

Works Cited

Ardizzone, Tony. *Heart of the Order*. New York: Henry Holt, 1986.

Brady, Charles. *Seven Games in October*. New York: Little Brown, 1979.

Carkeet, David. *The Greatest Slump of All Time*. New York: Harper and Row, 1984.

Charyn, Jerome. *The Seventh Babe*. New York: Arbor House, 1979.

Cohler, David Keith. *Gamemaker*. New York: Doubleday, 1980.

Cooney, Ellen. *All the Way Home*. New York: Putnam, 1984.

Coover, Robert. *The Universal Baseball Association, J. Henry Waugh, Prop.* New York: Signet, 1968.

Doctorow, E. L. *Ragtime*. New York: Random House, 1975.

Everett, Percival L. *Suder*. New York: Viking, 1983.

Greenberg, Eric Rolfe. *The Celebrant*. 1983. New York: Penguin, 1986.

Gregorich, Barbara. *She's on First*. New York: Contemporary Books, 1987.

Harris, Mark. *Bang the Drum Slowly*. 1956. New York: Dell, 1973.

———. *The Southpaw*. Indianapolis: Bobbs-Merrill, 1953.

Hays, Donald. *The Dixie Association*. New York: Simon and Schuster, 1984.

Hough, John Jr. *The Conduct of the Game*. New York: Harcourt Brace Jovanovich, 1986.

Kahn, Roger. *The Seventh Game*. New York: New American Library, 1982.

Kennedy, William. *Ironweed*. New York: Penguin, 1984.

Kinsella, W. P. *The Iowa Baseball Confederacy*. New York: Ballantine, 1986.

———. *Shoeless Joe*. Boston: Houghton Mifflin, 1982.

Kluger, Steve. *Changing Pitches*. New York: St. Martin's, 1984.
Lorenz, Tom. *Guys Like Us*. New York: Viking, 1980.
McManus, James. *Chin Music*. New York: Crown, 1985.
Magnuson, James. *The Rundown*. New York: Dial, 1977.
Malamud, Bernard. *The Natural*. New York: Dell, 1952.
Mayer, Robert. *The Grace of Shortstops*. New York: Doubleday, 1984.
Morgenstein, Gary. *The Man Who Wanted to Play Centerfield for the Yankees*. New York: Atheneum, 1983.
Neugeboren, Jay. *Sam's Legacy*. New York: Holt, Rinehart and Winston, 1974.
Parker, Robert B. *Mortal Stakes*. Boston: Houghton Mifflin, 1975.
Plimpton, George. *The Curious Case of Sidd Finch*. New York: Macmillan, 1987.
Pomeranz, Gary. *Out at Home*. Boston: Houghton Mifflin, 1985.
Ritz, David. *The Man Who Wanted to Bring the Dodgers Back to Brooklyn*. New York: Simon and Schuster, 1981.
Rosen, R. D. *Strike Three, You're Dead*. New York: Signet, 1984.
Roth, Philip. *The Great American Novel*. New York: Holt, Rinehart and Winston, 1973.
Sheed, Wilfred. *The Boys of Winter*. New York: Knopf, 1987.
Small, David. *Almost Famous*. New York: W. W. Norton, 1982.
Snyder, Don J. *Veteran's Park*. New York: Franklin Watts, 1987.
Stein, Harry. *Hoopla*. New York: Knopf, 1983.
Vogan, Sara. *In Shelley's Leg*. St. Paul, Minn.: Graywolf Press, 1985.
Willard, Nancy. *Things Invisible to See*. New York: Knopf, 1984.

The Bench Warmer with a Thousand Faces: Sports Fiction and the Democratic Ideal

ROBERT W. COCHRAN

Having paved the way for the favorable critical reception of sports fiction in America, baseball fiction deserving of consideration as serious literature is now being practiced by its third generation of authors. Ring Lardner, the patriarch and a generation unto himself, was followed rather directly by Mark Harris, though perhaps scarcely at all by Bernard Malamud, Robert Coover, and Philip Roth, all authors of the very first rank, each of whom has written just one baseball novel. To these four second-generation worthies must be added Eliot Asinof, for both his novel *Man on Spikes* (1955) and his study of the Black Sox scandal, *Eight Men Out* (1963). Distinguished offspring of *Eight Men Out* are W. P. Kinsella's *Shoeless Joe* (1982), Eric Rolfe Greenberg's *The Celebrant* (1983), and Harry Stein's *Hoopla* (1983), as well as an Off-Broadway play, Lawrence Kelley's *Out!*

Now, with splendid contributions from an ever-growing list of authors that includes—in addition to Kinsella, Greenberg, and Stein—Barry Beckham, David Carkeet, Donald Hays, John Hough, Jr., Robert Mayer, Philip O'Connor, George Plimpton, and Nancy Willard, novels and short stories with baseball as an ingredient have emerged in great profusion but not so much that at least some meaningful patterns may be discerned.

As sports fiction—baseball fiction, especially—has come of age in the 1970s and '80s, the worth of the common citizen has emerged as a major theme. It is as though several authors had anticipated a pronouncement Thomas Boswell made as a Parthian shot in a syndicated column released during the summer of 1988: "One reason that baseball films and fiction almost always fail is that hyperbole rarely works except in reality." Realizing before the appearance of Boswell's column that the point is sound, many serious authors of sports fiction have concentrated on protagonists who are not star athletes and on plots that do not follow a pennant drive or a Super Bowl week as ready-made scaffolds for organization.

Sport no doubt initially does invite a literary treatment of extremes, since the sports world of action on the field affords on the one hand a realm of heroes and hero worship, of romantic promise and of pastoral setting, and on the other, of worn-out arms, torn-up knees, and careers that at best are brief when compared to a lifespan, which in its turn is altogether too brief. And, since both literature for juveniles, whether past or present, and moving pictures for a mass audience, even to the present day, continue to supply a presumably yearned-for, literal, scoreboard victory, it follows that a sobering, corrective sense of tragedy would seem to be the remaining line to be followed in serious literature. Or, if not precisely tragedy, then certainly the high road of elevated significance and cosmic proportion. And so it is with Malamud's *The Natural,* Coover's *Universal Baseball Association,* and Roth's mock-heroic *The Great American Novel.* It is all the more heartening, then, that what today has been arrived at is a settled sense of coexistence between sport and art, born of a confidence that the honest pursuit of accomplishment in whatever human endeavor, and of fidelity to self under whatever sorts of pressures, need offer no apology for themselves.

Of the many trends and themes emerging from the extraordinarily rich sports fiction of the last two decades, a pronounced emphasis has been given to expressions of faith in democracy. Such a faith is not likely to attach to the star athlete, or at any rate certainly not to the star athlete while he or she is on the playing field, living life "all the way up," as Hemingway's Jake Barnes says of bullfighters. From a competitive realm that features Tom Boswell's "hyperbolic" reality—a realm of potential soaring heroes and Casey-at-the-Bat goats—several authors of fine fiction have created protagonists who occupy an intermediate position between the star on the field and the fan in the bleachers—a coach, an umpire, a sportswriter—in the service of large democratic themes. Eschewing the literary equivalents of Ruth and DiMaggio, these authors concentrate on the journeyman ballplayer, or the professional player as exploited chattel, or the successful high school player become big-league umpire, or the unsuccessful prep school player become sportswriter—or the boy on the sandlot—in a demonstration that sports (and again, especially baseball) supply sustaining threads in the fabric of American life. The upshot of this emphasis is the clear implication that the outlook of Arthur Miller in "Tragedy and the Common Man," as the playwright titled his celebrated companion-piece to *Death of a Salesman*, can be revised; that perhaps in the present generation the Willy Lomans of the Republic can be helped to recognize in themselves the carpenters and farmers they are meant to be and can learn to take pride and pleasure in their work, so that further tragic waste can be averted. The fathers will no longer need to fill their sons "so full of hot air [that the sons] could never stand taking orders from anybody," as Biff Loman so accurately describes his condition, having fallen from the perilous heights of stardom as a high school quarterback. Perhaps with the proper perspective the Biff Lomans of America can derive solid satisfaction from being "a dime a dozen" and can come to assess their personal value in less-demeaning figures of speech. In a nation still largely gauged to the Waterman and Peters model of a "search for excellence" as the only lifetime pursuit that can lead to authentic success, these authors of sports fiction assert that a place must be found for the ordinary achievements and enjoyments of the average citizen.

It may be instructive to return to Boswell's 1988 column, and in conjunction with it, drop back in time to the 1984 movie *The Natural*, starring Robert Redford, and to Bernard Malamud's 1952 novel, *The Natural*. In his essay composed on the occasion of the one-hundredth anniversary of the popular favorite "Casey at the Bat," Donald Hall reminds us that we are the Mudville crowd, first cheering on our hero and then agonizing over his failure. In that same position, the reader of Malamud's novel hopes along with the character Iris Lemon that Roy will break out of his slump, as for a time, with Iris's encouragement, he does. But of course Roy does not succeed finally in the novel, just as of course he must be made to succeed in the movie version, happy endings remaining *de rigueur* in sports films.

Malamud's title should be appreciated for its ambiguity: Roy Hobbs not only has a natural, God-given talent for baseball—first as a pitcher whiffing the Whammer and then as a major league hitter— but Roy *(roi)* Hobbs *(habitants)* also is emphatically and perhaps even particularly susceptible to human error. Still, Roy is one of the select few superb athletes for whom Harriet Bird reserves her silver bullets. Unlike Robert Redford's Hobbs, Malamud's does not (cannot) slug a dramatic game- and pennant-winning home run. Malamud's Roy has erred, has failed to learn a valuable lesson from his personal history, and so has been condemned to repeat that error.

Having undergone the torture of being gutshot by Harriet Bird, Roy nonetheless becomes an enthralled New York Knight for a second time, this time enthralled by the "sick-breasted" Memo Paris. Hobbs is a tragic figure, and he gains tragic stature by recognizing that he has failed to learn. The prideful Roy Hobbs considers it beneath his dignity to settle for and to settle down with Iris Lemon, very pointedly because Iris is a thirty-three-year-old grandmother. The only bride acceptable to the great Roy Hobbs is a veritable Marilyn Monroe. Malamud sees his audience as a society bedazzled by beauty contests, a society where wives are chosen for a surface pulchritude that can enhance their husbands' images and further their husbands' careers.

Malamud's keen interest in this topic is shown also in his short story "The Girl of My Dreams," in which the protagonist early in the story admits that he prefers a "looker." Eventually he learns enough to save his soul and his writing career by embracing his plump and middle-aged but doting and supportive landlady. And Mark Harris shares this concern of Malamud's in the third of his Henry Wiggen novels, A Ticket for a Seamstitch.

Since athletic-star talent and movie-star beauty are not vouchsafed many of us, what evaluation of self is possible in a star-struck, media-hype, personality-cult society, authors of the third generation of American sport fiction seem to be asking and answering. In this undertaking they are following the lead of Malamud and Harris but with a more positive approach and a more firm, because longer developed, outcome. The topical approaches are essentially two in number: first, the removal of belittling stereotypes—those handy putdowns so frequently seized upon in a young and diverse nation of immigrants, whatever the arrival date, but now to be overcome through efforts at consciousness raising. A special subheading here features the upgrading of the reputation of have-nots through revision of accepted history of the Black Sox scandal of 1919, from the stunned condemnation of the players during the 1920s and beyond to the more recent identification of owner greed as the root cause of betrayal of the public trust. In addition to the attempt to remove blinding stereotypes, a second pronounced approach has been the explicit celebration of ordinariness. Ordinariness is, of course, by definition the normal human condition; it is also, or so it might be argued, a basic tenet of our Founding Fathers' ringing declaration. If the self sung by Richard Ford in The Sportswriter is no exuberant Walt Whitman, Ford is no less the celebrant of the democratic "word En-Masse" than was the good gray poet of a century and more ago.

The first image of the protagonist in respectable baseball fiction is that which is referred to familiarly today as the "dumb jock," ironically revealing in his own self and voice his coarseness, ignorance, and even stupidity. This style-setting protagonist is patronized by the reader, who cannot match the narrator's accomplishments on the field but who can share a laugh with the author at the character's expense and so cut the mighty down to size, whether hero or goat. In avoiding extravagant praise of the literary pioneer on the one hand and condescension toward him on the other, it is to be noted that Ring Lardner initiated with his busher, Jack Keefe, a tradition of the athlete as narrator that has been followed with distinction by Mark Harris with his "author" Henry Wiggen—and in altered but still indebted form by, among others, Jay Neugeboren with his chapters of "slave" narration by Mason Tidewater in *Sam's Legacy,* Harry Stein with his fictional George (Buck) Weaver of the historical Black Sox in *Hoopla,* and John Hough, Jr., with his umpire, Lee Malcolm, in *The Conduct of the Game.*

In assessing reader reaction to Lardner's character, Walton R. Patrick is surely correct when he says, ". . . the Keefe stories . . . had the appeal of humor to one class of readers and of satire to another . . ." (47). That is, some readers saw but others failed to notice the extent to which Lardner distanced himself from his busher by means of the epistolary technique, just as patently as the Southern-gentleman authors in the tradition of Old Southwest humor identified themselves with—indeed, virtually *as*—the narrator-observers within their stories. Formal and articulate, these narrators relayed to their audiences, in cacographic spelling and fractured grammar, entertaining tales of ring-tailed roarers and latter-day Mrs. Malaprops. In founding the literary tradition of the athlete who as first-person narrator was often made to look decidedly foolish, Lardner fixed in print the stereotype of the athlete as limited in experience, education, intelligence—any or all of the above.

In his novel *Hoopla,* from the vantage point of the 1980s, Harry Stein assigns his fictional character George D. Weaver an attitude that humanizes and upgrades in perceived intelligence and sensitivity one of the infamous Black Sox of 1919 (even if not the greatest player among them—Shoeless Joe Jackson had a doubly great grievance against Charles Comiskey, the skinflint owner, and the pitcher Eddie Cicotte was a heavily-mortgaged farmer). Stein's choice of the historical Weaver for a fictional role rests on Weaver's having been aware of the World Series fix but having been unable to bring himself finally to participate in it; yet he was banned all the same by the inflexible and self-righteous first commissioner of baseball, Judge Kenesaw Mountain Landis. And so Stein's Weaver is emphatically a character with whom the reader can sympathize, warily at first and then ever more fully as Weaver's moral decency is seen both in and of itself and in marked contrast to the opportunism and amorality of the novel's alternating narrator, columnist Luther Pond. What Stein has his George Weaver say of baseball reporters in general and of the author of *You Know Me Al* in particular can well be imagined to be the opinion held by an athlete of whatever era:

> Us ballplayers did not call him Ring, but Old Owl Eyes. . . . When that book came out, there was all kinds of gas about how Old Owl Eyes was a great genius, and how fine it was that for the first time us ballplayers were not made out to be heroes, but just regular guys, and that in the book was what we were really like. Well, we did not ask to be heroes in the first place, but only got that way on account of the scribes themselves. . . . But this is how it always was with the writers, anyway. They were the ones that were really simple-minded, not us. (160–61)

A particularly well-contrived playing upon negative stereotypes is a story by W. P. Kinsella entitled "The Valley of the Schmoon." The story is not so incidentally a tribute to the comic genius Al Capp, whose "Li'l Abner" comic strip lends the story its title and whose unhappy final years contribute to the story's point. That point is delayed until the final sentence, in a switch reminiscent of Mark Twain's early work "The Dandy Frightening the Squatter," reminiscent even though Kinsella doubles the twist of the Twain reversal of expectations. What the two stories have in common is that in each the relatively elitist figure gets his comeuppance from the supposedly unsophisticated, apparently outclassed bumpkin. In "The Valley of the Schmoon" the joke is played on the highly educated, well-paid rookie ballplayer who is the increasingly alarmed passenger in the narrator's car; the joke is even more on the reader, however, who may grow a bit uneasy at the improbability of the story's premises but who is forced to admit that he or she has been outfoxed by Kinsella—a realization delayed until the reader has encountered the twist revealed in the final, uncompleted sentence.

Once the reader has finished the story and has viewed it in retrospect, he will appreciate how shrewdly the old coach must have maneuvered the rookie into what the rookie comes to fear is a potential death seat. Reminiscing about the old days, pretending to think he may be repeating himself, and explaining that he intends to commit suicide one day by crashing his car into an interstate overpass, the old-timer frightens the rookie into jumping from the car at his first opportunity and running off up the highway, away from what he regards as a despairing has-been whose life has degenerated into meaninglessness. But Kinsella has skillfully planted in the old coach's monologue three salient details. First is the story of how Babe Ruth as a rookie pitcher was victimized by Red Sox veterans into sleeping with his pitching arm in a sling to strengthen the arm before his pitching debut. Second is the information that in addition to being highly paid, the Mariners rookie is a college graduate, the fiancé of a psychologist and the son of a Shell Oil executive—in short, enviably well connected. And third is the narrator's assertion that his wife Lucy, whom he admits he still loves and toward whom he says he bears no grudge, divorced him to marry an owner of "six Ace Hardware stores." Then, as the rookie streaks down the highway in the story's penultimate moments, the narrator imperturbably follows up his "Geez, was it somethin' I said?" with words that demonstrate that the narrator is well aware that it was and that Kinsella has tricked the reader:

> Rookies. They never learn. Hell, I'd been in the majors for three years before I ever heard the word *sophisticated*. Let's see, by the time I get to Seattle it will be four A.M. That'll be seven in the East. I can phone Lucy before she goes to work. . . . (118)

Lucy is still the coach's wife, it dawns on the reader; the coach's tale of woe is an elaborate fabrication; and the coach's excuse for stopping here poses a threat to the rookie only because the coach has cunningly counted on the rookie to be attentive to the details of the coach's announced plans to commit the perfect, undetected suicide. Thus Kinsella shows the reader up as the true rookie, hooked on the stereotype of the old-time ballplayer as a maudlin and nostalgic recaller of the good old days and as a hopelessly naive revealer of his own considerable shortcomings.[1]

Readers. Maybe now they'll learn.

A second image of baseball fiction after that of the dumb jock is perhaps, properly speaking, not an image but rather an issue, at least once one proceeds beyond Malamud's Roy Hobbs and into characters created by the third generation of writers. This second image or issue is the hero, best exemplified in the words assigned by Eric Rolfe Greenberg to his fictional adaptation of the real-life sportswriter Hugh Fullerton, words about the hero Christy Mathewson that Fullerton addresses to the protagonist of *The Cele-brant,* Jackie Kapp:

> "Have you ever considered what he is to himself? What it's like to be Christy Mathewson? . . . The world makes you a god and hates you for being human, and if you plead for understanding it hates you all the more. Heroes are never forgiven their success, still less their fail-ure. . . . I want him to throw a no-hit game tomorrow, not for his sake but for mine. And don't you want the same, so you can cover him in glory? We're the worms that eat at the bodies of the great." (196)

Once readers have progressed beyond these two isolating con-ceptions of the performer on the field—conceptions of the stupid, self-absorbed athlete and of the supposedly superhuman hero—once the ground is cleared or raked smooth and level, one can read the current stage of some of the best sports fiction, where the human subjects are more nearly you and me (our name is Legion) and the topic our relationship to the game rather than the game itself. Among many of the works of the third generation of sports fiction, the protagonists are not the spotlighted stars. Even apparent exceptions, the fictional Buck Weaver of Harry Stein's *Hoopla* and the slugger Hog Durham of Donald Hays's *The Dixie Association,* for instance, are Ishmaels—outcasts whose survival as self-respect-ing human beings derives from their acceptance of figurative Quee-quegs and hence of themselves.

In this second but foremost of the two games involved in sports fiction—the game of literature—the reader is not mere spectator. He or she is invited to identify so closely with the protagonist as to be a virtual participant. Perhaps the most remarkable feature of Hough's *The Conduct of the Game* is that even while Hough pays tribute to the fictional tradition preceding him—and especially to Harris—he lets his protagonist, emphatically a common man, ex-hibit his decency and his intelligence as the teller of his own tale. Hough has carried the implications of the theme of faith in democ-racy to its logical conclusion, whereas in earlier decades, first Lardner and then Harris distanced themselves from their charac-ters.

A most influential figure in the shift away from author conspiring with his reader to laugh at the athlete is Eliot Asinof, himself once a professional baseball player. Both in fiction, with *Man on Spikes,* and in nonfiction, with what Harry Stein authoritatively calls the "seminal" *Eight Men Out,* Asinof began what has amounted to a revisionist interpretation of baseball history. From this perspective, the inherent dignity of the individual in a democratic society is emphasized in the playing off of the protagonists against baseball executives and even exalted commissioners. Thus the reader's identification with the main character is twofold. First, athletic identification with the protagonist feeds, and feeds upon, beguiling dreams of stardom that the reader has carried over from childhood. Next is a far more realistic political and economic identification with the fictionalized Buck Weaver or Joe Jackson or the wholly fictional Mike Kutner, in these novels set in an era when professional athletes were poorly paid. Just as the Black Sox figures provide instances of the underdogs exploited by a power-drunk owner, so is Asinof's Kutner of *Man on Spikes* as surely a man on a bed of spikes as he is an athlete wearing spiked shoes.

A second gain that Hough makes over Lardner and Harris is in the low-key but deep-rooted way he finds for relating Lee Malcolm's experience to the reader's experience. The national pastime is very often touted for its broad appeal, an appeal that cuts across levels of income and taste. Hough's appeal is different, but it is as surely democratic and also less suspect as an instance of shared experience:

> Now Pam and I sat down in the dark, cool grass along the first base line, exactly where I'd plunked down after a ball game with Joey and Howie Gladding and Robert Nailer and the rest. When had it ended? What day in our lives had we played here for the last time? There had been one final game, one last swing of a bat, one last out made, and we'd mounted our bikes and pedaled home in a spring dusk for the last time ever, without knowing it. I wished I could remember that time. (57–58)

Hough carries the protagonist out of any team lineup and into a role in the game that the reader might be able to learn to perform, the role of arbiter. And then that protagonist is also victimized by the members of baseball's power structure.

In *The Conduct of the Game,* Hough brings to life not a major league ballplayer (Lee Malcolm's older brother Joey, dead at age 18 in a car crash, is the Dimaggio-like "natural" athlete) but rather a quite good (all-conference) high school outfielder who becomes for a brief period a major league umpire. This is not the stuff of romantic dreams. The story Lee Malcolm tells of himself concerns not the materials of boyhood fantasies, but instead the requisites for solid achievement. Lee's career choice is not the goal of starry-eyed, red-white-and-blue-blooded American boys; it is not to be sneered at, however—most readers (fans), at one time or another, probably here agreed with the outraged fan who screams "Kill the umpire." Hough's novel is not set on the plane of tragedy, but Lee Malcolm qualifies as a hero of sorts, a hero of properly scaled-down democratic proportions. In trying to qualify as a major league umpire and succeeding, and in fulfilling his obligations to the game of baseball and his responsibilities to others and to himself, Lee Malcolm remains true to his own better nature.

Hough exhibits a marked awareness of themes developed by his predecessors in this literary subgenre. The most obvious indebtedness is to Harris and his *Bang the Drum Slowly*. From the treatment of Lucinda Fragosi in the opening chapter of *Conduct of the Game*—the hapless butt of schoolbus joking until Lee's brother Joey, the star athlete, calls a halt to the youthful callousness—the practice of "ragging" is condemned, in a clear echoing of Henry Wiggen's final utterance in *Bang the Drum Slowly*: "From here on in I rag nobody." The list of underdogs not to be ragged is long, if not absolutely exhaustive. In addition to Lucinda of the novel's prelude section, it includes alcoholics in the person of Lee's father, Frank; little guys like Eddie Snyder, a would-be umpire; jocks assumed to be stereotypically stupid ("[Pam] said Coach Maretta was dumb. He wasn't." [47]); blacks (baseball star Ron Chapman); gays—a former English teacher who is now Lee Malcolm's umpiring partner, Roy Van Arsadle; and, most importantly, just plain Janes and Bills like Lee's girl friend Vicky Vadnais and the first-person narrator himself. No reader will fail to see this stress pattern, and no reader of Mark Harris will fail to recognize it as an expansion on the lesson Henry Wiggen learned from coming to see Bruce Pearson's human worth during Bruce's final playing season, before he died of Hodgkin's disease.

Hough makes Lee Malcolm life size rather than the mythic larger than life. Nor does Hough invert the heroic; he does not reduce his protagonist to feckless cosmic pawn. Malamud's Roy Hobbs fails, both publicly as a hero and privately as a man. And Lee Malcolm would seem to a public within the novel to fail (were any public reaction included by Hough, which it is not)—for Lee is forced to resign after just his rookie year as a big-league umpire. Knowing the "inside story," however, which no newspaper reporter will ever even try to dig out, the reader sees Lee as unquestionably a successful human being. If the stage of *The Conduct of the Game* is not elevated and if the style is less than pyrotechnic, neither are the forces of temptation and manipulation at all distant for the reader. No translation is required: the character Pam Rogers recalls to the reader his own physically toothsome but ultimately undesirable high school crush, and the commissioner behaves like the reader's own high-handed, image-protecting boss.

The ultimate villain of *The Conduct of the Game* is not greed, as represented in the Black Sox novels and, rather allegorically, in *The Natural* by the team owner Judge Goodwill Banner and the one-eyed gambler Gus Sands. The ultimate villain of Hough's work is respectability, particularly in the person of the commissioner of baseball. The commissioner appears in a cameo role also facilitated by the revisionist view of the Black Sox scandal. The commissioner as a kind of latter-day unyielding Judge Landis represents society in hounding Van Arsdale to his death (whether that death is suicide or accident) and in requesting Malcolm's resignation. Thus Hough, like Asinof, Kinsella, Stein, and Greenberg, exposes immorality on what passes for the high road of integrity in representations made in print to hoodwink the public.

For all his championing of the common man, Hough does not emerge as a sentimentalist. Vicky Vadnais's father, the owner of a neighborhood bar, is a particularly well-drawn working stiff, utterly convincing in his love for his daughter and in his hope that Lee will become his daughter's husband. If Lee does not, Mr. Vadnais knows that Vicky will in all probability marry a longtime suitor who simply is not worthy of her.

The protagonist's fundamental decency as depicted in *The Conduct of the Game* is in essence an adult version of the cloyingly didactic school-sports novel written for a juvenile audience. But for that very reason, in these secular, iconoclastic and dry-eyed times, the portrayal of such decency places enormous demands on the author, since, without constant application of taste and vigilance, wholesomeness readily turns saccharine and silly.

In "K-Mart," like "The Valley of the Schmoon," one of the best of several fine stories in Kinsella's collection *The Further Adventures of Slugger McBatt,* the first-person narrator raises the besetting question of where the line is to be drawn between sports fiction and fiction that is not to be so categorized:

Jamie Kirkendahl [the narrator when he was a boy] would say this is not a story about baseball. Perhaps I [the narrator as an adult and a professional writer] should let you [the reader] be the judge of that. (78)

The reader has little difficulty in judging, thanks to such passages as the following:

I suppose it was sometime in my twenties when I realized that my *baseball days,* those three summers I spent in Northside, had so far been the best days of my life. That time when baseball was like the sun lighting my days. . . . My suspicions, shadows, gray, disturbing, like animals skulking about the edge of a camp, came in the form of disturbing thoughts about Cory, mixed with pleasant reveries about baseball. I dreamed of the long, sunny afternoons on the field where our endless game went on from the time the dew left the grass until it was too dark to see the ball. . . .

I loved those times, the tense, uncaring heat of August, the air thick, sweat drizzling into my eyebrows. I remember grabbing the bottom of my damp T-shirt, pulling it up and wiping my forehead, drying my eyes before heading for the plate. I remember squinting through a haze of perspiration from my spot in right field, the earth aerated by cheeky prairie dogs who peeked and chittered all the long, lazy afternoons. (85)

The question with respect to this story, and often elsewhere, may be debatable; yet what matters is not whether the answer given is that this is or is not a story about baseball but how one qualifies the response. In any case, the reader is forever, and properly so, in the presence of a passage from Wright Morris's *The Huge Season,* which Mark Harris chose as the epigraph for *Bang the Drum Slowly:*

He wiped his face with the towel again. "Old man, a book can have Chicago in it, and not be about Chicago. It can have a tennis player in it without being about a tennis player. . . ."

Kinsella's "K-Mart" both is and is not a sports story, which is but another way of saying that although third-generation writers of sports fiction may profitably tantalize with the question, any strict division between "life" and sport as provinces for fictional treatment would represent precisely that benighted attitude which the current generation of authors has striven to overcome. In "K-Mart," Kinsella uses sandlot participation in baseball as a reference point for poignant recollection of the narrator's adolescent years. The result is a nicely understated preference for a sandlot ball field over the same acreage after it has become a site of commercial development. The story also produces, more personally, a well-modulated tribute to Corrina Mazeppa, the daughter of immigrants and a high school dropout. The spiritual business that the story transacts is the restoration in retrospect of Cory's teenage virtue, whereupon her life is viewed as sadly wasted even well before her untimely death.

Many readers will wish to raise Kinsella's "K-Mart" question about Richard Ford's excellent novel *The Sportswriter*. Indeed, it is probably fair to say that many will argue that *The Sportswriter* is not a sports novel at all. To those readers, the relatively slight attention paid directly to sports in the novel, and that almost exclusively from the angle of reportage and commentary, will buttress the position that Ford's novel does not fall within the purview of sport literature. But *The Sportswriter* has something to say about the place of sport in American life and about the function of sport in personal relationships. Still more valuable are its periodic definitions of sportswriting as opposed to what first-person narrator Frank Bascombe terms "real writing." Even more particularly, in Frank Bascombe's insistence on his own (and the reader's own) ordinariness, *The Sportswriter* takes its place very comfortably in the company of the work of Harris, Stein, Kinsella, and Hough, to name just a few of the authors whose works are indubitably to be labeled sports fiction.

Ford does not attempt to analyze athletic events in close, technical fashion. Such a feature is unlikely in a present-day sports novel. In calling *The Celebrant* "simply the best baseball novel ever written," Kinsella presumably expresses his admiration for Greenberg's rather astonishing success in interweaving illuminating and evocatively detailed accounts of action on the field (although these are re-creations of actual major league games) with *The Celebrant*'s further intricacies. Among Greenberg's accomplishments are his impressive handling of social, economic, and sports history; his establishing of the mutual admiration beteen the fictional Christy Mathewson and the totally fictional protagonist of the novel, Jackie Kapp; and his paralleling of Mathewson's sports performance "gems" with Jackie Kapp's artistic designing and rendering of gemstones in the creation of celebratory jewelry.

The experience of reading *The Sportswriter* is one of anticipating developments that would tidy up Frank Bascombe's life, or at least some significant part of it, only to have those anticipations checked by what does or, more accurately, does not develop. The experience is nonetheless remarkably free of frustration for the reader, even though Frank Bascombe is such a convincingly decent fellow that the reader hopes time and again for some solution or resolution of Frank's state. It is a state that one is tempted to call suspended, but that temptation must be withstood. The reader of *The Sportswriter* may call to mind John Ciardi's invitation to honor twentieth-century poets because, unlike the fireside poets of an earlier day, they "won't tell us what they don't know."

Two literary parallels to *The Sportswriter* that suggest themselves are first, the Book of Job, Job's prime virtue being not the patience traditionally ascribed to him but rather a scrupulous intellectual honesty; and second, the distinction Eric Greenberg draws between baseball and life by having his fictional Christy Mathewson disagree with attempts to find analogies between the game of baseball and life:

> "After all, baseball isn't anything like life. . . . In truth, nothing in the game appealed to me as much as its unreality. Baseball is all clean lines and clear decisions. Wouldn't life be far easier if it consisted of a series of definitive calls: safe or out, fair or foul, strike or ball. Oh, for a life like that, where every day produces a clear winner and an equally clear loser, and back to it the next day with the slate wiped clean and the teams starting out equal." (86–87)

Like life, *The Sportswriter* is inconclusive, although Ford's novel ends inevitably; ends, that is, in a fashion absolutely consistent with its meaning. While Frank Bascombe would also reject the help offered Job by the comforters and while Ford will not say what he does not know, what he does know more than suffices. Indeed, it positively rewards.

Accustomed as the reader of modern literature is to stories of the unlived life, Ford's very title—*The Sportswriter*—will recall to many the Walker Percy title *The Moviegoer*. Ford's title, like Percy's, will at first suggest some such generic title as *The Bystander*. The story, the reader supposes, is to be one of a lack of commitment recognized too late (Joyce's "The Dead" or "A Painful Case," James's "The Beast in the Jungle") or providentially reversed by love *(The Moviegoer)*. This latter expectation is particularly strong, and particularly well counteracted, in the novel's Easter chapter, chapter 9, which ends with Frank's feeling himself "saved in the only way I can be *(pro tempore)*" (238).

Each of several solutions to a predicament of personal isolation appears to be a distinct possibility in *The Sportswriter*. Each time Frank Bascombe thinks of the death at age nine of his beloved son Ralph, and more especially each time Frank hears sounds of grief emanating from the cemetery beside his house, the likelihood seems great that Ford will have Frank profit from another's moving exhibition of genuine grief, just as Henry James had his cold and withdrawn John Marcher learn true emotion. But Ford's recurrent use of Ralph's death at the age of nine ends with Frank's saying, ". . . I realized that my own mourning is finally over. . . . Grief, real grief, is relatively short, though mourning can be long" (374). Forewarned as he has been by Frank's belief that Joyce's conception of epiphanies is "a good example of [literary] falsehood" (119), readers have only themselves to blame for their mistaken assumption.

The possibility that love will provide a release from what the reader may regard as Frank's emotional predicament is never the issue in Frank's relationship with the Lebanese woman Selma Jassim, neither while he teaches for a term at Berkshire College nor when he calls her on the telephone during what seems to be his time of crisis late in the novel. Much more likely is a reconciliation with "X", as Frank regularly refers to her, the ex-wife he still loves and who still loves him. X is a fine golfer, though, and has returned to serious play following her divorce from Frank. Once he has combined a working definition of what it means to be a sportswriter according to Frank's lexicon with the detail that Frank as a teenager was unable to develop into a competent first baseman, Ford can slip in as unobtrusive symbolism the fact that X plays golf so well. A gentler hint at the incompatibility of two people who once were married and who still love one another is hard to imagine. And so when Frank missteps with X after Walter Luckett's suicide, the reader understands that a reconciliation is not possible.

Among the other many women in Frank's life, only Vicki Arcenault and Catherine Flaherty require comment. Vicki looks particularly promising: she has the same first name as Vicky Vadnais of Hough's *The Conduct of the Game* and, similarly, a French last name; she has the same physical attractiveness, straightforward speech, and self-possession as Hough's Vicky; and her father, although he has graduated from Texas A&M with a degree in engineering, now works as a toll-taker in a booth on the New Jersey Turnpike. Present in only one scene in the novel, Wade Arcenault wins the respect of Frank Bascombe and of the reader in very much the same manner and to the same considerable degree as Mr. Vadnais does in *The Conduct of the Game*.

Catherine Flaherty is the late arrival in *The Sportswriter*. At last report she is trying on medical school for size and seeing Frank from time to time, while he, too, in an even more unhurried way, is deciding what he'll do next, and even whether he'll do something other than what he is now doing, which by accepted American standards is not very much. Among the fringe benefits of Frank's current sojourn in Florida is his meeting and enjoying the company of several pleasant, respectable but quite undistinguished relatives (Buster Bascombe, for one self-explanatory name) from both his father's and his mother's sides of his family. It is significant that these Florida retirees are presented more sympathetically than are X's affluent parents in Michigan.

This preference for prototypical retirees, at ease with themselves, over X's parents, who effect a late reconciliation only because they are afraid of dying alone, is but a very minor detail contributing to the major theme of *The Sportswriter:* the celebration of the ordinary and Frank's calm but repeated insistence on his own ordinariness. Very early, Frank describes human experience as "the normal applauseless life of us all" (10). A characteristic observation later in the novel is "for my lights they thought too little of themselves and didn't realize how much all of us are in the very same boat, and how much it is an imperfect boat" (220). Or again, "We've all felt that way, I'm confident, since there's no way that I could feel what hundreds of millions of other citizens haven't" (375). Frank does acknowledge that "None of our lives is really ordinary; nothing humdrum in our delights or our disasters" (107). Still, Frank does not simply insist upon but he wholeheartedly and even cheerfully accepts the notion that "Anyone could be anyone else in most ways. Face facts" (81). In Frank's particular case, this sense of self is in no wise a diminished sense. Even though the reader will wish to rate Frank higher than he rates himself, Frank's refusal to be self-congratulatory is one of his great virtues.

Again, in Frank's case his sense of his own ordinariness seems to others to prevent his developing his literary career beyond the single collection of short stories he has published and the one novel he loses. Branding "transcendent themes in life" a "lie of literature and the liberal arts" (16), Bascombe disappoints those well-wishers, mostly academics, who expect more from him. But Bascombe speaks somewhat ambiguously of those he considers "real writers." While he respects them, he is mistrustful of their tendentiousness.

Bascombe derives genuine satisfaction from his sportswriting, although here again Ford plays upon reader expectation by arousing conventional pieties and then methodically confounding them. Early in the novel the plot builds toward an interview Frank is to conduct with Herb Wallagher, a former professional football lineman who is now a paraplegic. Well after the unproductive interview has occurred, an interview during which Frank learns that Herb is no longer retained by the Detroit Lions as a source of inspiration and comes to see that Herb is, quite simply, "crazy" and no inspiration to anyone, the sportswriter toys briefly with trying to salvage the story that he was sent to get from Herb. But Frank's professional judgment is sound; there is no story here. Unquestionably, Frank knows his trade: his description of how to compose a good sports story,

> . . . put together some useful ideas, . . . just a detail or two to act as magnets for what else will occur to me in the next days, which is the way good sportswriting gets done (208)

would hold true for any successful piece of writing. It is hardly incidental that when the sportswriter must leave Haddam, New Jersey, doing so with no sense of where he is headed, he winds up in his office at the sports magazine's headquarters in New York City. The importance lies in his not finding himself by getting caught up (lost) in work but rather in his finding at his place of work—or being found at work by—Catherine Flaherty, a magazine apprentice who is an admirer of Frank's published sportswriting. That is, Frank does not take charge of his own fate, which is consistent with his belief that life does not allow anyone to do so, no matter how hard the struggle.

Including the predictable recognition of sports as "the perfect *lingua franca* for . . . crablike advances between successive boyfriends and husbands" (135) and as "always a good distraction from life at its dreariest" (186), Ford goes well beyond a consideration of the function of sports in American society. Introduction of *The Sportswriter*'s theme comes very early in the novel, in a sentence fragment among enumerations by his ex-wife of "mistakes" she believes Frank makes in concentrating his life too narrowly: "Sportswriting and being an ordinary citizen." (13) If that moment comes too early for more than speculation, the reader need not be tentative for very long; for *The Sportswriter* as a whole says that sportswriting, as opposed to sports performance at some high level of competition, is a very valuable enterprise for coming to grips with impermanence: "(Muslims, let me tell you, are a race of people who understand impermanence. More so even than sportswriters.)" (224) Frank judges that when he was still an aspiring "real writer" he had become

> . . . stuck in bad stereotypes. All my men were too serious, too brooding and humorless, characters at loggerheads with imponderable dilemmas, and much less interesting than my female characters, who were always . . . free spirited and sharpwitted. (46)

Now, as a sportswriter, Frank studies athletes, people he regards as typically "within themselves," by which he means that they are self-possessed but also that that admirable confidence in their own ability is confidence only within a severely circumscribed arena.

This progress from "bad stereotypes" to emancipation from the tendency to pigeonhole others is given summary statement in a passage midway in the novel, in which virtually all the chief recommendations of the work are included:

> At least as a stranger to almost everyone and a sportswriter to boot, I have a clean slate almost every day of my life,[2] a chance not to be negative, to give someone unknown a pat on the back, to recognize courage and improvement, to take the battle with cynicism head-on and win. (152)

When Walter Luckett, a character who also strongly rejects cynicism as a *modus vivendi,* embraces suicide as his only recourse after he has disappointed himself by engaging in a homosexual relationship, Frank's honest curiosity (which leads him to inspect Walter's living quarters after the suicide) and firm refusal to assume a guilt that another might readily have assumed are typical of the man and are saving graces. The inclusion of Walter and his suicide are the author's dismissal of that desperate "alternative" for Frank. Well after Walter's suicide has been reported, Frank provides an analogy between sport and life that is based on Frank's common sense and on his common experience as one of life's bench warmers:

> It takes a depth of character as noble and enduring as willingness to come off the bench to play a great game knowing full well that you'll never be a regular; or as one who chooses not to hop into bed with your best friend's beautiful wife. Walter Luckett could be alive today if he knew that. (341)

One reservation must be expressed. The poet John Berryman once said that one is gripped by Hamlet because Hamlet is a "poet." The critical point is well taken, surely, telling because of its paradoxical nature. With Richard Ford's Frank Bascombe, a kind of additional turn has been given this screw of the voice that an author gives to his or her character. Any character who argues so eloquently the point of his own ordinariness is, in Berryman's terms, too much a poet to be ordinary. But Frank Bascombe's ordinariness has, in the late twentieth century, a salutary effect startlingly similar to the effect of Hamlet's tragic stature. In either instance, the reader or viewer, common or uncommon, can only feel elevated by the shared humanity that such a revealed human being compels the thankful reader to acknowledge. And finally, it is well to remember what Frank Bascombe has thought, "The world is a more engaging and less dramatic place than writers ever give it credit for being." The sentence immediately preceding this literary accolade to the world is a warning against the tendency to stereotype: "But that is a man of bad stereotype, the kind my ["real"] writing career foundered over and probably should have" (261).

In creating Lee Malcolm, his first-person narrator, John Hough, Jr., breaks free from the distancing of Ring Lardner from his "busher," Jack Keefe; from the self-muzzling that Mark Harris felt to some extent he underwent in speaking through his "author," Henry Wiggen; and from the respectable and realistic voice of the fictional George Weaver as imagined by Harry Stein. Malcolm organizes his story precisely as his author organizes it (or vice versa)—no gap exists between the two, to be exploited for the reader's amusement—so that *The Conduct of the Game* is a thoroughly impressive work and a work devoid of the slightest hint of condescension of the author toward his character. Still, the words of Lee Malcolm are not very memorable or highly quotable. In this characteristic lies a descriptive distinction between two fine sports novels, *The Conduct of the Game* and *The Sportswriter,* each celebrating human ordinariness. One is written in a style the reader may think he or she could achieve, although he or she emphatically could not; the other in a style not soon to be equaled by any writer, no matter how accomplished. The voice of one illustrates the worth of the common citizen; the voice of the other accepts and champions that worth. Each celebrates it.

Notes

1. The old catcher's nickname, "Comic Book," recalls the story of Yogi Berra's looking up from his comic books to ask his road-trip roommate, Bobby Brown, how the plot of the book Brown was reading—Gray's *Anatomy*—turned out. In the days of such apocryphal stories, it was assumed that Yogi stumbled onto his many Yogi-isms. That was before Yogi managed and coached, and decidedly before he reviewed not just game films but feature films, in mufti and in front of audiences.

2. That is, Bascombe achieves precisely what Greenberg's Mathewson yearns for: a transference from sport to life in general.

Works Cited

Ford, Richard. *The Sportswriter.* New York: Vintage, 1986.
Greenberg, Eric Rolfe. *The Celebrant.* 1983. New York: Penguin, 1986.

Harris, Mark. *Bang the Drum Slowly.* 1956. New York: Dell, 1973.
Hough, John, Jr. *The Conduct of the Game.* San Diego: Harcourt Brace Jovanovich, 1986.
Kinsella, W. P. *The Further Adventures of Slugger McBatt.* Boston: Houghton Mifflin, 1988.
Malamud, Bernard. *The Natural.* New York: Noonday, 1952.
Patrick, Walton R. *Ring Lardner.* New York: Twayne, 1963.
Stein, Harry. *Hoopla.* New York: St. Martin's, 1983.

The Reflexive Vision of Sport in Recent Drama and Film

RONALD K. GILES

Critics have well remarked the long apprenticeship that sports served in the movies from the 1920s through the 1960s, when the idea of sport generally followed an inspirational conception, especially in its biographical version—*The Pride of the Yankees* (1942) and *The Stratton Story* (1949), for example. Numerous, too, are the purely fictional films of the inspirational type that followed the athlete-meets-girl formula, along the prototypal lines of Harold Lloyd's role in *The Freshman* (1925). These are films that, in a sense, exploit sports, offering an often humorous, sentimental interpretation of the American Dream story. More recently, critics have begun to acknowledge the maturing vision of sport in drama and film, particularly over the last two decades. This maturity has grown out of the progress sport has made from backdrop spectacle to full aesthetic component, as dramatists and directors alike have discovered, in Wiley Lee Umphlett's words, "how to integrate, in a meaningful and significant way, the inherent drama of sport into the larger drama of human relationships" (114).

Martin Scorsese's *Raging Bull* (1980) stands as a preeminent example of the dramatic possibilities of sport, in this case boxing, as it merges with the dynamics of character and theme. Scorsese weaves the brutal fight scenes into the fabric of his film so that they contribute directly to the movie's thematic message—what Joyce Carol Oates calls an attempt "to invite injury as a means of assuaging guilt, in a Dostoyevskian exchange of physical well being for peace of mind" (25). This exchange clearly manifests itself when, after violently abusing his wife and brother, the titular hero Jake La Motta takes a beating in defense of his middleweight crown—that is, until the last round when, after "playing possum" (as the radio announcer calls it), he quickly dispatches his opponent. Such is the directoral skill with which Scorsese brings boxing into the foreground as organic action, as part of the linear development of the plot. But the fight scenes sometimes accomplish more than just thematic complement; they reveal and extend the central character's personality and flaws in both reflexive and predictive ways. In one instance, for example, La Motta's wife happens to refer, in general conversation, to Jake's next opponent as "good looking." This seemingly harmless comment provokes La Motta to unleash an irrational fury, which he ruthlessly directs at his opponent's face, as if the face itself must pay for its unwitting appeal to Mrs. La Motta. In this way, *Raging Bull* goes beyond the matter of thematic relevance and achieves a reflexive dimension, returning to the sport itself, not for conventional dramatics (us vs. them, winners vs. losers, fair vs. foul play), but for the metaphorical, psychological, or mythical qualities that the sport may recursively contribute to plot, character, and meaning. And it is this reflexive quality, this doubling back, that distinguishes a number of recent plays and films about the idea of sport and its dramatic ramifications.

In an essay on sports in American film, Frank McConnell says that "films about sports are always about the idea of sports, about the mythology of sport, if you will: what it means to us, why we care so much about it, why it *matters*" (37). Jason Miller's play *That Championship Season* (1972), which Miller adapted and directed for its screen version (1982), may well qualify as the purest recent example about the idea of sport, for the movie does not show the principals—Tom, Phil, James, and George—in athletic competition but rather reveals the ways in which the game of basketball has mattered to them long after the team won the 1957 Pennsylvania High School Basketball Tournament.

In broad outline, the plot is about the annual reunion of four team members with their coach in order to celebrate the occasion implied in the play's title. The mysteriously absent Martin, the fifth member of the team, receives reverentially delivered praise as a "perfect" player, the one who hit the critical shot. However, as the story develops, the team's former sense of unity begins to rupture under the stress of various revelations: political ambitions, cronyism, philandering, racism, and the emerging recognition that the title is tainted because the coach ordered Martin to injure the opposing team's star, a black center. As the film moves toward its climax, Tom—the most disillusioned of the remaining team members—picks up the coach's constant mouthing of basketball metaphors for ironic counterpoint. When the coach urges his middle-aged players to use "teamwork" in their shady political tactics, Tom sarcastically cheers: "Go Gentiles!" In this case, the dialogue reaches back metaphorically to the sport in order to coordinate, and thus expose, a current immorality with a past one. The tensions finally resolve to a general catharsis, with each member of the team admitting his personal addiction: Tom to alcohol, Phil to wealth and women, James to ambition, and George to personal and political bigotry. At this point, the sport or game itself can function reflexively, recalling its prominence as a turning point and solidifying the team again. To this end, Miller's script calls for the coach to play a record of the closing seconds of the championship game, with the players, in the words of the original play, "transfixed by the memory" (128). The game may not be a testament to renewal and commitment—the trophy will always be tarnished—but it does bear witness to a fact of their lives: the game as the mainspring of manhood, as the collective point of reference. In McConnell's words, "What it means. . . . Why it *matters.*"

A more recent basketball film, *Hoosiers* (1986), also reveals the reverberant quality that sports are now contributing to dramatic impact. Again, it is not just a matter of integrating the game into the film, as in a cause-and-effect chain—although this happens, too, as the small-town team under the command of its new coach (Gene Hackman) begins to play, and win, using his system. And, certainly, there is thematic significance in the victories, as the new coach helps to rehabilitate one player's alcoholic father (Dennis Hopper) and to restimulate the interest of an emotionally bruised but outstanding player. These developments pointedly contradict the contention of a teacher (who becomes the coach's love interest) that "people never change." But, by the movie's end, the sport serves more than just these admittedly important causal and thematic connections. With the championship depending on the final basket, the coach tells the team to set up the star as a decoy and let another player try to score. The players balk, in effect defying the coach who has earlier claimed that his word is law. Relenting, he calls a play to let the star of the team take the last desperate shot. People do change, even coaches. But this time the change occurs strictly within the context of the sport-inspired moment, reaching back into the story to remind us that there is one last missing dimension to character: the coach himself must be pulled under the main thematic blanket.

A climactic scene, similar to the one in *Hoosiers,* occurs with even finer moral effect in *Personal Best* (1982), where, once again, the movie finds within the sport itself not only thematic relevance but also psychological resolution, resulting from the foreshadowing dialogue. *Personal Best* follows the intensive training of two women attempting to make the 1980 Olympics track team, while also trying to accommodate their homosexuality. As both writer and director, Robert Towne realizes his vision on film, with Mariel Hemingway (as Chris) and Patrice Donnelly (as Tory) creating the dynamics of character that intensify Towne's thematic point: one's real "personal best" depends on moral rather than athletic stature. Towne impressively orchestrates the climax so that the meaning coincides with the athletic competition, which is, in itself, a means for recursively completing the characterization. Under the stress caused by training and by Chris's attraction to a man, the women's emotional ties begin to unravel. Before the race that will decide the members of the pentathlon team, Chris and Tory discuss their leg injuries: Tory asks, "You know how hurt I am?" and Chris replies, "I know exactly how hurt you are." Ostensibly about the physical pain, the dialogue ironically but sympathetically masks Chris's concern for Tory's emotional anguish. During the race, Chris sprints ahead in order to tire another runner whom Tory can beat with a finishing kick. Thus, in one memorable scene, Towne brings the action, the characterization, and the theme to full expression: a dramatic fusion about winning, friendship, and moral risk. So the film, at its climax, incorporates sport as text (completing an organic part of the plot) and as reflexive subtext (recurring to the psychological dimensions of character).

Just exactly the opposite effect concludes *Fat City* (1972), John Huston's film about boxing that Leonard Gardner adapted from his novel of the same title. Opposite in the sense that the crucial thematic scene occurs not in the arena of competition but at a bar where the two boxers, Billy Tully (Stacy Keach) and Ernie Munger (Jeff Bridges), drink coffee and contemplate the bleak prospects of their boxing careers. In this movie about two small-time fighters, the idea of sport still works on a correlative principle, as Billy reflectively considers his past through Huston's freeze-frame technique: a series of stop-action shots of the old men idling time in the bar. The implication is clear: Billy and Ernie have nothing more than this colorless existence to anticipate. Huston's technique deftly recalls the blank look on Billy's face when, at the end of his comeback fight, the manager must inform Billy that he has won. More subtly, but in the manner of *That Championship Season,* the sport comes forward at the end to underscore, on the psychological level, what the enervating environment, the unlikable minor characters, and the prevailing tone have pessimistically suggested all along.

Gardner's screenplay changes the ending of the novel rather

drastically, where Ernie, hitchhiking home after an out-of-town bout, winds up temporarily alone on the desert after the two women with whom he is riding evict him from their car. The altered version for the movie, with Ernie sitting next to Billy, provides Huston with a powerful image, implying that Ernie will follow Billy's footwork to nowhere—the path along which, as Neil D. Berman says, "boxing becomes the means of a continuous, ungratified search for freedom and renewal" (17). Yet there is more, an ironic countercurrent in the image: a sense that a moment of ineffable comradeship bonds the two men. One may argue, in tribute to Huston's and Gardner's artistic merit, that despite its look at boxing's squalid underside, *Fat City* ends with a scene that is both pathetic and arresting: Billy and Ernie, together at the bar, savoring one of the best moments of their lives.

The idea of sport may, of course, legitimately function in light as well as serious film. If *That Championship Season* advances the sport through time by means of a phonograph record, *The Best of Times* (1986) humorously brings an old football game forward in order to replay it, "to remake history" as Jack Dundee (Robin Williams) says. Dundee claims to have a moral purpose: "to lift . . . out of lethargy" the small California town suffering from the gloom of a defeat by Bakersfield thirteen years earlier when Dundee dropped a winning touchdown pass. Dundee wants, of course, to redeem himself athletically, but he also hopes to reclaim himself personally, salvaging the self-esteem lost to his domineering father-in-law who obnoxiously supports the rival team. They replay the game on two levels: in a major key that settles the athletic conflict; and in a minor, reflexive key that resolves the off-field tension within the family. Thematically considered, this film is about what everyone would like to do: transform to success the failure that continues to torment. If, indeed, the film promotes the redemptive idea of sport—on both a physical and affective plane—then credit should go to the writer, Ron Shelton, and the director, Roger Spottiswoode, who conflate the two levels of conflict within the sporting event.

The redemptive idea, on a serious level, is the thematic force behind the story of Bruce Pearson, the catcher whose fatal illness inspires the New York Mammoths to the World Series championship in Mark Harris's novel *Bang the Drum Slowly* (filmed in 1973, from a screenplay by Harris). The members of the team, as they learn of Pearson's illness, atone for their "ragging" of the simple country boy who has been an easy mark for their jests. In his essay on the book and the film made from it, C. Kenneth Pellow points out the thematic significance of the illness to the team's players:

> It becomes a maturing factor in their lives, a presence that reminds them to make the most of the gifts they possess, to extend some respect to all of those around them who are also dying, and a reminder to them to do with intensity whatever it is they do best. (61)

The film generally follows the plot of the book, but there is a major change in the final game scene where the gravely sick Pearson (Robert De Niro) is "catching by habit and memory, only knowing that when the pitcher threw it you were supposed to stop it and throw it back" (276). In the book, the game ends when the rain stops play, with the bewildered Pearson just standing by himself in the rain until Pearson's roommate, a pitcher named Henry Wiggen who is also the narrator, runs back to assist his friend to the dugout. The rain-shortened game reflects Pearson's disease-shortened life, and thus the book does not capitulate to the temptation to make the team's crucial victory coincide with the final throes of Pearson's physical breakdown. The movie, however, telescopes these two events and shows Pearson's struggle to survive the big game that ends with a slow-motion sequence in which the disoriented catcher cannot find a pop-up, eventually caught by the first baseman—all played pathetically out to the sad strains of the theme song, "The Streets of Laredo," and the jubilant dance of the victorious Mammoths. Whatever the merits of the movie, its sentimental revision of Pearson's last athletic moment sacrifices the book's restrained but effective echo of his life.

On the other hand, another baseball movie—John Sayles's *Eight Men Out* (1988)—preserves the echo in a scene that recalls one of the movie's most dramatic moments. The scene in question occurs when Shoeless Joe Jackson, the great outfielder implicated in the Black Sox scandal of 1919, leaves the court where he has been on trial and confronts a boy who pleads with him to "Say it ain't so, Joe." (As William J. Baker points out, the encounter is "A fictitious concoction, [which] nevertheless represented the sentiments of baseball fans everywhere, whose faith in the game was momentarily shaken" [215].) Jackson, an illiterate man, was one of eight players permanently banned by the baseball commissioner, Kenesaw Mountain Landis. The movie's concluding scene, a wistful coda sometime after the main action and set at a bush-league game, shows Jackson playing baseball under an assumed name. Another banned player watches from the stands while two men speculate about Jackson's real identity. Finally, settling the question, the old teammate is able, *in effect,* to "say it ain't Joe." Though it recalls the earlier scene outside the court where denial was not possible, the old teammate's denial represents an ironic affirmation of Jackson's life, a matter hardly separable from baseball. Once again, one sees how, in the maturing evolution of the sport film, the on-field play may recall earlier dialogue or action for thematic or ironic resonance.

The foregoing analysis of sport in drama and film illustrates that the resonating effect could not occur if the setting were solely within the context of sports. That is, there must be a nonsport referent—dialogue, characterization, image, and so on—to which the sport itself may refer. For example, Jonathan Reynolds's play *Yankees 3 Detroit 0 Top of the Seventh* (1974) is set entirely within the game itself: the play opens and closes with the stage representing a baseball diamond, thus eliminating a reflexive dimension as herein defined. But that dimension is generally evident in the resurgence of sport films that, in addition to the ones analyzed, include among others, *All the Right Moves* (1983), *The Natural* (1984), *Bull Durham* (1988), *Everybody's All-American* (1988), and *Field of Dreams* (1989). The trend indicates that moviemakers are now fully recognizing the aesthetic, as well as dramatic, possibilities within the idea of sport.

Works Cited

Baker, William J. *Sports in the Western World*. Rev. ed. Urbana: University of Illinois Press, 1988.

Berman, Neil David. *Playful Fictions and Fictional Players*. Port Washington, N.Y.: Kennikat, 1981.

Harris, Mark. *Bang the Drum Slowly*. New York: Dell, 1973.

McConnell, Frank. "Being a Contender: Sports in Recent American Film." *National Forum* 62, no. 1 (1982): 36–38.

Miller, Jason. *That Championship Season*. New York: Atheneum, 1972.

Oates, Joyce Carol. *On Boxing*. Garden City, N.Y.: Dolphin/Doubleday, 1987.

Pellow, C. Kenneth. "Baseball in Fiction and Film: Mark Harris's *Bang the Drum Slowly*." *Arete* 4, no. 2 (1987): 57–67.

Umphlett, Wiley Lee. "The Dynamics of Fiction on the Aesthetics of the Sport Film." *Arete* 1, no. 2 (1984): 113–21.

"Who the Hell Are You, Kid?": The New Baseball Poem as a Vehicle for Identity

DON JOHNSON

Donald Hall says that "baseball has always been the preferred sport of American poets" (57), and although attempts by recent sport literature anthologists to highlight the broad range of sports embraced by American culture might mislead one, a comprehensive examination of the anthologies that have appeared in the last fifteen years supports Hall's assertion. For American *male* poets at least, baseball is the overwhelming choice, and a significant number of women have written baseball poems as well. But anthologists are, of necessity, relatively conservative, soliciting and accepting work that has already been judged worthy of respect. Hall's analysis of the baseball poem mirrors this conservatism. The poems he cites tend to fall into one of two general categories: examinations of the game's aesthetic potential (the "brief, exact lyrics" of Robert Francis, for example), or celebration of such heroes as Ty Cobb, Roberto Clemente, or Ted Williams.[1]

The contemporary baseball poem, found in literary magazines and individual collections rather than anthologies, continues to promote the grace and beauty inherent in the game, but today's open society, the media's insatiable appetite for scandal, and the candor of individual athletes have all but eliminated the popular baseball figure as hero. Consequently, the "new" baseball poem looks inward and backward rather than up and out. Rather than standing in awe at the pinstriped figures on the manicured grass at Yankee Stadium, the contemporary poet recalls his own experiences on the sandlot or the Little League field. His hero is not Wade Boggs, Don Mattingly, or Kirby Puckett, but himself.

In addition to the dearth of real heroes in contemporary American culture, the reasons for this elevation of self are manifold, having their roots in the current neoromantic attitude that dominates American culture and its art. These reasons are also beyond the scope of this essay. More important for my purpose here is the answer to the question, "Why baseball as a subject for poetic expression?" Interestingly enough, despite what I have referred to above as his literary conservatism, Hall rather off-handedly asserts that the reason for Americans' fascination with baseball might be "simply that all of us need regularly to revisit childhood" (62). The "new" baseball poem is essentially about childhood and the charmed circle of play at its core; and among all the games of childhood, baseball is the one most likely to have been experienced by the American male and thus most likely to appear in a meditation on things past. Other factors include the slow, meditative nature of the game itself, its emphasis upon ritual and memory, and its capacity for highlighting the confrontation between clearly identifiable individuals. Finally, one cannot ignore the prolific outpouring and cumulative influence of baseball literature, which makes the choice of baseball as subject matter not only legitimate but almost obligatory.

In defining the "new" baseball poem, I would like to examine four works: William Matthews's "The Hummer" from *A Happy Childhood;* Arthur Smith's "Extra Innings" from *Elegy on Independence Day;* Richard Jackson's "Centerfield" from *Worlds Apart;* and, to my knowledge, the only one of the four to have been anthologized, Dave Smith's "The Roundhouse Voices" from *Goshawk, Antelope.*

Of the four, only "The Hummer" lacks a first-person narrator. Still it presents an intimate view of childhood baseball, in this instance a solitary, almost solipsistic, game created, played, and umpired by the young boy in the poem who

> drew a strike zone
> on the toolshed door, and then
> . . . battered against it all summer
> a balding tennis ball, wetted
> in a puddle he tended under
> an outdoor faucet: that way
> he could see, at first, exactly
> where each pitch struck.

Better than any piece I know, this poem illustrates the paradox of inconsequence in sport, the notion that games become significant in inverse proportion to their association with the *real* world. The smaller the recognition and tangible reward associated with a particular game, the more significant it becomes *qua* game.

In this instance the game is wholly without significance beyond the confines of the moral framework the boy himself erects and adheres to. But in the later innings, when the door was "solidly blotched,"

> calling the corners was fierce
> enough moral work for any
> man he might grow up to be.
> His stark rules made it hard
> to win, and made him finish
> any game he started, no matter
> if he'd lost it early.

So fully is the boy drawn into his creation that he would have been the batter if he could have, "trying to stay alive." This last phrase carries with it the boy's realization that each out implies a death of sorts, one recorded in real games in the box score, "the obituary." Still the youthful pitcher "loved . . . mowing them down," as if he felt himself somehow beyond the bounds of mortality. But when it came time to administer the coup de grace, "the hummer,"

> it made him grunt to throw it,
> as if he'd tried to hold it
> back, but it escaped. Thwap.

The impulse for self-preservation (after all, the batter is the boy, too) conflicts here with the desire for resolution, but the finality of the poem's last syllable leaves no doubt that each game-winning strikeout pounds one more nail in the coffin of the boy's childhood.

The celebration of the childhood game is shadowed by the mature narrator's recognition that even the difficult, later-inning calls the boy made were simple compared to the complex decisions he would be responsible for in adulthood. This dual vision, a fusion of innocence and experience, is significant in many good poems, but it is critical to the effective sports poem. As M. L. Rosenthal observes, "that passion—to remember and retain what inevitably we must lose—is the most powerful sound of art" (19), and the central theme of sport literature is loss: loss of ability, loss of perspective, loss of innocence, loss of life, loss even of the ability to remember events that generated powerful emotions in the first place.

Rather than lamenting the loss of historical accuracy or resorting to the last refuge of statisticians who contend that "You could look it up," the poet capitalizes on the unreliability of memory by freely admitting the creative role of the imagination in reconstructing one's childhood. In the long title poem of *A Happy Childhood*, Matthews says,

> There's no truth about your childhood,
> though there's a story, yours to tend
> like a fire or garden. Make it a good one
> since you'll have to live it out, and all
> its revisions, so long as you all shall live,
> for they shall be gathered to your deathbed,
> and they'll have known to what you and they
> would come, and this one time they'll weep for you.

Childhood is, then, self-created. People become what they were, but what they were is not determined until the mature imagination has the capacity to construct what Gaston Bachelard calls "moments of illumination . . . moments of poetic existence" (100). Thus, the degree of poignance associated with the loss of youth is directly proportional to one's ability to heighten those moments.

The imagination's ability to illuminate the past and the contrast between history and the creative memory are the driving impulses of Arthur Smith's "Extra Innings," which begins with an idyllic memory highlighting the pastoral nature of the game:

> Back then the ballpark grass was so overgrown
> and sweet-smelling, I think
> I could have bellied down near the dugout
> And drowsed away the afternoon.

Having established the setting, Smith records his performance at the plate for a particular game, one for three.[2] What makes the game noteworthy is that his hit broke up a no-hitter with two out in the ninth and the opposing pitcher was "called up by the Mets" a few months later. "The rest, as we say, / is history," Smith says. "We say a lot / Of stupid things," because

> we know our bodies are not luminous
> like the stars,

> And so we make amends: we think ourselves luminous
> > the moment
>
> Sleep comes on, or after loving someone loved—
> > that warmth
> Radiating out like sound, a name called and carried off
> > on the air—or,
> Better, and far richer, because it happened once,
> > after breaking up
>
> A no-hitter by Tom Seaver, with two out in the ninth.

But after identifying his opponent as Tom Seaver, Smith then says he might have been "someone nameless like myself— / a landscaper, perhaps," who would remember not a spoiled no-hitter but a no-hitter accomplished.

Because of memory's capacity to re-create events, "neither of us / is wrong," Smith says. "Seaver has his stats,"

> And the rest of us are stuck with rearranging, cutting
> And mixing, working day and night, in dreams, in the dark
> > of a warehouse
> . . . .
> Trying to make it right, remixing, trying to accommodate
> > what happened with what
> Might have happened. And it never turns out true.
>
> The possibilities not to be trusted, but, rather,
> Believed in against the facts—whatever they are.

The poem ends with the assertion of the possibility that neither the batter's nor the pitcher's versions of the game were reliable, that the left fielder might remember the game ending with a fly ball that he had snared in a diving catch, that he had held the ball high over his head,

> > > the third out, the proof
> > That this, ah yes, this is what happened, the fans in
> > > his memory standing,
> > Roaring in disbelief, and the lovely applause lasting
> > > till he's off the field.

Despite the facts, the statistics, the history, or the memories of any of the other participants, each individual creates his own ver-

sion of heroism. The idea that the applause lasts only "till he's off
the field" underscores the significance of the sporting moment, the
heightened experience that allows for memory's interpretation.
Though Tom Seaver appears in "Extra Innings," his role is decidedly unheroic, the impulse of the poem determinedly reductive
insofar as the superstar is concerned. Seaver might not even have
been the pitcher who opposed the speaker in his youth, and if he
had been, his memories of the event would not have carried more
weight than the speaker's, the other possible pitcher, or the opposing team's left fielder.

   Unlike "The Hummer" or "Extra Innings," Richard Jackson's
"Centerfield" is set in the present, but it quickly turns to the past as
the speaker waits for a long fly ball to come down. It has been hit
into the dusky shadows beyond the field lights, and as the speaker
waits for the ball to drop, he notes that the field makes backpedaling
"risky / but keeps pulling you as if further into your past."
   While waiting for the ball to materialize out of the darkness,
Jackson invokes the sandlot of his childhood in Lawrence, Massachusetts. He muses about "what we try to steal from our darkening
pasts,"

> how age means knowing how many steps we have lost,
> remembering that too many friends have died,
> and how love is the most important thing,
> if only we knew who to love and when.

The remaining two-thirds of the poem is an inventory of losses
couched in baseball terms. In reverie the poet has "slid / over the
outstretched arms of twenty years," and "can see Joey Gile
crouched at third base" waiting for a sniper's bullet to "snap like a
line drive into his chest." Then there was John Kearns who would
"swing and miss everything / from a tree in his backyard," and Joe
Daly who was "tagged . . . to a tree" by a tractor, and Gene
Coskren, "fooled by a hit and run in Syracuse." The poet even
recalls an aunt who loved baseball. A victim of cancer, she died
thinking there was "no one to bring her home."
   The final stanza of "Centerfield" becomes blatantly self-reflexive
and establishes the poem as more than a nostalgic collection of
puns. Jackson, who has already drawn the reader into the poem
with the use of the second person, involves the reader more deeply
by admitting that "this is a poem"

> that could go on being about either death or love,
> and we have only the uncertain hang time
> of a fly ball to decide how to position ourselves,
> to find the right words for our love,
> to turn towards home as the night falls, as the ball,
> as the loves, the deaths we grab for our own.

By inviting the reader into the poem as, in effect, cocreator, Jackson moves one step beyond the assertion of the memory's creative capacity. Finding the "right words for our love" means that we rely on our active imaginations to carry us out of the past into a creative present. We become more than what our memories tell us we were. Recognizing the inevitability of loss, we become what we say we will become, the central figures in our own myths, not merely reliving a past but creating a present in response to that past.

In stark contrast to the speaker in "Centerfield," Dave Smith in "The Roundhouse Voices" questions the validity of words as a recompense for grief. At one point his speaker bitterly asserts that "words are all we ever were and they did us / no damn good." The lines are addressed to an uncle laid out in his casket for burial. A father surrogate, the uncle had taught the speaker as a young boy how to play baseball. Technically, they *played* softball, but references to "the Mick" and taking a "hard pitch" make it clear that the softball was a concession to the boy's inexperience and the unique setting of their games, a railroad line's roundhouse.

Like "Centerfield," "The Roundhouse Voices" is replete with baseball terminology, "diamonds," sliding, pinstripes, stealing, and so on, but Smith's poem is a narrative and the relationships are far more dramatic. Because the game took place in the roundhouse where the uncle worked, the boy had to sneak in, eluding the watchful eyes of the company guard who would pursue him with the question, repeated with slight variations four times in the poem: "Who the hell are you, kid?" Eluding the guard becomes as much a part of the game and the lesson for life as the pitching and the catching, and as the poem develops, the guard comes to represent the restrictions and limitations the child will encounter in the adult world: work, the ownership of property, management by arbitrary authority, and, ultimately, death.

With his uncle's encouragement, the boy taunts the guard, giving him "the finger,"

> just to make him get up
> and chase me into a dream of scoring at your feet.

In his innocence the boy exults in the ritual defeat of repression, is perhaps even lulled into a false sense of security when the guard succumbs to a heart attack, making evasion unnecessary. But as an adult, leaning over his uncle's tools, he realizes that he learned the wrong lesson from the guard's disability, that even the uncle's instruction was a betrayal of sorts in that it led him to face life too optimistically. "I gave him [the guard] every name in the book, Uncle," the grieving nephew says, "but he caught us / and what good did all those hours of coaching do?"

All that coaching failed to prepare the speaker for the ultimate defeat that death brings. He stands at his uncle's casket, holding the dead man's hand, "trying to say back that life, / to get under that fence with words . . .", but the gesture is futile. "Even the finger I give death is words / that won't let us be what we wanted," he says. And in this instance, words are "no damn good."

The poem ends with the nephew saying that he has had enough of words, and he has brought them back to the uncle's bier

> where the tick and creak of everything dies
> in your tiny starlight and I stand down
> on my knees to cry, *Who the hell are you, kid?*

Each time the question is asked in the poem it takes on slightly different meanings. Initially it might have been a legitimate question on the part of the guard, but after repeated encounters with the boy it had to have become essentially rhetorical. The guard would have known the boy's identity and would have meant, in effect, "What are you doing in my life?" In its final iteration the question is certainly genuine. The nephew, disillusioned and needing direction, is uncertain of his own identity. If all the games, all the coaching, all the words were inadequate preparation for life, then what could he be? How could he go on?

From one point of view, one might argue that the poem itself answers the question that art's ability to preserve experience, however bleak, is ample recompense for suffering. In this light, one might answer the speaker's question by saying, "You're a poet, and this fine poem gives the lie to your assertion that 'words are no damn good.' Your complaint is like Coleridge's claiming in 'Dejection: An Ode' that his 'genial spirits fail.'" Such a resolution would do violence to the poem, however. Unlike "Centerfield," "The

Roundhouse Voices" is not meant to be optimistic. Its speaker is genuinely bewildered, at a loss to understand or explain who or what he is. The resolution comes later in other poems in *Goshawk, Antelope*.

More important here is the fact that the question arises at all, that the inquiry as to the speaker's identity must be seen against the backdrop of his childhood experiences as a ballplayer. Like Matthews, Arthur Smith, Richard Jackson, and countless other contemporary poets, David Smith examines these experiences in an effort to determine their effect on what he has become. Like most "new baseball poets" he might refer to "the Mick" or another of baseball's immortals, but in his poem, like the others, the real hero is himself.

Notes

1. For a distinction between the participatory and nonparticipatory sports poem, see David Evans, "Poetry and Sport," *Arete* 4, no. 2 (1987): 141–45.
2. I am aware of the fact that in discussing these poems one might make distinctions between speakers and poets. In this study, however, I have chosen to ignore these distinctions.

Works Cited

Bachelard, Gaston. *The Poetics of Reverie: Childhood, Language and the Cosmos*. Translated by Daniel Russell. Boston: Beacon, 1969.
Evans, David. "Poetry and Sport." *Arete* 4, no. 2 (1987): 141–45.
Hall, Donald. *Fathers Playing Catch with Sons: Essays on Sport*. San Francisco: North Point, 1985.
Jackson, Richard. *Worlds Apart*. Tuscaloosa: University of Alabama Press, 1987.
Matthews, William. *A Happy Childhood*. Boston: Little, Brown, 1984.
Rosenthal, M. L. *Poetry and the Common Life*. Oxford: Oxford University Press, 1974.
Smith, Arthur. *Elegy on Independence Day*. Pittsburgh: University of Pittsburgh Press, 1985.
Smith, David. *Goshawk, Antelope*. Urbana: University of Illinois Press, 1979.

Women's Sports Poetry: Some Observations and Representative Texts

BROOKE K. HORVATH
SHARON G. CARSON

As readers of this volume should be aware, the past several years have seen sport literature emerge from the ghetto of subliterature to critical respectability. Critical esteem no longer depends on the extent to which one can make the case that a "sports" poem or novel is not really about sports, or is worthwhile despite the fact that it has sport as its subject. Today, discussions of sport literature's aesthetic success can drop the qualifying adjective and judge a text in terms of the expectations and evaluative criteria brought to bear on it while recognizing that sport literature does retain a claim to an area of experience that is this literature's business to explore fully.

Yet despite this growing critical interest, women's sport literature—especially women's sports poetry—continues to suffer neglect. The reasons for this situation are not so hard to fathom. Most critics attracted to sport literature are men, women poets have written fewer sports poems than have male poets, and sports poems feature women less often than men, partly because women have been excluded from those sports—professional baseball, football, basketball, boxing—which have most often received poetic treatment and which most interest the majority of critics (principally because these sports, especially baseball, have been most often and most successfully treated in fiction). In literature as in life, sports remain primarily a male enterprise. Thus, as Michael Oriard says in his "Brief History" of the feminist sport novel,

> from the 1920s until the 1970s [women] were largely excluded from what seemed an essentially masculine world of sport. They were not excluded from sport itself, of course, but from that sporting world in which sport mattered as more than physical health, that world where

116

sport was viewed as a training ground, where sport was thought to teach valuable lessons for conduct in life generally, where sport embodied a cultural myth and ideology. (9)

Moreover, women's sport literature has doubtless been ignored in part because the feminists, literary and otherwise, have paid scant attention to sport. There is, for example, no full-scale work of feminist theory treating women and sport, despite the American society's obsession with sport, despite sport's significance as a locus of those societal values and attitudes of which Oriard writes.

All of which is not to deny a wealth of relevant material—in the biographies and autobiographies of successful female athletes, in the pages of *Ms., Women's Sport and Fitness,* and general-interest magazines as well as in scholarly journals such as *The Journal of Sport Psychology, The Journal of Sport and Social Issues,* and *The Journal of Sport Behavior,* among others. Yet with the focus of attention elsewhere, little of this material is immediately useful to the would-be critic of women's sports poetry. Consequently, in the space allotted here, we cannot offer, as we might wish, anything like a complete theoretical foundation upon which to erect readings of individual poems.

Given, then, our space limitations and our principal desire—to introduce readers to some very good sports poems by women—we will, as a sort of prolegomenon to a proper study of the subject, simply draw upon a few provocative comments for insights into what might be said to characterize a female response to sport, a set of sporting values forming an alternative to the habitual ones espoused and/or embodied in male writing about sport, to see if these ideas provide a useful lens through which to view a handful of poems by women that deserve to be better known and more often taught, poems that ought to be taken into account in any effort to grasp what is happening in sport literature today.

Let us begin with Bonnie Beck's 1980 essay, "The Future of Women's Sport: Issues, Insights, and Struggles." The bit of verse with which Beck opens her essay succinctly reveals her orientation:

> PERHAPS,
> Before there were Gods there were Goddesses;
> Before there was Man there was Woman;
> Before there was Sport there was Play;
> Before Roboticized-Automatons there were Life-
> Living/Loving-Free-Spirited/Joyful Humans-Be-ing,
> and PERHAPS, there will be again. (401)

In brief, Beck sees sport as it exists today—which she labels "NowSport" or "ManSport"—to be a product of a male mindset and as such "reflect[ing] the dominant values of both patriarchy and capitalism" (401). "Male-dominated" and "for-profit," Man-Sport fosters "sexism, racism, ageism, and classicism" (402), creating a sporting world "hellbent on a Death-March at the end of which lies robotocized existence and nonSelves . . ." (405). With its unhealthy commitment to violence, competition, ends over means, and thanatos over eros, ManSport "contribute[s] strongly and effectively to the gradual but persistent demise of Living/ Loving, Free-Spirited, Joyful, Creatively energized Humans Be-ing" (406), and for Beck, women appear all too eager to plug into this male-defined sports world, to join in this nation's "Death-March (with NowSport leading the way)" (407) rather than seeking to realize the alternative she calls "NewSport" or "JoySport": a playful, communal "abandon/reunion of comtesting . . . that is, playing with others in the quest for Self-Knowing, Self-Be-ing, Self-Creation, universal Spiraling, Spinning, Connecting . . ." (401). Valuing the life-affirmative beauty that springs from creative energy employed "to create new patterns of movement/forms of moving/ ways of moving that emphasize Wholeness/Integration/Con-nectedness" (409), Beck's vision is one of play as an end in itself with cooperation replacing agon, "life-energizing" activity replacing competitive violence both physical and psychological, participation for all regardless of ability replacing selection on the basis of talent: "play for the enjoyment of playing, with winning and extrinsic rewards being only incidental to the experience of playing hard, sweating profusely, scoring a goal, [and] bond-ing with other women" in "an environment conducive to healthy com-test-ing . . ." (406).

Having taught Beck in several college sport literature classes, we know that her essay will strike many readers as outrageous (her aggressively hostile and divisive language, so at odds with her ostensible message, is in large part to blame), giving voice not to a truly female alternative conception of sport but to hopelessly idio-syncratic wishful thinking to which few others will want to pledge allegiance. Yet consider the following pairs of poems, chosen more or less at random from those available in Tom Dodge's *A Literature of Sports:* Maxine Kumin's "Morning Swim" and Robert Francis's "Swimmer"; James Dickey's "In the Picket" and May Swenson's "Watching the Jets Lose to Buffalo at Shea."

Kumin's poem describes a solitary swim in a quiet foggy lake at dawn. Opening with the speaker's account of how, "oily and nude," she gives herself trustingly to the unknown, to the misty uncertainty of the lake, "Morning Swim" evokes memories that come to fill her "empty head" with thoughts that despite the "fuzzy" dark, arrive with all the domestic comfort and familiar warmth of a terry cloth robe (feelings echoed by the poem's rhythmic tetrameter couplets):

> Into my empty head there come
> A cotton beach, a dock wherefrom
>
> I set out, oily and nude
> Through mist, in chilly solitude.
>
> There was no line, no roof or floor
> To tell the water from the air.
>
> Night fog thick as terry cloth
> Closed me in its fuzzy growth.
>
> I hung my bathrobe on two pegs.
> I took the lake between my legs.

Although the next stanza briefly introduces a note of potential hostility ("invaded and invader"), this attitude is quickly diluted in the smoothing immersion of the swimmer's body into the lake, to which she soon acclimates herself. Her swim becomes both a source of erotic pleasure ("I took the lake between my legs"); and later: "water fell / Through all my doors") and a means of establishing communion with nature:

> Invaded and invader, I
> Went overhand on that flat sky.
>
> Fish twitched beneath me, quick and tame.
> In their green zone they sang my name
> And in the rhythm of the swim
> I hummed a two-four-time slow hymn.

With this last line, the religious dimension of the swimmer's activity breaks the poem's surface as a romantic transcendence through union with nature, a sensual-spiritual experience healing the split between body and soul and giving rise to thoughts of God. This becomes the poem's dominant mood to its conclusion, her sense of oneness and harmony emphasized by the mingling of her breath with the lake water and by her conviction that her bones "drank water" even as she feels herself that water's source:

> I hummed *Abide With Me*. The beat
> Rose in the fine thrash of my feet,
>
> Rose in the bubbles I put out
> Slantwise, trailing through my mouth.
>
> My bones drank water; water fell
> Through all my doors. I was the well
>
> That fed the lake that met the sea
> In which I sang *Abide With Me*.

In "Morning Swim," in short, are depicted many of those characteristic attitudes and values attributed by Beck and others to a female (if not strictly feminist) perspective: a dilution of egotism and absence of competition and violence; an affirmation of joy, health, self, and communion; the portrayal of a positive body image; a freedom from stifling regimens or fears of failure; a peaceful coexistence with and love for the other (here, the lake and its fish). Indeed, one might conclude that "Morning Swim" is not finally a sports poem at all (insofar as it does not involve rule-governed competition) but rather a poem celebrating seriously playful physical activity as an end in itself whose end is joy. To this point we will return.

By way of contrast, consider Robert Francis's "Swimmer":

> Observe how he negotiates his way
> With trust and the least violence, making
> The stranger friend, the enemy ally.
> The depth that could destroy gently supports him.
> With water he defends himself from water.
> Danger he leans on, rests in. The drowning sea
> Is all he has between himself and drowning.

Although the poem speaks of "trust and the least violence," of gentle support, it is the potential for violence, the imminence of death by drowning, that dominates the scene. Emphasizing the disharmony between man and sea (a more threatening locale than a lake) through the irregular rhythm and the absence of rhyme, the poem stands at a distance from its subject ("Observe how he . . .")

as though objectivity and a correct reading of the lesson to be learned matter more than a subjective re-creation of the experience itself. Success here lies in turning the sea's powers against it, in learning to inhabit danger, a strategy giving the lie to the speaker's description of the sea as "friend" and "ally." The achievement here is not communion with nature, not erotic-spiritual ecstasy, but a sense of triumph in danger overcome through pure mind and self-control, of disaster outwitted through skill and courage, of that invigoration which comes from successfully flirting with and cheating death. (For a discussion of the relation of sport to death, see Howard Slusher.)

The second set of poems may be addressed more briefly. In James Dickey's "In the Pocket," the same preoccupation with danger overcome through skillful confrontation and controlled violence that informs "Swimmer" appears once more. Plugging directly into one of the most familiar of football truisms—that football is metaphoric warfare—"In the Pocket" is a highly successful evocation through form and content of that chancy and chaotic moment when a quarterback drops back to pass.

> . . . my arm is looking
> Everywhere and some are breaking
> In   breaking down
> And out   breaking
> Across, and one is going deep   deeper
> Than my arm. Where is Number One hooking
> Into the violent green alive
> With linebackers? I cannot find him he cannot beat
> His man   I fall back more
> Into the pocket   it is raging and breaking . . .

Conflict, violence, destruction (of poetic line as of the offensive line), impending threat and death are clearly foregrounded; the poem speaks for itself:

> . . . my friends are crumbling
> Around me the wrong color
> Is looming   hands are coming
> Up and over between
> My arm and Number Three: throw it hit him in the middle
> Of his enemies   hit move scramble
> Before death and the ground
> Come up LEAP STAND KILL DIE STRIKE
> Now

In "Watching the Jets Lose to Buffalo at Shea," May Swenson perceives the same literal/symbolic violence and danger of which Dickey writes (and that are, after all, difficult to ignore) but turns immediately to the action's allegorical possibilities in a fashion quite distinct from Dickey's (who worked his own variation of sorts on this theme in "The Bee"). Here, the ball becomes a baby, the runner a father, the field life's dangers, and the endzone a cradle of safety:

> Sent aloft by a leather toe,
> a rugged leather baby
> dropped from the sky and slammed
> into the sling of your arms.
> Oh, the feel of that leather bundle.
> Oh, what a blooper and fumbler
> you are, that you couldn't nest it,
>
> that you lost and couldn't nurse it,
> long enough to lay it
> in the cradle of grass at the goalposts.

We leave it to the reader to make what he or she will of the runner-father's failure and of the implications of a man's lavishing such solicitude upon a "leather baby"; regardless, what is striking is Swenson's perception of the scene in such familial terms.[1] If nothing else, the poem would seem to urge readers to keep their priorities straight—that a player's failure finally matters less than a father's—and to see sport not only as a metaphor for war and aggression but, in the face of such unpleasantries, as a reminder of the need for similar care and concern in the world beyond the endzones.

Readers may feel that we have stacked the deck in our choice of poems, and no amount of protesting on our part is likely to alter this opinion. (Actually juxtaposing these poems was a happy moment of serendipity when our sport literature students turned in disgust from Beck to test her ideas against whatever poems they could find in their text.) It is therefore worth noting that Beck's contentions are corroborated elsewhere—for instance, in Marcia Westkott and Jay J. Coakley's "Women in Sport: Modalities of Feminist Social Change." Summarizing and synthesizing the answers forwarded in response to the question of why women should want to gain access to sporting activities and organizations that have excluded them, the authors present as one of two principal responses what they designate "the critical argument."[2] This response rejects patriarchal institutions and their activities. In particular, it rejects the values and attitudes associated with male defined behavior: competition, aggression, inflexibility, and egotism. According to this argument, the goals of feminist social change are not to have girls and women emulate "macho" behavior, nor to encourage females to participate in the institutions that require such behavior for survival or success. Those who reject male dominated institutions and behavior endorse the creation of alternative institutions that permit the freedom for women to define their own goals and modes of operating. . . . (32)

Briefly, the critical argument rejects the present sports world again because of its negative effects on participants (and, one imagines, on spectators as well). It fosters a set of distorted values that "often turn individuals into anxiety-ridden failures or cynical, egotistical sport specialists" (37). Further, sport's unhealthy emphasis on winning—"on the quality of performance and the outcome of contests" (38)—transforms what should be a playful, life-enhancing activity into an overly rigid, work-oriented chore and devalues "the goals of improved health, self-esteem, and [positive] body image" (39) while wrongheadedly translating success on the field into an index of one's worth as a human being. Finally, with the pressure to win joining hands with the present coaching practices, sport encourages not assertiveness and autonomy but "responsiveness, dependence, and self-doubt . . ." (39). As Harry Edwards has remarked, advocates of the critical argument would, all things considered, prefer to see women's athletics not mirror existing programs but develop real alternatives wherein "the younger generation can be socialized with values stressing cooperation rather than antagonism, participation and self-actualization rather than confrontation and domination" (cited by Westkott and Coakley, 39).

From these brief summaries of Beck and of Westkott and Coakley—to which could be added others[3]—a set of alternative values and attitudes can readily be extrapolated. In addition to those suggested already, these values include self-identity and a self-awareness that specifically *includes* others rather than *excludes* them, as do the "rules" or the "game plan" of organized sport. This may be a strong theme because the rules of sport, like many of the rules of life, have so often excluded women. Other poems stress the pure joy of play and reveal an obvious preference for play as a more self-affirming and other-affirming activity than sport. And a final and recurrent theme in this poetry is a life-and-love-expanding coexistence with nature.[4] This key theme clearly implies that the natural world is superior to the human-made environment of sports, games, and "life by the rules," and suggests that an understanding of life involves not a struggle against it but cooperation with it. As Oriard remarks in his essay on Jenifer Levin's *Water Dancer:* "Not competition or mastery but surrender becomes a new kind of freedom. . . . To be a water dancer is neither to dominate nor be dominated but to live in one's body in the world" (18). Jenifer Levin's swimmer in *Water Dancer* becomes the prototype for all players who would achieve harmony and balance in the element of life.

Judith Wright's poem "Sports Field" illustrates the theme of self-identity that includes rather than excludes others. The poem's playing field functions as a clear metaphor for the duality of the natural and the artificial environment. As the poem opens, the reader sees the field at night, "naked . . . breathing its dew," and it is marked and controlled for the forthcoming game only by the appearance of the sun, "the great gold ball of day," which springs from the "dark hill." Wright emphasizes the autonomy of the natural world and its rhythms by using the sun as the golden ball "that no one ever catches." The children who come to play the game are born equally into the day with each other being all at first "gilt by the sun." However, this equality is soon shattered by the artificial provisions of the race, requiring that the children "shoulder one another; / crouch at the marks." The game divides and pits player against player, rather than achieving a union of children "gilt by the sun." For this activity, the field itself is "ruled": "measured and marked, its lanes and tapes are set." It becomes clear that this is a race, the race of life, and because of the rules, not everyone can win, so the children must be separated:

> the children pledged and matched,
> and built to win or lose,
> who grow, while no one watches,
>
> the selves in their sidelong eyes.

Thus, the "rules of the game" have become a substitute for the players' experience of themselves. They are watched in vain by spectators who love an illusion, because the only things that are real are the rules: "What's real here is the field, / the starter's gun, the lane, / the ball dropped or held."

Set toward the future, the children "run like running water," their pride and pain to be won only out of a "measured field," but the night and the field continue to glitter, "naked and perilous," a continuous reminder of the futility and transience of their games in contrast to the enduring rhythms of the sun and the night.

In stark contrast to Wright's "Sports Field" is Elizabeth Spires's poem "The Playground," wherein she eloquently captures the joy and pleasure of play for its own sake. Here the speaker is "drawn by shouts / of the children playing tug-of-war and crack-the-whip." Their joy becomes for both children and speaker a lifeline: "the lines alive, *taut*." The children demand entrance into this play, this life, through her body, and as she stretches her arms to grasp a child on each side, she becomes a link in the chain. The chain grows as DNA grows, becoming a line of time:

> caught in a line
> snaking backward and forward
> until it joins, like time, at either end
> and mends invisibly,
> the face of the child on either side of me
> pale as a star
> as each holds my hand tightly
> begging to enter the world and live a little while,
> my body the instrument of passage.

Here Spires captures the innocent grace and symmetry of the threads of life, weaving all into a single pattern, a pattern of patterns, which overrides human-made rules, even the rules of time itself:

> We play
> as the clock strikes
> *one*, then *two*, then *three*,
> . . . .
> no thought to the waning moon.

Spires pictures the joy of childhood play as a dream—a state of grace that cannot last—and like Wright, she grieves that it is ultimately lost in the rush toward the future:

> . . . . the world inverted
> like a dream I'll wake alone from in the
> morning, the bed's cold sheets
> thrown off like so many obligations,
> as they pull me toward them and I pull away,
> the future bearing down so quickly upon us.

Jan Mordenski's "For Athletes, Poets, and Lovers" carries this key theme of separation from the self and from others because of rules over into adult love relationships, again in the context of a football game. There is a gender division at the first line of scrimmage:

> After the draft, there is
> the line of scrimmage, the moment
> that stretches long white arms to the left
> and the right dividing the world in half.

Unknowingly, all have "padded ourselves with elaborate protections" against the other—a ritual of isolation. Here the reader imagines not only football pads but the more impenetrable garments of "masculinity" and "femininity." And once people have insulated themselves, and step out on the field, they are on their own:

> There is no cheering from the stands;
> the air stands still and green
> as a referee from training while we
> try to read the opposition, the strategies,
> the strengths, the potential for effectual pain.

Unlike those of an actual football game, the signals for this game come to the players like the shadows of Plato's cave—never direct, always heard from behind, always futile:

> Somewhere from behind I hear signals being called,
> a litany of attempts that have failed or half-failed

Although none of the signals makes sense, the reader keeps hoping for one that does: "a new number, a number that will work." Amid this confusion, people keep trying: "in order to catch, / take hold, and run with the one small thing / that still matters in this game." Here Mordenski uses the image of the football to suggest that the large things that should matter—such as love, tenderness, and communication—don't, and the small things that shouldn't matter—such as power, status, and wealth—do.

Finally, even the goal becomes an illusion, and just as the signals for the game have been heard only vaguely, so the goal is seen only as an abstraction, "not the goal, / but a picture of the goal," and in the player's attempts to seize this goal he sees only "a picture of my hands as they stretch to meet it." Here the sport imagery emphasizes the distance and isolation of the players, even lovers, from one another, and the futility of human relationships played by "the rules of the game."

Linda Mizejewski's poem "Season Wish" is an even more poignant statement about the arbitrary rules of human relationships. This time, however, the game is between a father and daughter. The daughter is reminiscent of the little leftout Sasha Davis in Alix Kate Shulman's *Memoirs of an Ex-Prom Queen*. Oriard notes that Shulman finds in "playground grade-school games a metaphor for the male appropriation of the larger world" (15).

"Season Wish" brings home the whole history of the female as an offering, an object to be traded, bought, purchased, exchanged, bartered, stolen, or sacrificed for some artificial social or material gain. Like Rapunzel, the little girl in "Season Wish" is also "traded to the gods for wheat or rain." Every spring, her father takes her "out at dusk, to lots the boys had left," to see if she could become the "missing son." The father hopes that there might be some "magic in the glove or sneakers or wooden bat." The little girl understands very painfully her father's attempt to transform her through some mystical baseball alchemy:

> The cap, perhaps, might keep my hair
> forever clipped; holding the glove
> against my chest might stop
> my breasts; and if I learned
> the grip and stance, perhaps my wrists
> would thicken, hard, around the bat.

The father becomes the priest in this ritual of sacrifices and transformation, as he "made the diamond out of stones he piled like altars into three small mounds."

Year by year, the father continues this ceremony in other ways. Just as he tries to make her fit into the sandlot where she knows she does not belong, he tries to make her fit into the "real" world, from which she has also been excluded:

> Year by year he built for me
> the things he thought
> a man one day would want me for:
> investments, a name
> the family business—stock
> to insure a fair exchange
> for a man who might try
> to be a son.

But her father always fails at the spring trades, and is never able to transform her:

> I always came back being
> still a girl who couldn't play
> the way he'd hoped. . . .

Being "still a girl," she is denied access to any game. Read the rules.

But if left to herself this same little girl would play for all she was worth, and this is the message of Alice Fulton's "Fierce Girl Playing Hopscotch." This poem is a celebration of the value of play above and around and beyond and between all rules, play that carries people into the future, with messages about who they are. The speaker in the poem looks into the past at herself as a girl:

> I am what you made to live in
> from what you had: hair matted as kelp, bad schools.

Unlike the adult speaker observing her past, the girl is so engrossed in play that she is oblivious to her future:

> Oh you will never know me. I wave and you go
> on playing in the clouds
> boys clap from erasers.

Playmates are gone from this future without play:

> Where's the kid called Katydid? The moonfaced
> Kewpiedoll? The excitable pouting
> Zookie? The somber O-Be-Joyful?

But the "lost girl" of the speaker's memory continues to play hopscotch, while the adult fulfills the promise of the child, but now believing in the anagrams and magic chants that once led her down the walk: "Name of father, son, ghost. Cross my heart and hope." The hopscotch ritual of childhood becomes the social ritual of self-identity and survival in adulthood as the sea of chalk changes to "loam and gold."

The little lost girl of hopscotch dancing in a sea of chalk, the players in tug-of-war, and the children "gilt by the sun" keep resurfacing with a central message already noted in Maxine Kumin's "Morning Swim." It is the idea that a peaceful cooperation among people and a faith in the natural world will expand and redeem loves. This is once again the theme of our final poem, Linda McCarriston's "Riding Out at Evening." The poem begins quietly, with a feeling of companionship between horse and rider, moves into a life-affirming love for particular others, and rises mystically into a love-expanding affirmation of the whole world. Dusk at the beginning of the poem is pictured as a sanctified time when "everything blurs and softens." As the fields and hills pull up "the first slight sheets of evening" and the rider "on horseback takes it in" she becomes one with the dusk—not an intruder, "but kin passing, closer and closer to night." It is in this peaceful union with the evening that the rider begins her blessing of her surroundings, "alone, wishing, or praying for particular good to particular beings."

The horse at once becomes a symbol of the rider and a vehicle of transcendence carrying her into flight:

> The horse bears me along, like grace,
> making me better than what I am,
> and what I think or say or see
> is whole in these moments, is neither
>
> small nor broken. For up
> out of the inscrutable earth, have come my body
> and the separate body of the mare:
> flawed and aching and wronged.

Horse and rider experience the power of their weakness and the strength of their separateness. And "we, as one, might course over the entire valley, over all valleys, as a bird in a great embrace of flight." Like the myth of Bellerophon and the winged horse Pegasus who triumph over the monster of havoc, they triumph over the grief of the world with tenderness:

> as a bird in a great embrace
> of flight, who presses against her breast,
> in grief and tenderness,
> the whole weeping body of the world. . . .

It was by way of a similarly tender image that Kenneth Patchen once described art as a pair of magic shoes that take one where one has never been before. If not all sports poems by women exhibit the alternative values about which we have been speaking, if some

130   BROOKE K. HORVATH AND SHARON G. CARSON

seem indistinguishable from poems written by men insofar as attitudes toward and perceived significance of sport are concerned,[5] women's sports poetry nonetheless continually offers itself as a pair of magic shoes, as a strong and graceful horse, ready to carry the reader into regions of experience he or she may never have visited before. We hope this essay proves useful enroute.

Notes

1. A positive focus on family values was one early modification of the traditional male sporting myth made by women writers in the years before a fully female alternative began to assert itself, according to Oriard (11–14). Indeed, an emphasis on family—fathers and daughters, mothers and their children, husbands and wives (as well as other male-female relationships and dreams of such potentially familial relationships)—accounts for the subject matter of many sports poems by women. In addition to several of the poems discussed here, see, for example, Betty Adcock's "The Sixth Day," Nancy Jones's "Running Blind," Mabel M. Kuykendall's "Baseball Pitcher," and Louise Glück's "The Racer's Widow," all in Tom Dodge's *A Literature of Sports.*

2. The other response discussed by Westkott and Coakley is "the assimilationist argument," according to which "feminist change is defined in terms of women gaining access to culturally valued spheres of action rather than changing those cultural values and actions" (32).

3. Here is not the place to offer a working bibliography of useful sources for the further study of women and sport. Beyond the bibliography in this volume, we would direct the reader's attention to Oriard, whose essay deserves to be read in its entirety; to the work of feminists Mary Daly and Marilyn French; and to the extensive lists of references appended to the Beck and Westkott and Coakley essays.

4. A feature of a number of women's sports poems we have not considered at length but that deserves mention at this point is the direct criticism of male-defined sport behavior. See, for instance, Babette Deutsch's "A Bull," Louise Glück's "The Racer's Widow," and Barbara Howes's "In Autumn," among others, in Tom Dodge's *A Literature of Sports.*

5. From Beck's perspective, such nonalternative poems would be the products of women who have fully assimilated male values and attitudes. Also of interest in this respect are the recently reconceptualized Jungian notions of anima and animus as discussed, for instance, in Bettina Knapp's *Women in Twentieth-Century Literature,* which applies a number of Jungian concepts to a spectrum of literary works. As Knapp explains, the anima (or female principle of all personalities, female and male), once characterized as the source of emotionalism, helplessness, vanity, and the like, is now described positively as nurturing, caring, feeling, creative, and life enhancing (with the animus representing intellect, rationality, heroism). Such concepts might help, among other things, in positing a female perspective on sport not exclusively the possession of women and thereby in accounting for masculine values and attitudes in certain sports poems by women as well as feminine characteristics in sports poems by men.

Works Cited

Beck, Bonnie. "The Future of Women's Sport: Issues, Insights, and Struggles." In *Sport in Contemporary Society,* edited by D. Stanley Eitzen, 401–14. 2d ed. New York: St. Martin's, 1984.
Dickey, James. "In the Pocket." In *A Literature of Sports,* edited by Tom Dodge, 389–90. Lexington, Mass.: Heath, 1980.
Dodge, Tom, ed. *A Literature of Sports,* Lexington, Mass.: Heath, 1980.
Francis, Robert. "Swimmer." In *A Literature of Sports,* edited by Tom Dodge, 416. Lexington, Mass.: Heath, 1980.
Fulton, Alice. "Fierce Girl Playing Hopscotch." *Poetry,* March 1985, 340.
Knapp, Bettina. *Women in Twentieth-Century Literature: A Jungian View.* University Park: Pennsylvania State University Press, 1987.
Kumin, Maxine. "Morning Swim." In *A Literature of Sports,* edited by Tom Dodge, 413–14. Lexington, Mass.: Heath, 1980.
McCarriston, Linda. "Riding Out at Evening." *Poetry,* June 1982, 153–54.
Mizejewski, Linda. "Season Wish." In *Baseball Diamonds: Tales, Traces, Visions & Voodoo from a Native American Rite,* edited by Kevin Kerrane and Richard Grossinger, 37–38. Garden City, N.Y.: Anchor-Doubleday, 1980.
Mordenski, Jan. "For Athletes, Poets, and Lovers." *Arete: The Journal of Sport Literature* 4, no. 1 (1986): 56.
Oriard, Michael. "From Jane Allen to *Water Dancer:* A Brief History of the Feminist (?) Sports Novel." *Modern Fiction Studies* 33 (1987): 9–20.
Slusher, Howard S. "Sport and Death." In *Sport Inside Out: Readings in Literature and Philosophy,* edited by David L. Vanderwerken and Spencer K. Wertz, 752–55. Fort Worth: Texas Christian University Press, 1985.
Spires, Elizabeth. "The Playground." *Poetry,* October 1983, 33.
Swenson, May. "Watching the Jets Lose to Buffalo at Shea." In *A Literature of Sports,* edited by Tom Dodge, 410–11. Lexington, Mass.: Heath, 1980.
Westkott, Marcia, and Jay J. Coakley. "Women in Sport: Modalities of Feminist Social Change." *Journal of Sport and Social Issues* 5, no. 1 (1981): 32–45.
Wright, Judith. "Sports Field." In *A Literature of Sports,* edited by Tom Dodge, 425–26. Lexington, Mass.: Heath, 1980.

II

The Supplemental Literature— Criticism, Philosophy, Autobiography, Biography, History, and Special Studies

. . . we believe our sports-crazed society places too much un-thinking value on sport and directs too little critical thought toward serious, interpretive, sport-related literature.

Hence this call for tough-minded critics willing to chart and navigate the river of sport-related literature flowing out of the lake of sports. Our goal is to recruit and encourage critics who will investigate, study, discriminate, and evaluate the hazards, beauty, and wealth of the river of sport literature.

—Fred Boe and Lyle Olsen,
"Navigating Huck Finn's
River," in *Arete: The Journal
of Sport Literature* (Fall 1984)

The Inception and Reception of a Journal: The Story of Sport Literature's Search for a Voice and an Identity

LYLE I. OLSEN

As every graduate student knows, the overcrowded shelves in academic libraries are lined with the serial volumes of scholarly journals that probe the esoteric findings of the various disciplines in solemn and ponderous depth. Early in 1984, researchers began to take notice of a new entry. Surprisingly, the subtitle identifying this journal had to do with "sports," a subject many academicians contend should be perused only in the newspaper along with their morning coffee, certainly not a subject worthy enough to be considered for scholarly analysis.

In spite of such an attitude, it is worth noting that the critical reviews of the first two issues of *Arete: The Journal of Sport Literature* (1983–84) were quite favorable, though they did not always appear in the most august of publications. For one example, Professor Jarold Ramsey of the University of Rochester wrote in the "Booktalk" department of *Sports Illustrated* for 6 August 1984:

> Athletics and imaginative literature have been intersecting, sometimes memorably, at least since Homer sang the story of the Greeks' funeral games for Patroklos. Now, with a good kind of inevitability, we have the first two issues of *Arete: The Journal of Sport Literature* . . . edited by Lyle I. Olsen and Alfred F. Boe, both of whom are professors at San Diego State. . . . The journal is a logical response to the recent discovery of sport as a legitimate subject of intellectual inquiry from many angles—sports and religion, sports and myth, the sociology, politics, economics, psychology of sport. . . .

Nonetheless two basic questions still remain—why another scholarly journal when librarians in universities across the country have been asking faculty to help them reduce their proliferating journal holdings? And more to the point, why a journal devoted to a supposedly ephemeral subject such as sports? Following is my response to these questions, actually the story of how a journal for sport literature came to be.

Early in the 1970s, I was encouraged to teach in one of the subdisciplines of physical education: the sociocultural area of sport studies. Though most instructors' interest here lay more in art, history, and sociology, I soon became aware that the literature of sport was my primary interest although I was overwhelmed by the wealth of material that could be classified as sport literature. Not only was this an exciting discovery, I soon realized that the amazingly diverse literature of sport contained a mother lode of untapped potential for the serious study of sport in society.

Nonetheless, from the start of my work in the sociocultural area of sport, I encountered nagging frustrations. By the end of the 1970s, I had enough experience teaching sport history and sociology to realize that I wanted to include more sport literature in my course than was feasible if I were to maintain a balance between art, history, sociology, and literature. I was also displeased with the lack of respect I encountered whenever I advocated sport as a subject for serious, scholarly study in the humanities area.

When I finally began teaching a course on the literature of sport I discovered, however, that teaching sport literature could be both rewarding and frustrating—rewarding because of the wealth and depth of the material but frustrating because I kept turning up (usually by chance) more and more articles, novels, and source material that I could have used in my course if I had only known they were available. Furthermore, I soon realized that my idea of how sport literature should be studied came as a shock to many of my students. It seems that they had not enrolled in the class expecting to study such novels as Robert Coover's *The Universal Baseball Association, Inc.*, John Updike's *Rabbit, Run,* Bernard Malamud's *The Natural,* or Mark Harris's *The Southpaw.* In fact, the students were surprised and dismayed to learn that they would be held responsible for turning in critiques and producing research papers, and that in addition, they had to contend with a course textbook by sport literature pioneer Wiley Lee Umphlett entitled *The Sporting Myth and the American Experience: Studies in Contemporary Fiction* (1975). It was evident that the students had enrolled expecting classroom time to be devoted to no more serious subject matter than discussions about the merits of Yogi Berra as the Yankees' manager or who should play quarterback for the San Francisco 49ers.

But to be honest, I had not been trained to teach the material I had on hand, so early in the 1980s I started looking for help—someone, somewhere who could guide me through the vast accumulation of material in the field. Perhaps there was a professional organization that could help me become knowledgable of the best work being done in the area of sport literature, I reasoned.

After beginning my quest for professional competence, every time I located a new source, it would lead me to other journals further afield. I concluded that gems about sport literature were scattered (and buried) in many diverse publications, and as a result I was learning about my best sources through happenstance. A typical example occurred when a student submitted a critique of an article from the *Journal of Popular Culture;* that article led me to Walter Harrison at Colorado College who, as it turned out, was preparing to coordinate a session on sport literature at an upcoming popular-culture meeting. Though this method proved semisuccessful, I realized that my system of acquiring information was, at best, piecemeal.

After listening to me voice my problems, some colleagues advised me to attend the next meeting of the North American Association of Sport History (NASH). Listed on the early notices of the NASH program were Allen Guttmann of Amherst College and Robert J. Higgs of East Tennessee State University—two leaders in the budding field of sport literature. Unfortunately, neither was able to attend, but Richard Keller of Emporia State University was on the program, and this gentleman turned out to be just what my sagging morale needed.

Professor Keller, who presented an excellent paper, "Coaches in Fiction," also coordinated a stimulating sport literature session, and I was, in a word, elated. This was my first formal encounter with such people as Mary McElroy and Kent Cartwright from Kansas State University, Richard Crepeau from the University of Central Florida, and Gerry Redmond of the University of Alberta in Edmonton—reputable scholars who had analyzed and debated the finer points of sport literature. So for the next few days, I cornered the experts, and they were kind enough to answer all the myriad questions I had about sport literature. How much poetry did they teach? What articles did they use along with the novels? How extensive were their reading lists? Would they recommend the use of a textbook, and who else did they know teaching sport literature?

Sometime during that first meeting, Dick Keller recommended that I contact Tom Dodge at Mountain View College in Dallas, further suggesting that I adopt his excellent anthology, *The Liter-*

ature of Sport. Then Dodge, in turn, introduced me to more people who were writing and teaching in the area. Thus I became involved in "networking" before I realized what the concept meant. From this random type of contact I learned about Neil Isaacs, Chris Messenger, Neil David Berman, Mike Oriard, Don Johnson, David Vanderwerken, and a host of other English professors who were presenting sport literature papers at different meetings or working on books in the field.

With renewed enthusiasm I returned to my teaching, but the basic questions and frustrations persisted. How could a person keep finding out more about this growing field? If so many scholars were working in this subdiscipline, how many more were out there who had yet to present papers at meetings? To what sources could a person go to acquire more information? It soon became obvious that I was searching for something that did not exist—an established clearinghouse, a forum for the exchange of information and research about sport literature.

So what does a frustrated teacher of sport literature do if no forum exists? He considers taking the bull by the horns and starting one. In the meantime, though, I had been making a list of the scholars working in this literary subdiscipline, and it had grown into an impressive lineup, both in size and expertise. Then in 1981 the *Journal of American Culture* came out with its special issue, "Focus on Academics in Sport," edited by Melvin Friedman, and it suddenly dawned on me what was needed—a regularly published, wide-ranging journal featuring fiction, poetry, criticism, and reviews focused on sport literature, one that would encourage, stimulate, and foster an alliance of sport and the humanities.

Since everyone I had contacted up to this time knew at least four or five more professors (previously unknown to me) who were also teaching or writing about sport literature, it was obvious that an impressive underground existed. And every professor (with absolutely no exception) whom I continued to contact was interested in sharing names, information, and articles. In talking with these dedicated teachers, who had designed and fought for their own courses in sport literature, I felt a strong bond of fellowship, and for this reason I considered these men and women as "special." So I decided to determine if there were enough committed scholars around to start a journal devoted to sport literature.

However, I first had a major hurdle to surmount: who was going to publish such a journal? Before I started canvasing the field to see if interested colleagues were willing to be involved in my project, I needed to locate a university press that would print their work. So I met with Roger Cunniff, the founder and editor of the San Diego State University Press, who seemed surprisingly receptive to my proposal. During our meeting he outlined the major problems I would face and sketched a rough plan for starting up a journal. Most importantly, however, Cunniff indicated that he would be interested in printing the journal if I could meet the requirements he had set forth. In a short while I was back in my office figuring out what the next step was to get this enterprise underway.

First we had to have a scholarly as well as a financial base. From my list I was confident we could start with an organization of at least 150 men and women who were involved in some area of sport literature. From the special feeling I sensed in talking with these individuals, I assumed that they were as interested as I was in becoming members of a formal sport literature forum.

Next I determined that we had to have a first-class product. Since sport as an academic topic had always been suspect, I figured it would be up to contributors from academic circles to help make it respectable. Would the best qualified (thirty men and women) around the United States and Canada, then, write an article and/or be an editor for the first or second issue of a new journal devoted exclusively to sport literature? The first person I called was Dick Crepeau at Central Florida. He not only agreed to write an article but also act as an associate editor. His enthusiasm motivated me immediately to telephone Jack Higgs at East Tennessee State, who in turn strongly recommended that I call Allen Guttmann at Amherst. So in just a couple of afternoons and evenings of calling, I had twenty-nine of the first thirty people I called committed to writing articles, reading submissions, and acting as editors.

During this process of recruiting writers and editors for the first two issues, the format of the journal had been taking shape. A consensus of the associate editors decided on a strong fiction section along with a pithy poetry forum to enliven and balance the scholarly essays. Following the lead of other quality journals, we planned specialty departments devoted to topics such as book reviews and journal surveys so that our readers would be apprised of what was going on throughout the field. A unique feature of the journal was to be the "classics" department. This resulted from my discovery that many of the associate editors used works by ancient classical authors in their sport literature courses. After checking with classicist David Young at the University of California, Santa Barbara, I telephoned his first choice for editor, one of the leading experts in the field, Tom Scanlon at the University of California, Riverside. After a visit to Riverside, we had an Ancient Sport Literature section and editor.

When I finally sat back to consider what I had accomplished, the scope of it all was frightening. But after I called Roger Cunniff and told him of the response, he gave me more encouragement and advice. We had enough articles for the first two issues of the journal, he said. Now we needed to organize a local editorial staff and a sport literature membership base to finance the operation. Recruiting help from colleagues Susan J. Bandy, Ralph Grawunder, and Richard Wells in the San Diego State University (SDSU) Physical Education Department, I started out with them on both tasks simultaneously.

I knew from the high praise of his students that Fred Boe had taught a sport literature course at SDSU. And since I was attending a Hemingway class taught by James Hinkle, I asked for his help in recruiting local editors. There were some quality concern issues to be settled at first in determining what we meant by sport literature in an editorial sense. Fortunately, Jim Hinkle knew Michael Oriard's work (from an earlier job search), and I presented Jim a copy of Christian Messenger's *Sport and the Spirit of Play in American Fiction: Hawthorne to Faulkner*. The combination of books, research, and articles dealing with sport literature by these two outstanding scholars convinced Hinkle that this would be a serious literary venture and helped establish an editorial stance.

Subsequently, Professor Hinkle contacted a small group of his English Department colleagues he thought would be interested, and a meeting was arranged. It turned out that they were more than interested; they were highly enthusiastic, and the first meeting with Boe, Hinkle, Fred Moramarco, and Larry McCaffery resulted in more progress. In fact, they were all willing to help after I explained what had been accomplished and committed up to that point: (a) the arrangement with Roger Cunniff and the San Diego State University Press to print the journal; (b) the commitment of twenty-nine scholars to write pieces and function as associate editors; (c) a rough sketch of the departments and sections that would make up the magazine; and (d) plans for a sport literature organization that would be the business and financial umbrella for all the production aspects of the enterprise. Following several more meetings, Fred Boe settled in as the person in charge of the fiction section while doubling as the associate editor. Fred Moramarco agreed to start the Book Review Department, and Jim Hinkle volunteered to do the final proofreading. With these decisions, I concluded that the creative and scholarly aspects of the proposed journal had been placed in competent professional hands, and so my worries about its quality were laid to rest.

Just before the meeting with the English faculty at SDSU, I had also been fortunate enough to recruit a poetry editor. Both James Whitehead of the University of Arkansas and James Dickey of the University of South Carolina recommended Bruce Weigl at Old Dominion University in Norfolk, Virginia. Following a telephone call and a letter or two, the journal now had a first-class poetry editor.

From this point on in setting up the editorial operation, Fred Boe and I would meet and discuss our remaining needs. Following each meeting I would telephone a couple of the experts Fred had recommended (or we knew by reputation), and in the next day or so we would decide upon our choice. Usually our first choice would accept the task, and we'd have another section of the journal covered.

While the editorial staff was being recruited, my colleagues in physical education were busy setting up a tax-free commercial organization. As printing bills would soon be outstanding and an organization meeting was scheduled for the summer of 1984, we started the process of mailing thousands of flyers and handbills alerting everyone we thought would be interested that for only $30.00 they could join this fledgling venture.

Amazingly and, of course, fortunately, the Sport Literature Association was able to pay its first printing bills with the proceeds of this early call for members. And late in the summer of 1984 the SLA held its first annual meeting on the campus of the University of California at San Diego.

Before the first issue of *Arete: The Journal of Sport Literature* was published in the fall of 1983, the Sport Literature Association membership numbered approximately 500 (inclusive of individuals and institutions). Judging from the reception letters, Fred Boe (who produced the lion's share of work putting together the first issue) and the associate editors had done an outstanding job. Naturally, some criticism was forthcoming, as in the following by Jarold Ramsey (*Sports Illustrated,* 6 August 1984):

> To be sure, not all of *Arete* 1 and 2 measure up. Several of the essays here are afflicted by what seems to be an occupational hazard of the sport-lit field: a glib pop-myth/pop-existential discourse in which everything in an athletic contest from the heroics to the liniment used by participants becomes symbolic of some larger truth. . . .

But far and away the critical response was closer in spirit to a comment by Wayne Swanson in a *Los Angeles Times* review (11 June 1984):

> Together, Olsen and Boe have created a journal that holds sports literature to a high standard. Theirs is not a forum for sports stories about how the home team gave 110 per cent, overcame adversity and won the state championship. Rather, it is a forum for literature that incorporates sports into its world view.

To bring matters up to date, I should make a comment here about the recent change in the journal's title in that the threat of a law-suit has forced us to settle on a new name. It seems that a small specialized publication of the School of Social Work at the University of South Carolina has been using the title *Arete* for about fifteen years. Although we thought the whole matter ridiculous (there's obviously no area of conflict or competition between the two journals, as our full title makes clear), San Diego State's lawyers did not and insisted that we capitulate. Beginning with the Spring 1988 issue, therefore, the journal has been known as *Aethlon: The Journal of Sport Literature*.

Regardless of name change, though, I wish to reassert our original intent of striving to encourage, stimulate, and foster the alliance of sport with the humanities. Of the themes that have inspired memorable writing in our culture, sport certainly is not the least—and to remind our readers of this fact through the publication of quality literature is what *Aethlon: The Journal of Sport Literature* is all about.

The Agonic and the Edenic: Sport Literature and the Theory of Play

ROBERT J. HIGGS

At the beginning of the 1960s the intellectual historian René Wellek rendered a service to the study of literature by identifying the major critical approaches of the time and showing how they developed internationally. From a systematic viewpoint, Wellek wished to provide "some principles of selection" for "mountains of printed matter" (344). Such an effort, he says, was unique and quite different from that of Northrop Frye who in 1957 with his *Anatomy of Criticism* had aimed at "an all-embracing theory of literature . . . of the most grandiose pretensions." To Wellek, "a more modest view of the function of criticism seems . . . wiser" (361). Frye, Wellek argues, sees art as truth and uses criticism as a means of epistemology while Wellek himself sees art as beauty and criticism as a tool for aiding in aesthetic understanding and appreciation.

While Wellek tends to favor "formalistic, organistic, and symbolistic aesthetics rooted in the great tradition of German aesthetics from Kant to Hegel" instead of a study of "attitudes, feelings, concepts, and philosophies" in poetry and fiction, the point of his essay is to identify and describe the main critical trends that have developed in the twentieth century, though all have roots in the past. These forms of criticism are (1) Marxist, (2) psychoanalytic, or Freudian, (3) linguistic and stylistic, (4) organic, or formalistic, (5) mythic, or Jungian, and (6) philosophic and existential. In *Anatomy of Criticism* Frye had identified most of these forms, expressed his own preference for manifold or "polysemous" meaning, and issued a caveat for the student of literature:

> The modern student of critical theory is faced with a body of rhetoricians who speak of texture and frontal assaults, with students of history who deal with traditions and sources, with students using material from psychology and anthropology, with Aristotelians, Coleridgians, Thomists, Freudians, Jungians, Marxists, with students of myths, ritu-

als, archetypes, metaphors, ambiguities, and significant forms. The
student must either admit the principle of polysemous meaning, or
choose one of these groups and then try to prove that all the others are
less legitimate. The former is a way of scholarship, and leads to the
advancement of learning; the latter is the way of pedantry, and gives us
a wide choice of goals, the most conspicuous today being fantastical
learning, or myth criticism, contentious learning, or historical criticism
and delicate learning, or "new" criticism. (72)

At the time of his article Wellek spoke of "survivals, leftovers,
and throwbacks" such as "impressionistic description," "arbitrary
pronouncements of taste," and "historical scholarship," and while
he had all the major trends fairly well catalogued for the moment,
neither he nor Frye nor anyone else could have predicted what
would arrive on the scene in the next two and a half decades. In a
1987 article in *The New York Times Magazine* entitled "The Tyranny of the Yale Critics," Colin Campbell summarizes what has
happened since that time:

> During the 1960s romantic poets such as Shelley and Romantic critics
> such as Harold Bloom came in like typhoons, and the new critics faded.
> A lot of other forces also appeared: Sartre, Marx, Freud, Jung,
> Nietzsche, Wittgenstein, Heidegger, Lévi-Strauss. In came the struc-
> turalists and the declaration of the late French critic Roland Barthes of
> the death of the author. . . . In came feminism. (28)

In, too, came the biggest storm of all—deconstructionist criticism, which Wellek recently attacked: "The doctrine of 'the prison
house of language' (words referring only to other words) is absurd,"
he argues. He has also written that "the blurring of the distinction
between poetry and critical prose, the rejection of every idea of
correct interpretation in favor of misreading, the denial of all literature of any reference to reality are all symptoms of a profound
malaise" (Campbell, 47). There are also attacks on deconstruction
by leftist critics, says Campbell, who see it as an "empty, elitist,
bourgeois game."

In turn, there are attacks upon the left and the right, especially by
Harold Bloom. At Yale today, he says, "there are various covens
and sects and various new orthodoxies of a self-righteous kind."
There are "purple-haired semioticians," deconstructionists, of
course, "fourth-rate reactionaries," "fierce neo-Marxists," "New
Stalinisms," "vicious feminisms," and "punk ideologies." But
"What all true believers in one system or another have failed to
learn," says Bloom, "is that there is no method except yourself.

Ideologists of every description hate the self. . . . They all deny that there can be such a thing as an individual" (28).

In his humorous survey of what's happening at Yale, Bloom makes no mention of the theory of play, but it too has prospered at Yale in league with deconstruction, which for Jacques Derrida is based "on the infinite freeplay of signs" (Hans, 307).[1] The "play" of Derrida, however, is quite different from that of Hans-Georg Gadamer, who along with Bloom was one of the commanders leading the attack on the New Criticism. As James Hans has observed:

> If we . . . recognize play as the central process in human and natural activity, and if we come to value the contributions of both Derrida and Gadamer to our understanding of the role of play in human life, we are left ultimately, I think, with a perspective which makes Gadamer and Derrida mirror images of each other, that we are seeing how the concept of play works from a hermeneutic, continuous point of view and from a deconstructive, discontinuous point of view and that both views are simply parts of the same process, that there is no hermeneutics without deconstruction and no continuity without discontinuity. (316–17)

Both men were influenced by Martin Heidegger, whose theory of play in turn has itself been contrasted and categorized by Richard Detsch in "A Non-Subjectivist Concept of Play—Gadamer and Heidegger versus Rilke and Nietzsche." There is also a strong element of play both in the overall manner of Harold Bloom and in his romantic criticism.

In fact, play theory today is everywhere on the intellectual scene. In "Toward a Critical Theory of Play," Francis Hearn endorses a spirit of play in all disciplines and throughout society:

> Ultimately, the celebration of freedom must receive rational articulation, the playful circumvention of conventional restraints must be committed to the search for truth. In short, play must be informed by critical discourse. At the same time, however, critical disourse, if it is to transcend the given, must be informed by play. Further, if the community of rational theorizers is not to devolve into a vanguard elite, it must be playful, for in play we learn to be equal. (160)

In religion there is a widespread theology of play, and I am not talking about muscular Christianity here. David Miller in *Gods and Games: Toward a Theology of Play* (1970) argues in two chapters that "Play Is Religion" and "Religion Is Play" and that one ought to regard "life as a children's game." In the same vein Robert E.

Neale, in *In Praise of Play: Toward a Psychology of Religion* (1973), concludes with a chapter called "The Crucifixion as Play." According to him the crucifixion is an extension of God's spirit of adventure, whereas Jürgen Moltmann in *Theology of Play* (1972) sees it as inconsistent with God's play.

Even in the new theories of science there is a bountiful playfulness as seen in such books as *The Tao of Physics* (1977) by Fritjof Capra and *The Dancing Wu-Li Masters* (1980) by Gary Zukav. Einstein himself appeared to be nothing less than a "true believer" in play as revealed in his response to an inquiry sent to him in 1945 about his working methods:

> Taken from a psychological viewpoint, this combinatory play seems to be the essential feature in productive thought—before there is any connection with logical construction in words or other kinds of signs which can be communicated to others. . . . Conventional words or other signs have to be sought for laboriously only in a secondary stage, when the mentioned associative play is sufficiently established and can be produced at will. (Koestler, 171)

In all these views there is a common theme, the desire for a better world, a creative world in which suffering will no longer dominate. There is a unified call almost for a genuine understanding of the self and nature, an assumption or belief that when human beings really know themselves and the world they will find that the essence of being is play, which of course means fair play and equality. It can even be said that play theorists in all disciplines want in some ways to return to Eden. All point to barriers that seem secondary or artificial—Derrida (and even Einstein) to language, Miller and Neale to sin, and Hearn to social classes. In Eden there were no words, no sin, and no economic order. There was, however, play, as Anne Herbert points out in her delightful essay about the fall of man in the *Next Whole Earth Catalogue*:

> At first we did have fun just like he [God] expected. We played all the time. We rolled down the hills, waded in the streams, climbed in the trees, swung on the vines, ran in the meadows, frolicked in the woods, hid in the forest and acted silly. We laughed a lot.

Then enters the snake, who introduced "scoring," that is, sports:

> It was different after that. We yelled a lot. We had to make up new scoring rules for the games we played. Other games like frolicking we stopped because they were too hard to score. By the time God found

out about our new fun, we were spending about forty-five minutes a day in actual playing and the rest of the time working out the score. God was wroth about that—very very wroth. He said we couldn't use his garden anymore because we weren't having any fun. We said we were having lots of fun and we were. He shouldn't have got so upset just because it wasn't exactly the kind of fun he had in mind. . . . Really, it was life in Eden that didn't mean anything. Fun is great in its place but without scoring there's no reason for it. God has a very superficial view of life and I'm glad my children are being raised away from his influence. We were lucky to get out. We're all very grateful to the snake. (31)

There is no doubt about it: play is in, but sports are not exactly out. There is just confusion as to what the connection is between them, or put another way for purposes here, between sport literature and the theory of play. Are sports part of the universe of play, as Roger Caillois observes, or are they fundamentally antagonistic to the very idea of play? Is play implied in the term "sport literature," and, if so, is it inherent in the term "sport" or the term "literature" or both? Since literature is an art and since play is central to art and science, as Koestler effectively argues, it almost goes without saying that play is essential to creative writing of any type. How, though, does "play" relate to "sport"? One knows that they are different, though they are usually spoken of in literature in the same breath.

For instance, in *Samson Agonistes* the Philistines "are only set on sports and play." In their "idolatrous rites" are "sword players, and every sort / Of gymnic artists, wrestlers, riders, runners, / Jugglers and dancers, mummers, mimics . . ." (1323–25). In "The New England Holiday" section of *The Scarlet Letter,* Hawthorne, after describing the virtual absence of play ("no rude shows of a theatrical kind"), goes on to say that still the people smiled, "grimly," and watched the "sports" that the colonists had witnessed and shared in long ago" in the county fairs and village greens of England" (221), showing in his comments upon wrestling his knowledge and use of Strutt's *Sports and Pastimes of the People of England.* Lewis Carroll, too, saw the connection between sports and play but wrestled with the distinctions. Though he is talking primarily about hunting, that is, sport as opposed to sports or athletics, the question he raises in the Sylvie and Bruno books will serve here and is perhaps more relevant today than ever: "How can I get the idea of Sport into your innocent mind?" (Blake, 168) One way he attempts to do this is by relating Bruno's rationalization of his game with "Mouses": "I teaches the Mouses new games: the Mouses like it ever so much. . . . Sometimes little accidents happens: sometimes the Mouses kill theirselves!" (171) In the same vein Carroll once told a little girl that Alice was about "malice." Still, in spite of everything he has shown to undermine it, including sport and "exclusive sports" such as cricket, "he never completely abandons the ideal of the innocence of play" (173).

At this point I want to argue that there are two sides to the theory of play that I call the "Edenic" and the "agonic." I have already indicated an Edenic aspect of play—simple, free, nonegalitarian, and noncompetitive, which many bright minds thoroughly endorse and which is applauded by all. There is, however, a less conspicuous side of play theory, an agonic side, a competitive or score-keeping aspect that is analogous to the idea of contests (agon) that lies at the heart of the sport literature tradition. Sports imply competition and, of course, prizes and rules, and wherever there are prizes and rules there are questions of performance (excellence or *arete*) and behavior (ethics). This is not to say that play is not concerned with these matters. But so often in the idea of what is normally called play, emphasis is placed upon communion instead of individual struggle or achievement—or failure. To paraphrase Herman Melville, in no world but a fallen one could sports exist; play, on the other hand, existed in the unfallen one and the fallen, though it keeps reminding over and over that its true home is prelapsarian Eden. Sports point not toward an undifferentiated world of green pastures and murmuring brooks but toward a heavenly city where the winners walk eternally on streets of gold. Play emphasizes pleasure and being; sports meaning and becoming. Thus in sport literature the focus is always upon contending individuals. In the theory of play the focus is upon systems of language and laws of nature or social orders that inhibit the freedom that unfettered play promises to all. Until one can know with more certainty than is now the case just what the nature of Eden is or the heavenly city, sports and play should be considered in both a symbiotic and antagonistic relationship. The tendencies of human nature that both represent are not mutually exclusive. Students of sport literature can learn much from the theory of play as currently reflected in various fields; by the same token, the literature of sport is now in an excellent position to inform critical play theory with endless texts confirming some aspects of play theory while casting doubts upon others but in any event providing an opposite pole for a dialectic that can only advance understanding on all fronts.

Harold Bloom may lament that yet another theory claiming more attention is the last thing needed, but the truth is that play theory has abounded at Yale for some time in the guise of deconstruction, and even in Bloom's own critical manifesto. The challenge now is to understand play theory, especially its relationship to sport literature. It might be argued that one is a subject or genre while the other is a theory, but I do not believe that is quite the case, either. Sport literature is a mode as well as a genre, constantly reflecting in fiction, nonfiction, and poetry some aspect of the world of play. That scholars can now talk confidently about critical interpretations of sport literature is perhaps the surest sign of its success to date. A tremendous body of quality writing is required before one can even begin to discuss it in terms of critical schools.

Bloom and Gadamer, two noted thinkers who have helped to widen critical possibilities, reflect both Edenic and agonic aspects of play. The competitive elements in their works are submerged, even disguised, but they are present nevertheless. Both illustrate a polysemous method that incorporates sporting metaphors in their attack upon the old fortress of New Criticism, Bloom by showing that every poet competes with those who have preceded him and Gadamer by showing that an involved audience is central to both art and play. One shows the inevitability of influence and the other the need for spectators, both of which are as essential to sport as they are to the play of poetry and drama. They succeed in these efforts, however, subtly, with only brief reference to sports or athletic metaphors.

In Gadamer's *Truth and Method* the apparent emphasis is upon an idea of play that seems to be at odds with the essence of athletics, goal, purpose, and strain or agony, as seen, for example, in the following comments:

> Play obviously represents an order in which the *to* and *from* motion of play follows of itself. It is part of play that the movement is not only without goal or purpose but also without effort. It happens as it were by itself. The ease of play, which phenomenologically refers only to the absence of strain, is experienced subjectively as relaxation. The structure of play absorbs the player into itself, and thus takes from him the burden of initiative, which constitutes the actual strain of existence. This is seen also in the spontaneous tendency to repetition that emerges in the player and in the constant self-renewal of play. . . . Nature, inasmuch as it is without purpose or intention, as it is, without exertion, a constantly self-renewing play, can appear as a model of art. Thus Friedrich Schlegel writes: "All the sacred games of art are only remote imitations of the infinite play of the world, the eternally self-creating work of art." (94)

Here clearly is the Edenic view of play, play as innocent and simple, noninstrumental and re-creative, like nature itself. Like Koestler, Gadamer believes that play is the central activity of nature and art, which would mean that the critic should have some understanding of how play "works" and perhaps how works "play" in order to practice his own craft, especially if he or she would be creative, too. Of course, what Gadamer and Koestler have to say in this regard applies immediately to the creator of sports fiction and stories, where the play of the mind is essential, and everyone knows from personal experiences or endless accounts of others where play or nature seems to take over in a contest and replace the player in a sense. *The Psychic Side of Sport* by Michael Murphy and Lea White contains numerous instances of the rhythms of a game controlling, or seeming to control, those of the participants as if nature was itself at play, which is not to imply that Gadamer is trying to justify psychic phenomena.

In spite of the application of what Gadamer has to say to literature and sports, his language is not that of athletics but that of play, which furnishes his examples, especially the theater he focuses upon as an example of the game in which "the difference between the player and the spectator is removed." Richard Detsch is not exactly correct when he says that "the game played on the sports field serves Gadamer as an analogy of a work of art, notably in the particular instance of the 'Schauspiel.'" Gadamer just barely mentions sports (Gadamer, 98) and says that they tend to rob games of "their playful character" by becoming a "show" (Detsch, 157). Even by concentrating on the stage instead of the athletic field, Gadamer conveys the crucial role of spectators in sports as well as art. An athlete has always been one who competes for a prize in a public place and so to a degree does the author—perhaps the author of a sports story is someone seeking a prize in a public place for a story about someone seeking a prize in a public place. This is not an accusation of vanity but a statement of the natural instinct to compete and to observe and applaud competition.

Gadamer does not tell the reader, though, just why it is that a theater audience complements the play character of the game on the stage while sports spectators have the opposite effect. There is more going on here presumably than the fact that in a drama one wall has been replaced by an audience while in a stadium all the walls are down, which, it would seem, would allow for greater audience involvement as is often the case. What is suggested is that Gadamer sees some sort of fundamental difference between a sports spectator and a theatergoer, as no doubt there usually is.

Nevertheless, in neglecting the world of sports as he does, even avoiding definition, Gadamer reflects an ancient distinction and perhaps to some degree a bias common to patricians down through the years. William J. Baker explains what that essential difference was and is:

> Under the Romans sport became a show, a dramatic staged event for the purpose of diversion. The Latin word *ludi* was distinctly Roman. Whereas the Greek word for athletics, *agon,* meant a contest, *ludi* was a game in the sense of an amusement or entertainment. The same word was used for the players and actors in the theater: *ludiones.* It was a far cry from the Greek athletic ideal. (31)

Though "ludic" can convey the idea of tragedy as well as comedy, there is, even in tragedy, the sense that the audience is watching something un-real, an en-actment, a re-creation. Though every athletic contest is also a re-creation in which players follow a text, the struggle of the athlete on the playing field or in the arena is real, and while no two games can ever be the same, the outcome of a dramatic text is forever fixed. Hence the ludic, or playful, conveys the notion not of actual strain but imitation of truth or beauty or both. In athletic events there may also be beauty and there often is, but the goal of the athlete is simply winning a prize in a public place through physical skill. Thus with its ties to drama, "ludic" is closer to the notion of Edenic than agonic in the sense that what is happening on stage is amusement and entertainment as all the world was all the time in the Garden. Eden was a stage set with God as writer, director, and producer. All Adam and Eve had to do was to follow or mime the lines until they decided to "compete" for knowledge. Even Huizinga's *Homo Ludens,* as the name implies, generally neglects athletics, focusing upon the politer forms of play elements in culture.

What is minimized by a concentration on actual theater or the theater of the mind and language is both an appreciation of physical excellence *(arete)* and a sense of the ethical questions that specialized excellence raise for any society. What is sacrificed in part is a concern for *arete,* which has broad applications but which is rooted in physical excellence and the contest *(agon).* According to H. D. F. Kitto,

> It *[arete]* may be limited by its context; the *arete* of a race-horse is speed, of a cart-horse, strength. If it is used in a general context, of a man it will connote excellence in the ways in which a man can be

excellent—morally, intellectually, physically, practically. Thus the hero of the *Odyssey* is a great fighter, a wily schemer, a ready speaker, a man of stout heart and broad wisdom who knows that he must endure without too much complaining what the gods send; and he can both build and sail a boat, drive a furrow as straight as anyone, beat a young braggart at throwing the discus, challenge the Phaecian youth at boxing, wrestling or running; flay, skin, cut up and cook an ox, and be moved to tears by a song. He is in fact an excellent all rounder; he has surpassing *arete*. . . . (172–73)

For the Greeks the contest *(agon)* "was a means of stimulating and displaying human *arete*. . . . It was *arete* that the games were designed to test—the *arete* of the whole man, not a merely specialized skill" (172–73). In play theory the attention is not upon willed achievement of individuals and the questions of cultural values raised by those efforts but upon the game in relation to nature, not upon *contests* but *contexts*. In Gadamer "the real subject of the game is . . . not the player, but instead the game itself" (Gadamer, 95–96); "for Derrida we can no longer even speak of knowledge or truth but only of infinite interpretations based on the infinite freeplay of signs" (Hans, 307). "The world," Hans concludes in his article on Gadamer and Derrida, "is a world of play to the end of it" (317).

It is also a world of words to the end of it, as the poet Wallace Stevens intimates in "The Pure Good of Theory":

It is never the thing but the version of the thing:
The fragrance of the woman not her self
Her self in the manner not the solid block,

The day in its color not perpending time,
Time in its weather our most sovereign lord,
The weather in words and words in sounds of sounds.

(332)

It is no accident that Harold Bloom is a great admirer of Stevens, one of the most imaginative and playful of all poets. Bloom himself is apparently a delightful player, "a free-floating professor of the humanities" who as a teacher is "known as sage, genius and comic rolled into one—Zarathustra cum Zero Mostel" (Campbell, 26). Grandly eclectic, he ranges over literature, philosophy, and psychology, looking not only at the text of poems but at poets in context of their times and influences. In "A Manifesto of Antithetical Criticism" he writes: ". . . for poems arise out of the illusion of freedom, out of a sense of priority being possible. But the poem—unlike the mind in creation—is a made thing, and as such is an achieved anxiety" (Bloom, 96). Illusion, as Roger Caillois points out, comes from "in-lusio," which means "beginning a game" (19). In the view of Bloom, "the ephebe or beginning poet" starts a game by imitating others, but if he is to avoid drowning he must learn to swim as did the ephebe in ancient Greece who also learned other sports useful in military service (Gardiner, 150). The choice of the ephebe as metaphor is revelatory both of the two modes of play—the Edenic, or imitative, and the agonic, or heroic—and of Bloom's theory of the anxiety of influence.

Like T. S. Eliot, Bloom appreciates both individual talent and tradition, and sees an invariable competition between them, as he says in *The Anxiety of Influence:*

> When a potential poet first discovers (or is discovered by) the dialectic of influence, first discovers poetry as being both external and internal to himself, he begins a process that will end only when he has no more poetry within him, long after he has the power (or desire) to discover it outside of himself again. Though all such discovery is a self-recognition, indeed a second birth, and ought in the pure good of theory, to be accomplished in a perfect solipsism, it is an act never complete in itself. Poetic influence is the sense—amazing, *agonizing* [italics added], delighting, of other poets, as felt in the depths of all but perfect solopsists, the potentially strong poet. For the poet is condemned to learn his profoundest yearnings through an awareness of other selves. The poem is within him, yet he experiences the shame and splendor of being found by poems—great poems outside him. To lose freedom in this center is never to forgive, and to learn the dread of threatened autonomy forever. (Bloom, 26)

There is always a childlike play in the artist, but Bloom is explicit in the argument that what the artist is compelled to do—or else drown in the influence of precursors—is to surpass the state of imitation (Edenic) and become heroic (agonic).

If the artist, then, is to be measured against the best that has been penned, the excellence of which he is painfully aware, then the role of the critic, to evaluate, to score as it were, is also agonic to a degree. *The Anxiety of Influence* is to literary criticism what Allen Guttmann's *From Ritual to Record* is to sport studies. It shows that the poet, like the athlete, is in competition with previous performances and both are constantly trying to break records. Criticism, like sportswriting, is not just keeping records, but glorifying and debunking, as the case may be, a keeping of score and story of how the game was played. The spirit of play ripples through the criticism of Gadamer and Bloom, but a long agonic shadow falls over what they have to say about truth and method and aesthetics and anxiety.

Prior to the publication of *Truth and Method*, Roger Caillois in *Man, Play and Games* raised sports *(agon)* to the same level of theater *(mimesis)*, gambling *(alea)*, and whirling *(ilinx)*—all of which were part of the universe of play. He also posited two "ways of playing" (53)—*ludus* (tension and skill) and *paidia* (spontaneity and naturalness)—running through these quadrants of play in opposite directions. What Wellek and Frye did for criticism Caillois did for play. Wellek has made clear what he would do with deconstruction as hermeneutics, but it cannot be inferred how Caillois would deal with it or the fanciful play in the solipsistic poetry of Wallace Stevens or the free-wheeling criticism of Harold Bloom. Perhaps another category called "Aesthetic Games" is needed for Caillois's taxonomy of play. In any event, Caillois made a tremendous contribution to the study of sports and play, in some ways more of a contribution than Huizinga's. Whether or not one agrees with his classifications, he wrestled with definitions and provided a usable framework for critical study. One of the works drawing upon Caillois's pioneering efforts was Christian Messenger's *Sport and the Spirit of Play in American Fiction* (1981), which treats with considerable sophistication the aesthetics of play and the cultural values raised by forms of competition in American society. Published by Columbia University Press, which also lent its distinguished imprint to Allen Guttman's *From Ritual to Record*, the book is further testimony to the growing respectability being accorded the critical study of sport literature.

There is a problem here, though, that one has to consider, and that is the tendency to fall into a restricted vision of the old New Critics. For example, Messenger attacked my own book, *Laurel and Thorn: The Athlete in American Literature*, for, among other reasons in his view, creating "an unsophisticated art-versus-life dichotomy, opposing the aesthetic to the cultural, in contrast with virtually all recent criticism that confirms the union of the two in any relevant critical discourse. Furthermore, sport and play have intrinsically aesthetic properties that cannot be ignored by critics of sports in literature" (Messenger, 120).

It is open to debate whether all "recent criticism" has advocated a union of the cultural and aesthetic at the time I was writing my book (1981), but even if that were the case there is no reason why I or anyone else should follow the prevailing critical pattern. Just as

Messenger was considering the aesthetic and the cultural, so I was primarily focusing upon the cultural, as I stated. His approach was "polysemous," but so was mine since within that area I was considering two traditions, as he acknowledged in a footnote by saying that I appeared to be "seconding" Arnold's Hellenism and Hebraism. In a sense I was doing that by looking at the Christian-Hellenic synthesis and drawing upon the work of Otto Rank for my structural metaphor as well as the thought of Ernest Becker, looking also at athletes from the world of the drama. What is at issue is the question of pluralistic criticism in sport literature and whether as an established discipline critics will fall into some of the same errors as in the past. It wasn't as if I were taking an entirely new route in this century. There are a number of distinguished works that have taken similar approaches, for example, Werner Jaeger's *Early Christianity and Greek Paideia* (1965), both of which traditions in the title reflect agonic themes from different perspectives. One cannot do everything. The more the attention upon play and aesthetics, the less that can be said about agony and ethics. The realms are not unbridgeable, but the focus should never be narrowly defined. There are many choices in "polysemous" criticism.

That sport literature has arrived at a stage where critical debate can occur is a healthy sign. What needs to be remembered, though, is that there are many paths around Parnassus that cross at several points, sometimes going in opposite directions. Critics need to be tolerant of those taking other routes, for they simply see another side of the mountain. Critics should also share insights with those from other camps. Periodic gatherings such as the joint meeting of the Sport Literature Association (SLA) and the Philosophic Society for the Study of Sport at Texas Christian University in 1987 and the joint meeting of SLA with The North American Society for the Study of Sport History in 1989 at Clemson University have been steps in the right direction. Critics do not have to worry about loss of definition of their discipline by such reaching out and sharing, for whatever critical force sport literature associates with, there will always be at its center stories of sports, stories of physical contests dealing with the individual sense of worth and quality in an imperfect world—stories of *arete*.

Notes

1. I wish to thank George Buck for bringing this article and others to my attention. Students of philosophy and language would want to read his . . . *Might*

Be with a 480-item bibliography: Dignity Books, 2500 Lakemoor Drive, Knoxville, Tennessee, 37920.

Works Cited

Baker, William J. *Sports in the Western World*. Totowa, N.J.: Rowman and Littlefield, 1982.

Blake, Kathleen. *Play, Games, and Sport: The Literary Works of Lewis Carroll*. Ithaca: Cornell University Press, 1974.

Bloom, Harold. *The Anxiety of Influence: A Theory of Poetry*. New York: Oxford University Press, 1973.

Caillois, Roger. *Man, Play, and Games*. Translated by Meyer Barash. New York: Free Press, 1961.

Campbell, Colin. "The Tyranny of the Yale Critics." *The New York Times Magazine*, 9 February 1986, 20–28, 43, 47–48.

Capra, Fritjof. *The Tao of Physics: An Exploration of the Parallels between Modern Physics and Eastern Mysticism*. New York: Bantam, 1977.

Detsch, Richard. "A Non-Subjectivist Concept of Play—Gadamer and Heidegger Versus Rilke and Nietzsche." *Philosophy Today* 29 (Summer 1985): 156–70.

Frye, Northrop. *Anatomy of Criticism: Four Essays*. Princeton: Princeton University Press, 1957.

Gadamer, Hans-Georg. *Truth and Method*. New York: Continuum, 1982.

Gardiner, E. Norman. *Greek Athletic Sports and Festivals*. London: Macmillan and Co. Reprint. Dubuque, Iowa: Brown Reprints, 1970.

Guttmann, Allen. *From Ritual to Record: The Nature of Modern Sports*. New York: Columbia University Press, 1978.

Hans, James S. "Hermeneutics, Play, Deconstruction." *Philosophy Today* 24 (Winter 1980): 299–317.

Hawthorne, Nathaniel. *The Novels and Tales of Nathaniel Hawthorne*. Edited by Norman Holmes Pearson. New York: Random House, 1937.

Hearn, Francis. "Toward a Critical Theory of Play." *Telos* 30 (Winter 1976): 145–60.

Herbert, Anne. "Snake." *The Next Whole Earth Catalog*. Edited by Stuart Brand. New York: Random House, 1980.

Higgs, Robert J. *Laurel and Thorn: The Athlete in American Literature*. Lexington: University Press of Kentucky, 1981.

Kitto, H. D. F. *The Greeks*. Baltimore: Penguin, 1951.

Koestler, Arthur. *Act of Creation: A Study of the Conscious and Unconscious Processes of Humor, Scientific Discovery and Art*. New York: Macmillan, 1964.

Messenger, Christian Karl. "After Strange Gods." *Review* 5 (1983): 119–24.

———. *Sport and the Spirit of Play in American Fiction: Hawthorne to Faulkner*. New York: Columbia University Press, 1981.

Miller, David. *Gods and Games: Toward a Theology of Play*. New York: World, 1970.

Milton, John. *Complete Poetical Works of John Milton*. Edited by Harris Francis Fletcher. Cambridge, Mass.: Houghton Mifflin, 1941.

Moltmann, Jurgen. *Theology of Play*. Translated by Reinhard Ulrich. New York: Harper and Row, 1972.

Neale, Robert E. *In Praise of Play: Toward a Psychology of Religion*. New York: Harper and Row, 1973.

Stevens, Wallace. *The Collected Poems of Wallace Stevens.* New York: Knopf, 1961.

Wellek, René. "The Main Trends of Twentieth-Century Criticism." In *Concepts of Criticism.* New Haven: Yale University Press, 1963.

Zukav, Gary. *The Dancing Wu-Li Masters: An Overview of the New Physics.* New York: Bantam, 1980.

Sport, Art, and Aesthetics: A Decade of Controversy (1978–88)

DANIEL J. HERMAN

For almost 2,000 years, philosophy has been concerned primarily with highly intellectual areas of thought such as epistemology, metaphysics, social and political philosophy, ethics, and aesthetics. During all this time, little attention was paid to matters of everyday life and concern. The upsurge of existential philosophy and phenomenology in the 1940s is to be primarily credited for redressing this long neglect. Heidegger in Germany and Sartre and Merleau-Ponty in France were philosophically responsible for restoring man to his true place—the world of everyday living. Man's incarnation, his facticity, and his persistent awareness of a physical self gave birth to philosophical investigations centering chiefly on man's relation to his body, a pursuit that previously had been deemed of low respectability. As a result, philosophers began to turn their attention to the existential and phenomenological aspects of sport.

The publication in 1969 of Paul Weiss's *Sport: A Philosophic Inquiry* perhaps single-handedly gave birth to sports philosophy. This pioneering work made Weiss the founding father of the Philosophic Society for the Study of Sport, which attracted international attention, especially that of philosophers in the United States and Canada. With the first meeting of the Society in conjunction with the Eastern Division of the American Philosophic Association, it was formally recognized as a scholarly society, and in 1974 the first issue of the *Journal of the Philosophy of Sport* made its appearance, thereby bringing this new philosophical field of investigation into full bloom.

Consequently, a bountiful bibliography devoted to all areas of the philosophy of sport is now available to the interested reader and researcher, of which some of the most significant articles on aesthetics are included in the recently published anthology edited by William Morgan and Klaus Meier: *Philosophic Inquiry in Sport*.

I have chosen to discuss here the interrelationship of sport, art, and aesthetics because such a philosophical survey is perhaps more revelatory than any other in shedding light on the American concern for formulating a sport aesthetic that could have literary significance. If scholars are to formulate a "sport aesthetic" of literary import, then perhaps the analysis of the following philosophical debate may suggest some insights into an aesthetic relationship of sport and literature that will lead to a better understanding and appreciation of the various genres constituting the vast body of sport literature.

In 1978 the British aesthetician David Best published his magnum opus: *Philosophy and Human Movement*. In this highly controversial work, particularly from the American point of view, Best argues (at times convincingly) that sports of whatever kind can never claim to be art. The ground for this denial lies in his distinction between the aesthetic and the artistic standpoints and ultimately the common failure to distinguish between them, which has erroneously resulted in the position that sport is art. The source of this confusion, argues Best, is to ignore the fact that there are two kinds of sports—the purposive and the aesthetic. The first kind is the most encompassing: football, baseball, hockey, tennis, basketball, and so on, where the end is external to the means—for example, in the act of scoring goals no matter how the goal is scored. The second kind is more restricted: synchronized swimming, figure skating, gymnastics, diving, and dancing, all of which have an aesthetic component in so far as the performance of the sport must be accompanied by an economy of effort and movement. In other words, the aesthetic sports, in order to be successful, must be graceful or beautiful as an intrinsic characteristic of the activity, a characteristic that is lacking in the purposive sports, or if present, entirely accidental to them. In this sense, continues Best, the gap is partially closed between the aesthetic sports and the arts, but it will never be completely closed, for there remains a difference in kind and not merely of degree between them. The buttress for his arguing for this distinction is that in a work of art the end is inseparable from the means of achieving it, whereas in the aesthetic sport there remains, even though limited, an externally identifiable aim not to be found in art. Furthermore, an artwork, for the most part, is a genuine expression on the part of the artist of, for example, a moral or political conception of life, which is completely absent in any sport, both purposive and aesthetic. Actually, the distinction between means and end and the lack of distinction thereof has been misunderstood, according to

Best. If art, he argues, is to be nonpurposive, then can art be meaningful at all? The answer supposedly lies in the order of the priorities one attaches to art. If a particular work is evaluated (exclusively) in terms of achievement, then that particular work loses its intrinsic value, which, according to Best, is enough to eliminate all sports as works of art. To ask what is the purpose of any work of art whatsoever is self-defeating (if not outright contradictory), for the work of art speaks for itself. It is both the form and content of its expression. In short, every feature of a work of art is relevant to the aesthetic appreciation of it, whereas when an aesthetic sport is being judged, for example, there are effective alternative means of achieving the specified critical purpose.

In summary, Best's distinction between sport and art is that even in the aesthetic sports that aim at spectator satisfaction through expressing grace and beauty, even though that satisfaction may be intrinsic to that sport, sport must still be distinguished from art since the latter aims at the expression of life situations whereas the former does not.

However, American aestheticians were not to lay this matter to rest. In a fairly lengthy essay, "Beauty, Sport, and Gender" (1984), Jan Boxill raises four pointed objectives to Best's thesis that sports are outside of the unique and inviolable art form because (1) the concern for skill in the form of technical efficiency overshadows the essential art ingredients of style, grace, and form; (2) the strong desire for victory in sports overshadows the aim of beauty; (3) even if one of the aims of sport is beauty, it is not the sole aim; and (4) even when athletes consciously aim at beauty, they are not making any implicit or explicit statements about the human condition.

In countering Best's first point, Boxill argues that both technical efficiency and beauty in sport may be applied to the relation of the two in art. Citing examples from music, painting, and dance where the three are intrinsically related as in the aesthetic sports, Boxill demonstrates that that very relation destroys Best's arguments for a radical distinction between the two kinds of human endeavor.

In support of her second objection, Boxill disputes Best's contention that the strong desire for victory (ends distinguishable and external to the means) destroys sport as an art form since "to win at all costs" precludes and excludes that very sport from aesthetic experience by adducing the fact that some athletes would prefer to lose with a well-played game rather than to win with a poor performance.

The third point that Best makes in favor of excluding sport from art is that in the former, beauty may be aimed at but is not the sole aim, whereas in art such is the goal. Boxill reiterates Best's alleged position on this issue by directly quoting him: "The end [in sport] can be specified independently of the manner of achieving it *as long as it conforms to the rules of the games.*" In art, however, there can never be a change of expression without a corresponding change in what is expressed. Boxill argues, however, that just as in sport, the artwork, although aiming at beauty for the most part, nevertheless deviates from that goal so that, according to her, the spurious distinction between sport and art breaks down.

Finally, to Best's criterion that art aims at the expression of life situations that are totally absent from both kinds of sport in so far as the latter portrays human movements and not artifacts aiming at life situations, Boxill retorts that analogically between the artist and his artifact there exists the relation between the designer of sport and the rules that govern it. She says that the sport designers are definitely concerned with establishing rules designed to control raw talent in order to maximize economy of effort, thereby enhancing the grace and beauty of the sport in question. In addition, she adduces the fact that in the "new games," for example, the life situation of cooperation is stressed because it is felt that cooperation is what sustains a society.

The careful reader of Boxill's essay will not have failed to notice that notwithstanding her almost heroic effort to defend sport as art, she does not sufficiently heed Best's warnings that confusion about the relation between sport and art arises from not separating aesthetic experience from art properly so called. In his "Sport Is Not Art" (1985), Best categorically refutes Boxill's arguments. He does state explicitly that some sports are highly pleasing and rewarding in an aesthetic sense. However, to recognize this quality does not in any way imply or acknowledge that sport is art. Whence the source of this confusion then? Again and again, points out Best, it comes strictly from the failure to recognize the centrality of his argument, which is to separate the aesthetic from the artistic, which, he argues, have been hopelessly conflated by Boxill. Best cites his alliance with Joseph Kupfer who, in his "A Commentary on Jan Boxill's 'Beauty, Sport, and Gender' " (1984), rightly points out that many things have aesthetic value without being beautifully intended, such as landscape, sunsets, and so on.

Boxill again misrepresents Best when she accuses him of finding aesthetic values in sports but only as mere by-products of them and thus not intrinisically intended. This is again a misrepresentation of the Best position on aesthetic sport, which narrows the gap between sport and art but which still falls short of a complete indentification since the former can never lay claim to self-expression whereas the latter does.

In another commentary on Boxill's essay, B. C. Postow once again, according to Best, confuses the artistic with the aesthetic. But more importantly, in appealing to Wittgenstein's notion of family resemblances, the author attempts to identify competititve sports with works of art. This identification is again flatly denied by Best on the basis that even though resemblances may be found between two objects or activities, it does not follow that one is of the same kind as the other. By the same token, the very attempt at showing analogies between aesthetic sports and works of art is self-defeating and even contradictory since to claim that A is analogous to B implies that A is not B.

In "Context and Intention in Sport and Art" (1984), S. K. Wertz attacks Best's argument that it is the context of any action that determines its description. The context of, let us say, a movement provides a sense of place that originates and is sustained by its conventions and institutions being practiced by those who participate in them. Thus, two seemingly similar movements, a dance and a gymnastic sequence, are actually different because of the place of their occurrence. The dance is normally performed on a dance floor, whereas the gymnastic sequence takes place in a gymnasium with the clear implication that, according to Wertz's understanding of Best, the former is art and the latter sport. Such an analysis, says Wertz, is extreme, for it fails to take into consideration the intention behind the movement, which Best views in complete isolation from such intention. These movements, regardless of the author's intentions, do not contribute to their character. Thus, that a given set of movements is performed in a studio, gymnasium, or stadium determines them to be dance, gymnastics, and sport respectively. If, of course, this is what Best meant, the argument is ludicrous, for a considerable number of events taking place in studios, gymnasiums, and stadiums have little relevance respecting the intentions of the activities occurring in those places. A dancer, for example, may not have a studio readily available for her performance and thus may have to perform in a gymnasium instead.

Wertz's article elicited an irate reply from Best. In his previously cited article, "Sport Is Not Art," Best categorically denies that he ever meant to imply that movements, regardless of their author's intentions, are simply categorized by their physical settings. Referring back to his major work on human movement, Best claims to have specifically acknowledged the fact that a dance action, for example, can be such in a physical setting quite different from the normal. The source of Wertz's confusion is his misinterpretation of context as mere physical setting. What Best actually meant, a meaning significantly different from the one assigned to him by Wertz, is that the character of an action is inextricably related to the normal context of this occurrence, which does include the intention of the agent.

Last, in "Sport, Art, and Particularity: The Best Equivocation" (1986), Terrence Roberts accuses Best of evading the basic issues of the argument in that he [Best] describes art in exclusively particular terms whereas sport is described in general terms. Thus, according to Best, says Roberts, there is only one way to paint the painting or to express the emotion of sadness, whereas in purposive sport of whatever kind, a goal is a goal is a goal. This is unfair, according to Roberts, since to view goals generally is to arbitrarily separate them from the particular actions that constitute them. So separated, goals lose what makes them particular. But then the same can be said about expressions of sadness. Separated expressions of sadness lose their particularity. And so it must be in art as it presumably is in sport. In short, there are as many ways to express sadness as there are ways to score goals. Therefore, concludes Roberts, once the equivocation is righted, the differences between sport and art vanish and sport is art.

So far as this survey goes, a decade of controversy ends here but will undoubtedly continue. What Best has generally said during this time to his American opponents in categorically denying that sport is art is (1) to refuse to recognize sport as art is not denying sport's respectability; and (2) because art cannot be strictly defined, it does not follow that anything is art, for if that term could be hypothetically applied to anything and everything, it would amount to being applied to nothing, with the consequence that art would be meaningless and therefore any attempt to equate sport with art entirely self-defeating.

While sport can be considered as worthy a literary subject as any other in that it expresses itself through human experience, one's understanding of sport and its aesthetic relationship to literature may have to await the outcome of the philosophers' continuing debate over what really constitutes the aesthetic side of sport. An underlying task here has been to show how an integral part of everyday life has finally come into the philosophical limelight, and for this development one must be grateful to the sport aestheticians and their untiring search for meaningful relationships between art and sport.

Works Cited

Best, David. *Philosophy and Human Movement*. London: Allen and Unwin, 1978.
———. "Sport Is Not Art." *Journal of the Philosophy of Sport* 12 (1985).
Boxill, Jan. "Beauty, Sport, and Gender." *Journal of the Philosophy of Sport* 11 (1984).
Kupfer, Joseph. "A Commentary on Jan Boxill's 'Beauty, Sport, and Gender.'" *Journal of the Philosophy of Sport* 11 (1984).
Morgan, William, and Klaus Meier, eds. *Philosophic Inquiry in Sport*. Champaign, Ill.: Human Kinetics, 1985.
Postow, B. C. "Sport, Art and Gender." *Journal of the Philosophy of Sport* 11 (1984): 52–55.
Roberts, Terrence. "Sport, Art, and Particularity: The Best Equivocation." *Journal of the Philosophy of Sport* 13 (1986).
Weiss, Paul S. *Sport: A Philosophic Inquiry*. Carbondale: Southern Illinois University Press, 1969.
Wertz, S. K. "Context and Intention in Sport and Art." *Southwest Philosophical Studies* 13 (1984).

Athletes Displaying Their Lives: The Emergence of the Contemporary Sports Autobiography

MARY McELROY

One needs only to browse through a local bookstore to witness the remarkable popularity of the "athlete's own story" in print. Sports autobiographies appear in a variety of forms, concentrate on a number of sports, have authorized representation from both sexes, and at any given time, can be found on national best seller's lists. No longer reserved for the athlete nearing retirement, sports autobiographies may appear after one championship season (e.g., Phil McConkey and Phil Simms, *Simms to McConkey;* Jim McMahon, *McMahon*); after a singular triumph (e.g., Bart Conner, *Winning the Gold;* David Hemery, *Another Hurdle*); and in some cases, even after the athlete falls short of ultimate victory (e.g., Roger Clemens, *Rocket Man;* Dwight Gooden, *Gooden*).

However, the large number of sports autobiographies flooding today's book market coupled with their unevenness in writing have raised serious questions concerning the literary quality of such undertakings. Some critics even refer to autobiographical writing as "flawed biography," which may have prompted Bill Russell, in his popular self-portrait, *Second Wind,* to contend that his story is not like all of the rest:

> *Second Wind* is not simply one more autobiography of an athlete written with a hack sportswriter and filled with anecdotes about past athletic glories and pictures of the superstar in action. Indeed, basketball occupies less than half of this book. . . .[1]

The negative image associated with the sports autobiography is indeed unfortunate. Autobiographical writings offer the reading public a rare glimpse into the organized world of sport. Accordingly, the purpose of this essay is to explore America's fascination with stories about the personal and professional lives of sports figures. More specifically, it will attempt to identify the qualities that make for "successful" sports autobiography, and at the same time consider the problems that have relegated some of these sports-oriented writings to the ranks of "literary" mediocrity.

Definition and Classification of Sports Autobiographies

The sports autobiography, particularly during the last fifteen years, has become a "sounding board" for athletes, managers, owners, and numerous others involved in America's highly visible sports scene. The volume of personal writings by sports celebrities as revealed in the comprehensive listing of published works presented in the Appendix to this essay invites attempts to categorize the large and diverse array of these personal accounts. One such classification approach, first introduced by Gerald Kenyon, is known as the "primary and secondary modes of sport involvement," and is presented in Table 1.[2] The framework consists of two large categories: *producers,* those responsible for putting on the event; and *consumers,* those who "consume" or "enjoy" sports. The production mode is further broken down into primary, or athletic roles, and secondary, or roles of nonparticipants that may affect the outcome of the game. The consumption mode further classifies sports roles into spectators in attendance at the game (primary) and those who indirectly consume sports (secondary).

Covering a wide range of primary athletic roles and experiences, primary sports participants comprise the subject matter of the majority of sports autobiographies. Some athletes when writing about themselves have enjoyed several decades in a particular sport, while others put pen to paper after only one glorious season or, in rarer instances, after a not so glorious career, as in the cases of perennial minor leaguers Pat Jordan (*A False Spring*) and Rick Wolff, a former Harvard student (*What's A Nice Boy Like You Doing in the Bushes*).

Secondary producers have also contributed to the subgenre of autobiographical writings. Coaches, managers, owners, promoters, umpires, and particularly sportswriters are all well represented in the field of sports autobiography. Insights from seldom observed perspectives are also available, ranging from the writings of spouses of professional athletes (Bobby Bouton and Nancy Marshall's *Home Games;* Danielle Torrez's *High Inside*); to a professional golf

Table 1

Categories of Sport Roles Associated with Sports Autobiography

Producers

Primary	Secondary
Baseball	Coaches
Basketball	Managers
Football	Sport promoters
Golf	Athletic trainers
Tennis	Team owners
Track and field	Team physicians
Road racing	Sportswriters
Touring	Sports announcers
Bowling	Sport caddies
Auto racing	Athletic directors
Ice skating	Umpires
Gymnastics	Referees
Skiing	
Ice hockey	
Boxing	
Horse racing	
Equestrian events	
Triathlons	

Consumers

Primary	Secondary
Spectators	Television viewers
	Sport hobbyists

---

caddy (Michael Bamberger's *The Green Road Home*); to a football team's psychologist (Arthur Mandell's *The Nightmare Season.*) The sports spectator or "consumer" is not left out either, with such entries as Barry Gifford's *The Neighborhood of Baseball* and Joel Oppenheimer's *The Wrong Season,* both of which follow the plight of two fans and their "love affair" with their respective teams.

Kenyon's model allows one to focus on the many "sport-related" roles found in the contemporary sports autobiography; a second but less satisfying scheme concentrates on the motives of the author. Some autobiographers write for publicity or money, but others, compelled by interest in the social reform of sport, raise such issues as racial prejudice (e.g., Frank Robinson's *Extra Innings*), violence (e.g., Preston Pearson's *Hearing the Noise;* Bob

Chandler's *Violent Sundays*), or drug abuse (e.g., Hollywood Henderson's *Out of Control*). From a literary perspective, motives for writing autobiographies typically follow any of four forms: to chronicle, to confess, to expound, or to rebut one's public character, the latter motivation also known as an "apology." Motives, although critical to text evaluation, are somewhat limited as a classification tool since the contemporary sports autobiography is likely to include a mixture of goals and purposes, some of which are ambiguous and not always apparent to the reader.

Perhaps of greater importance is the recognition of sports autobiography's unique qualities that prompt one to consider exactly what constitutes a sports autobiography. As a starting point, one might define an autobiography as simply a narrative of the past experience of a person written by the person concerned. Such a restrictive definition, unfortunately, would exclude well over 90% of the sports books on the market. In most sports autobiographies, and for that matter in autobiographies generally, the author's own story is likely carved out by a professional writer after extensive consultation with the personality. Athletes rely on their physical prowess on the field but usually require assistance in translating their story from the playing field to paper; such a coauthored arrangement facilitates the athlete's communication with the reading public but, consequently, raises doubts concerning the authenticity of the work. How much did the athlete contribute to the work? Are the written words those of the athlete or those of the professional writer? Such questions are important and constantly relate to each and every sports autobiography that appears in the marketplace.

Sports autobiographies are sometimes confused with other forms of personal writing and, consequently, are judged according to an inappropriate set of expectations. For example, autobiographical writings differ markedly from the literary style of the diary. Diaries move through a series of events stressing what is important at the moment but at the expense of long-term reflection or the "unfolding" of one's life events. Pam Shriver, for example, in her book *Passing Shots,* uses daily entries to chronicle and detail the events of one full year on the professional women's tennis tour. The limitation of the diary format is perhaps best illustrated in Keith Hernandez's *If at First,* originally published after the Mets finished a close second to the St. Louis Cardinals in 1985, and revised one year later after the Mets won the World Series. The 1986 version included one additional chapter detailing the journey to the World Series; the rest of the book, however, remained unchanged. Although Hernandez's "revised life-story" provides the complete details of the success of the New York baseball team, the majority of the book, and thereby the reader, does not benefit from any new wisdom gained from the Mets' miracle season.

Other forms of personal writings concentrate externally on the people and places of the sports world, rather than internally, on the sports personality. Books such as Bowie Kuhn's *Hardball*, George Halas's *Halas by Halas*, and Willie Stargell's *Stargell* are better categorized as memoirs or reminiscences in that they say little about the writer. Books written by coaches and sports announcers often fit into this category of reminiscences or memoirs. Tim McCarver's *Baby, I Love It* or Ralph Kiner's *Kiner's Corner* focus on issues outside their experiences as television/radio sports announcers. Instead of addressing potentially more interesting topics such as the transition from ball field to press box, books written by these and other sports announcers usually concentrate on describing the people and places of sport from the "press box view." Likewise, books by coaches and managers, such as Davey Johnson's *Bats*, Sparky Anderson's *Main Spark*, and Earl Weaver's *It's What You Learn after You Know It All That Counts*, also disappointingly fail to tackle the larger issues relevant to coaching and managing roles.

One exception to the general failure of sports autobiographies written by coaches and managers is Alvin Dark's *When in Doubt, Fire the Manager*. Dark masterfully recounts the "paradoxes in the managerial career" of a very successful leader of the world champion Oakland Athletics by artfully revealing the vulnerability of a major league manager's existence, located somewhere between player and upper-level management, criticized by both, and trusted by neither.

Interaction between the Sports Personality and the Sports World

What is important to the ultimate success of sports autobiography is not the portrayal of events of the outside world but how such a world is viewed and shaped by the autobiographer. Through the "selection of facts," the use of language, and carefully detailed discussion, the reader becomes an active participant in discerning the author's personal interpretation of his or her important life events. The recounting of people and places provides the reader with finite detail, which is certainly necessary to "telling the whole story"; however, good sports autobiography must go far beyond the events of the outside world. The contribution that autobiographies offers is perhaps best summed up in the definition by Roy Pascal:

> [Autobiography is] . . . a sort of harmony between outward experience and inward growth or unfolding between incidents so that each circumstance, each incident, instead of being an anomalous fact, becomes a part of a process and a revelation of something within the personality.[3]

The unfolding of one's life in writing requires much reflectivity on the part of the autobiographer. Books written near the beginning of one's career (e.g., Dwight Gooden's *Gooden* and Earvin Johnson's *Magic*) or directly after one significant event (e.g., Mary Lou Retton's *Mary Lou* or Bart Conner's *Go for the Gold*), provide provocative sports reading, but the authors have not had sufficient time to appreciate and interpret the true meaning and impact of their successes for themselves and for the sports world. Chris Evert wisely declined to write her story in 1977, since a book "about a twenty-two-year-old tennis player seemed premature."[4] Five years later, filled with reflection and insight, she wrote the successful *Chrissie: My Own Story,* and in 1985, the less-well-received sequel, *Lloyd on Lloyd,* with British tennis player and former husband John Lloyd.

Personal athletic accounts that are either not based on lifelong achievements or are written while the athlete is too young, almost always fail to link the past and present in a meaningful way. The desire to get one's life story out while the "market is still hot" may result in publication of nonpolished material, but perhaps more consequently such "time-constrained" projects contribute to the production of shallow works destined for literary failure—although perhaps not financial failure.

This is not to say that all short athletic careers offer little insight into the world of professional sport. One remarkable exception is Michael Oriard's *The End of Autumn.*[5] Oriard, in this magnificently written exposé, takes the reader behind the scenes to the harsh realities of "big-time" football, first during his college years at Notre Dame and then during his brief career with the Kansas City Chiefs.

For the most part, however, the interaction between personality and the "social world" stresses the importance of the long-term sporting experience and brings me to my final consideration of what constitutes a good sports autobiography; that is, the potential importance of the role of sport in shaping the person's life. Is sports autobiography simply a biography about a sports personality, or must it convey something more about the personality's sport itself?

Oriard, in a recent review of sports fiction, defines the "sports novel" as one in which "no substitutes for sport would be possible without radically changing the book."[6] Requirements emphasizing the importance and uniqueness of sports experience seem equally appropriate for the sports autobiography. Diaries, reminiscences, and memoirs, while of interest to the avid sports fan, typically concentrate on the sports personality or the dynamics of his or her world of sport but rarely on both. Good sports autobiography, on the otherhand, gives the sport personality the reflectivity necessary to meaningfully interpret his or her own contribution to sport. Whitey Ford's *Slick* and Martina Navratilova's *Martina* were penned after a "lifetime" of the ups and downs of the baseball season and those found on the tennis circuit. Autobiographies by such long-term achievers as Willie Mays *(Say Hey)*, Reggie Jackson *(Reggie)*, Steve Garvey *(Garvey)*, Mickey Mantle *(The Mick)*, and Bill Russell *(Second Wind)* potentially provide a truer picture of the real and sometimes absurd world of sports.

Intimacy in Sports Autobiography

The sports autobiography asks the reader to judge the author on a personal level. The media coverage of today's sports makes available the "facts" of a sport personality's life but leaves the average reader wanting to know something more about these highly visible celebrities. James Olney describes this interest as a shift from "bios" to "autos," or a move from the life to the self.[7] Attempts at recounting successful sport seasons such as Gary Carter's *A Dream Season* and Sparky Lyle's *The Bronx Zoo* fall short of the mark, mostly because the details of their successful seasons have already been well chronicled in newspapers and periodicals. Rather, the reader searches for a personal communion with the athlete, and herein lies what I consider the most critical "test" of the effectiveness of the "successful" sports autobiography. Unlike the athlete's "bigger-than-life" public image, in order for the sports autobiography to work the reader must readily see him or herself in the athlete. The detailed descriptions of the athlete's interactions with others—families, parents, sexual partners—must allow the reader to temporarily "change places" with the athlete or at least momentarily become what Anna Burr has termed a "sympathetic peer."[8] The autobiographer cannot "win over the reader" by proving the hero worthy through athletic or other achievements. In fact, if not handled with care and sensitivity, the athlete's achievement may be interpreted as conceit and arrogance. Pascal, in *Design and Truth in Autobiography* (cited above), warns that good autobiographical writing must appeal to the reader's understanding and is successful only when the reader is "admitted into intimacy."[9] Not such an easy task for such visible and successful athletes as Jack Nicklaus *(On and Off the Fairway)* or Björn Borg *(My Life and Game)*. Martina Navratilova *(Martina)*, perhaps the best women's player in tennis history, still had to, and successfully did, convince the reader that she too struggled for friendship, identity, and acceptance.

Trust is also a key ingredient in the formulas for good sports autobiography. In biography, facts are verified by meticulous research, but in autobiography, the reader accepts the "author's facts" on faith. This trust sets up an emotional bond between author and reader, a forceful tie that will not be broken unless the author grossly betrays the relationship.

The use of the first person singular in the narrative also brings the reader closer to the athlete. Terminology such as "ours" and "mine" helps the reader to empathize with even such controversial sports figures as Jim McMahon *(McMahon)*, Jack Tatum *(They Call Me Assassin)*, Billy Martin *(Billyball)*, and Howard Cosell *(I Never Played the Game.)* Conversely, the use of the third-person format by John Lloyd and Chris Evert in their dual autobiography distanced the two sport celebrities from their readers.

Success and Failure in the Sports Autobiography

Success and failure, significant factors in competitive sport, not surprisingly also play a central role in the sports autobiography. Leverett Smith, in a recent analysis of the sports autobiographies of several baseball personalities, including Ty Cobb's *My Life in Baseball*, Ted Williams's *My Turn at Bat*, and Jim Brosnan's *The Long Season*, concluded that "failure" themes permeate their life stories. Similar to the protagonists in sports fiction, sports autobiographers also use failure and other humbling experiences to accentuate their humanness.[10] But unlike fictional sports heroes, sports autobiographies are ultimately winners. Unlike their fictional counterparts, it is not through their failure, but through their ultimate successes, that the reader comes to appreciate their sacrifice, perseverance, and sometimes courage.

Take for instance, Ty Cobb or Ted Williams, who are among the greatest players in baseball history; rendered autobiographically, their dimensions of failure are viewed only within their "successful sporting histories." Naturally, the highly visible athlete is not an unfamiliar figure to the reading public. In the cases of highly publicized athletes, such as Superbowl victors or those with long and illustrious sport careers, the audience is familiar with the ending of the story prior to reading the book. Therefore, when the athlete discusses failure along the way, the author and reader are absorbed in retrospective reflection, knowing that the ultimate result is achievement, not failure. Reggie Jackson *(Reggie)* describes how racial prejudices forced him to "strike out in the first big World Series of [his] life," but both author and reader recognize these setbacks as only temporary. Stories of Olympic triumph such as Nancy Lieberman's *Basketball My Way,* and Bruce Jenner's *Decathlon Challenge* or other sport successes, such as Ken Stabler's *Snake* or Ozzie Smith's *Wizard,* are also reinforcing. Like the traditional juvenile sports novel, the sports autobiography epitomizes the American concern with the "struggle for success" and provides reassurance that such things as "talent," "hard work," and "a willingness to try" are still alive and well in this complex and ever-changing world.

The underlying theme of "reinforcement of success" is often depicted in the form of the "athletic comeback." Rocky Bleier's *Fighting Back* typifies the struggle to overcome physical adversity, tracing his recovery from life-threatening war injuries to the resumption of his football career and ultimately, of course, to Superbowl victory with the Pittsburgh Steelers. Gene Littler's *The Real Score* and Danny Thompson's *E-6: The Diary of a Major League Shortstop* both focus on these athletes' bouts with potentially terminal illnesses. Other athletes such as Bob Welch in *Five O'Clock Comes Early,* Darrell Porter in *Snap Me Perfect,* and Lawrence Taylor in *LT: Playing on the Edge* accentuate these players' recovery from drug addiction problems and return to successful sport careers.

While the comeback motif relies—and is usually successful—in eliciting emotional reader response, not all such attempts qualify as good material for sports autobiography. Some "comeback stories" emphasize the courage of the athlete but totally ignore the place of the sporting world in such a trying experience. One such example is Darrell Stingley's *It's Good to Be Alive,* a recounting of the aftermath of the paralyzing football injury suffered by the young professional player. Stingley's poignant story emphasizes his acceptance of his injuries but fails to address the place of the sports world in such a tragedy. A victim of an automobile accident might have been easily substituted here for that of the sports performer.

Bob Welch's *Five O'Clock Comes Early,* on the other hand, successfully addresses the athlete's off-field struggle within the unique world of sport. The story about a highly successful young baseball player's bout with alcoholism, Welch's book shares his feelings of the athlete's invincibility felt during his early baseball years, a factor that he admits contributed to his lengthy denial of drug addiction. He sensitively discusses his decision to seek professional help and the mixed support he received from members of his family and the sports establishment. Autobiography titles such as Frank Gifford's *Gifford on Courage* or Orlando Cepeda's *High and Inside* nicely capture the essence of the theme of overcoming adversity. Likewise, Darrell Porter's *Snap Me Perfect* describes his ten-year battle with drugs and "baseball," and the eventual self-discovery that, not surprisingly, culminates in his winning of the World Series' Most Valuable Player Award in 1982.

Emergence of the Feminist Sports Autobiography

The number of quality autobiographies by female athletes has also increased during the last decade. Books such as Martina Navratilova's *Martina,* Joan Benoit's *Running Tide,* Lynda Huey's *A Running Start,* and Jane Blalock's *The Guts to Win,* in addition to the books by Evert and Shriver, differ significantly from those written in the late 1960s and early 1970s. Up until then, the female athlete's story usually relied on the theme of how women overcame the barriers to a "man's sporting world." The new feminist approach to women's sports autobiography, on the other hand, seriously addresses the real issues concerning women's involvement in sport. Topics such as heterosexual and lesbian relationships, mother-daughter friendships, and even interactions of these athletes with their own children represent issues that are crucial to the female athlete's pursuit of sport, and that are now being included in their recorded stories.

Unfortunately, women sports celebrities are usually assisted by male coauthors. Only the biographies of Virginia Wade *(Courting Triumph),* Joan Benoit *(Running Tide),* Nancy Lieberman *(Basketball My Way),* and Chris Evert *(Lloyd on Lloyd)* receive the scrutiny of female writers; the others, if not objectively handled, may be tainted by views of the female athlete's story as seen through the eyes of the male sports world.

Less Visible Sporting Accounts

The autobiographical approach has also brought less visible sporting activities to the forefront. For example, Bill Rodgers's *Marathoning* and Marty Liquori's *On the Run* likely contributed significantly to the increased popularity of road racing. Mike Plant's *Iron Will: The Heart and Soul of the Triathlon,* Jayne Torvill and Christopher Dean's *Torvill and Dean,* and J. T. Hubbard's seafaring adventure, *The Race,* likely will do the same for their sports. Carmen Salvino in his *Fast Lanes* portrays the daily and often monotonous grind of the bowling tour. These accounts highlight the struggles of athletic achievement within a sporting context heretofore not well known to the general public. While these athletes face many of the same problems as "athletes competing in the public eye," athletes of less visible sports have a unique opportunity to convey to the reader a deep personal commitment to their respective sports.

Conclusions

During the last decade hundreds of sports personalities have publicly shared their life stories, and today the American sports autobiography represents a major component of the preserved sports legacy. Sports autobiographies take many different forms; they are written with many different motives in mind, appeal to a wide range of readership, and as is the case with other forms of literature, some are better written than others. But in general, successful sports autobiographies follow a consistency in format, one that allows the athlete *retrospection* (time to ponder events occurring in the past) and *introspection* (ability to relate their inner feelings to an interested general public). Moreover, the interplay between the characteristics of the individual and those of the sports environment suggests that one should not judge the merits of such writings on traditional criteria such as those used for evaluating fiction. The athlete in autobiography sheds his or her "bigger-than-life" public image by communicating with the reading public on a personal level. As a result, the sports autobiography provides a particularly fertile field of information to social scientists, historians, psychologists, and philosophers alike. Through the telling of an athlete's own story in order to meet the ultimate literary challenge, that of successfully translating actions, ideas, and emotions from spoken words into written ones, the sports autobiography provides reading no sports scholar or devoted sports fan can afford to pass up.

Notes

1. Bill Russell and Taylor Branch, *Second Wind: The Memoirs of an Opinionated Man* (New York: Random House, 1979), book jacket.
2. Gerald Kenyon, "Sport Involvement: A Conceptual Go and Some Consequences Thereof," in *Aspects of Contemporary Sport Sociology,* ed. Kenyon (Chicago: The Athletic Institute, 1969).
3. Roy Pascal, *Design and Truth in Autobiography* (London: Routledge & Kegan Paul, 1960), 185.
4. Chris Evert Lloyd and Neil Amdur, *Chrissie: My Own Story* (New York: Simon and Schuster, 1982), 14.
5. Michael Oriard, *The End of Autumn: Reflections on My Life in Football* (New York: Random House, 1982).
6. Michael Oriard, "On the Current Status of Sport Fiction," *Arete: The Journal of Sport Literature* 1 (1983): 7–20.
7. James Olney, "Autos Bios Graphein: The Study of Autobiographical Literature," *South Atlantic Quarterly,* Winter 1978, 118.
8. Anna Burr, *The Autobiography* (Boston: Houghton Mifflin, 1909), 11.
9. Pascal, *Design and Truth,* 1.
10. Leverett Smith, "Versions of Defeat: Baseball Autobiographies," *Arete: The Journal of Sport Literature,* Fall 1984, 141–58.

Appendix

Comprehensive Listing of Sports Autobiographies, Diaries, Memoirs, Reminiscences: 1975–1988. [Editor's note: Other autobiographical works published prior to 1975 that influenced later publications in this genre, due largely to their controversial nature, are Jim Bouton's *Ball Four* (1970), Dave Meggyesy's *Out of Their League* (1971), Connie Hawkins's *Foul!* (1972), Chip Oliver's *High for the Game* (1971), and Bernie Parrish's *They Call It a Game* (1972). During this era, Jerry Kramer's *Instant Replay* (1969) and John Brodie's *Open Field* (1974) were among the few works reflecting an overall positive tone.]

Abdul-Jabbar, Kareem, and Peter Knobler. *Giant Steps: An Autobiography of Kareem Abdul-Jabbar.* New York: Bantam, 1983.
Alston, Walt, and Jack Torbin. *A Year at a Time.* Waco, Tex.: Word, 1976.
Alzado, Lyle, and Paul Zimmerman. *Mile High: The Story of Lyle Alzado and the Amazing Denver Broncos.* New York: Atheneum, 1978.

Anderson, Sparky, and Si Burck. *Main Spark: Sparky Anderson and the Cincinnati Reds.* New York: Doubleday, 1978.
Ashe, Arthur, and Neil Amdur. *Off the Court.* New York: New American Library, 1981.
Auerbach, Red, and Joe Fitzgerald. *On and Off the Court.* New York: Putnam, 1977.
Bamberger, Michael. *The Green Road Home: A Caddy's Journal of Life on the Pro Golf Tour.* New York: Contemporary Books, 1986.
Bannister, Roger. *The Four Minute Mile.* New York: Dodd, Mead, 1981.
Bench, Johnny, and William Brashler. *Catch You Later: An Autobiography of Johnny Bench.* New York: Harper and Row, 1978.
Benoit, Joan, and Sally Baker. *Running Tide.* New York: Knopf, 1987.
Bertrand, John, and Patrick Robinson. *Born to Win: A Lifelong Struggle to Capture the America's Cup.* Sydney: Hearst Marine, 1985.
Birdwell, Cleo. *Amazons: An Intimate Memoir by the First Woman Ever to Play in the National Hockey League.* New York: Holt, Rinehart, 1980.
Blalock, Jane, and Dwayne Netland. *The Guts to Win.* New York: Golf Digest, 1977.
Blanda, George, and Mickey Herkowitz. *Over Forty.* New York: Simon and Schuster, 1978.
Bleier, Rocky, and Terry O'Neil. *Fighting Back.* New York: Stein and Day, 1975.
Borg, Björn, and Eugene Scott. *My Life and Game.* New York: Simon and Schuster, 1980.
Borg, Marianna. *Love Match: My Life with Björn Borg.* New York: Dial, 1981.
Bouton, Bobbie, and Nancy Marshall. *Home Games: Two Baseball Wives Speak Out.* New York: St. Martin's, 1983.
Bouton, Jim. *Ball Four Plus Five.* New York: Stein and Day, 1981.
Bowa, Larry, and Barry Boom. *Bleep.* New York: Bonus Books, 1988.
Bradley, Bill. *Life on the Run.* New York: Quadrangle, 1976.
Bradshaw, Terry, and David Diles. *Terry Bradshaw: Man of Steel.* Pittsburgh: Zondervan Publishing House, 1979.
Broun, Heywood Hale. *Tumultuous Merriment.* New York: Richard Marek, 1979.
Brown, Paul, and Jack Clary. *P. B.: The Paul Brown Story.* New York: Atheneum, 1979.
Burke, Michael. *Outrageous Good Fortune.* New York: Little, Brown, 1984.
Burt, Jim, and Hank Gola. *Hard Nose: The Story of the 1986 Giants.* San Diego: Harcourt Brace Jovanovich, 1987.
Cannon, James. *Nobody Asked Me But. . . .* New York: Holt, Rinehart, and Winston, 1978.
Carew, Rod, and Ira Berkow. *Carew.* New York: Simon and Schuster, 1979.
Carson, Harry, and Jim Smith. *Point of Attack: The Defense Strikes Back.* New York: McGraw-Hill, 1986.
Carter, Gary, and John Hough. *A Dream Season.* San Diego: Harcourt Brace Jovanovich, 1987.
Cepeda, Orlando, and Bob Markus. *High and Inside.* South Bend, Ind.: Icarus Press, 1983.
Champion, Bob, and Jonathan Powell. *Champion's Story: A Great Human Triumph.* New York: Coward, McCann and Geoghegan, 1982.
Chandler, Bob, and Norm Chandler. *Violent Sundays.* New York: Simon and Schuster, 1984.

Clemens, Roger, and Peter Gammons. *Rocket Man*. Lexington, Mass.: Greene Press, 1987.

Cohen, Stanley. *The Man in the Crowd: Confessions of a Sports Addict*. New York: Random House, 1981.

Conner, Bart, and Paul Ziert. *Winning the Gold*. New York: Warner, 1985.

Cosell, Howard, and Peter Bonventre. *I Never Played the Game*. New York: Avon, 1986.

Cousy, Bob, and John Devaney. *The Killer Instinct*. New York: Random House, 1975.

Dark, Alvin, and John Underwood. *When in Doubt, Fire the Manager: My Life and Times in Baseball*. New York: Dutton, 1980.

Davis, Mervyn, and David Parry-Jones. *Number Eight*. New York: Pelham, 1977.

Dobler, Conrad, and Vic Carucci. *They Call Me Dirty*. New York: Putnam, 1988.

Donovan, Arthur, and Bob Drury. *Fatso: Football When Men Were Really Men*. New York: Morrow, 1987.

Ditka, Mike, and Don Pierson. *Ditka: An Autobiography*. New York: Bonus Books, 1986.

Dreisewerd, Edna. *The Catcher Was a Lady: The Clem Dreisewerd Story*. New York: Exposition, 1978.

Dundee, Angelo, and Mike Winston. *I Only Talk Winning*. New York: Contemporary Books, 1985.

Dunphey, Don. *Don Dunphey at Ringside*. New York: Holt, Rinehart and Winston, 1988.

Duren, Ryne, and Robert Drury. *Comeback*. Dayton, Ohio: Lorenz, 1978.

Durocher, Leo. *Nice Guys Finish Last*. New York: Simon and Schuster, 1975.

Dykstra, Len, and Marty Noble. *Nails*. New York: Doubleday, 1986.

Edwards, Harry. *The Struggle That Must Be: An Autobiography*. New York: Macmillan, 1980.

English, Alex, and Gary Delsomer. *The English Language*. New York: Contemporary Books, 1986.

Evans, Norm, and Edwin Pope. *On the Line*. Old Tappan, N.J.: Fleming H. Revell, 1976.

Fidrych, Mark, and Tom Clark. *No Big Deal*. Philadelphia: Lippincott, 1977.

Ford, Whitey, Mickey Mantle, and Joe Durso. *Whitey and Mickey: A Joint Autobiography of the Yankee Years*. New York: Viking, 1977.

Ford, Whitey, and Phil Pepe. *Slick*. New York: Morrow, 1987.

Garagiola, Joe. *It's Anybody's Ballgame*. Chicago: Contemporary Books, 1988.

Garvey, Steve, and Skip Rozin. *Garvey*. New York: New York Times Books, 1986.

Gifford, Frank, and Charles Mangel. *Gifford on Courage*. Philadelphia: Lippincott, 1976.

Glickman, Harry. *Promoter Ain't a Dirty Word*. Forest Grove, Oreg.: Timber Press, 1978.

Gooden, Dwight, and Richard Woodley. *Rookie*. New York: Doubleday, 1985.

Goolagong, Evonne, and Bud Collins. *Evonne: On the Move*. New York: Dutton, 1975.

Gorman, Tom, and Jerome Holtzman. *Three and Two*. New York: Charles Scribner & Sons, 1979.

Grier, Roosevelt. *Rosey: The Gentle Giant*. Tulsa, Okla.: Harrison House, 1986.

Griffin, Archie, and Dave Diles. *Archie: The Archie Griffin Story*. New York: Doubleday, 1977.

Guidry, Ron, and Peter Golenbock. *Guidry*. New York: Prentice-Hall, Inc., 1980.

Halas, George, and Gwen Morgan. *Halas by Halas.* New York: McGraw-Hill, 1979.
Hall, Donald, and Dock Ellis. *The Pitcher and the Poet.* New York: Coward, 1975.
Havlicek, John, and Bob Ryan. *Hondo: Man in Motion.* Englewood Cliffs, N.J.: Prentice-Hall, 1977.
Hayes, Elvin, and Bill Gilbert. *They Call Me the Big E.* Englewood Cliffs, N.J.: Prentice-Hall, 1978.
Heidenreich, Steve, and Dave Dorr. *Running Back.* New York: Hawthorne, 1979.
Heinsohn, Tommy, and Joe Fitzgerald. *Give 'em the Hook.* New York: Prentice-Hall, 1988.
Hemery, David. *Another Hurdle.* New York: Taplinger, 1976.
Henderson, Thomas, and Peter Knobler. *Out of Control: Confessions of an NFL Casualty.* New York: Putnam, 1987.
Holzman, Red, and Harvey Frommer. *Red on Red.* New York: Bantam, 1987.
Holzman, Red, and Leonard Lewin. *A View from the Bench.* New York: Norton, 1980.
Houk, Ralph, and Robert Creamer. *Season of Glory: The Amazing Saga of the 1961 New York Yankees.* New York: Putnam, 1988.
Hubbell, Ralph. *Come Walk with Me.* Englewood Cliffs, N.J.: Prentice-Hall, 1975.
Huey, Lynda. *A Running Start: An Athlete, A Woman.* New York: Quadrangle, 1976.
Huff, Sam, and Leonard Shapiro. *Tough Stuff: The Man in the Middle.* New York: St. Martin's, 1988.
Hunter, Jim, and Armen Keteyian. *Catfish: My Life in Baseball.* New York: McGraw-Hill, 1988.
Jackson, Reggie, and Mike Lupica. *Reggie: The Autobiography.* New York: Villard, 1984.
Jackson, Reggie, and Bill Libby. *Reggie: A Season with a Superstar.* Chicago: Playboy, 1975.
Jenner, Bruce, and Phillip Finch. *Decathlon Challenge.* Englewood Cliffs, N.J.: Prentice-Hall, 1977.
John, Tommy, Sally John, and Joe Musser. *The Tommy John Story.* Old Tappan, N.J.: Fleming A. Revell, 1978.
Johnson, Davey, and Peter Golenbock. *Bats.* New York: Putnam, 1987.
Johnson, Earvin, and Richard Levin. *Magic.* New York: Viking, 1983.
Johnstone, Jay, and Rick Talley. *Temporary Insanity.* New York: Contemporary Books, 1985.
Jones, K. C. and Jack Warner. *Rebound.* Boston: Quinlan, 1986.
Jordan, Pat. *A False Spring.* New York: Dodd, Mead, 1975.
Kardong, Don. *Thirty Phone Booths to Boston: Tales of a Wayward Runner.* New York: Macmillan, 1985.
Karras, Alex, and Herb Gluck. *Even Big Guys Cry.* New York: Rinehart and Winston, 1977.
King, Billie Jean, and Frank Deford. *Billie Jean.* New York: Viking, 1982.
Killanin, Lord Michael. *My Olympic Years.* New York: Morrow, 1983.
Kiner, Ralph, and Joe Gergen. *Kiner's Corner: At Bat and on the Air—My 40 Years in Baseball.* New York: Arbor House, 1987.
Knox, Chuck, and Bill Plaschke. *Hard Knox: The Life of an NFL Coach.* San Diego: Harcourt Brace Jovanovich, 1988.
Kopay, David, and Perry Deanne Young. *The Dave Kopay Story: An Extraordinary Self Revelation.* New York: Arbor House, 1977.

Kramer, Jack, and Frank Deford. *The Game: My Forty Years in Tennis.* New York: Putnam, 1979.

Kramer, Jerry, and Dick Schaap. *Distant Replay.* New York: Putnam, 1985.

Kubek, Tony, and Terry Pluto. *Sixty-one: The Team, the Record, the Men.* New York: Macmillan, 1987.

Lasorda, Tommy, and David Fiser. *The Artful Dodger.* New York: Arbor House, 1985.

Lee, Bill, and Dick Lally. *The Wrong Stuff.* New York: Viking, 1984.

LeFlore, Ron, and Jim Hawkins. *Breakout: From Prison to the Big Leagues.* New York: Harper and Row, 1978.

Lemon, Meadowlark, and Jerry Jenkins. *Meadowlark.* Nashville: Nelson, 1987.

Lieb, Frederick. *Baseball as I Have Known It.* New York: Coward, McCann and Geoghegan, 1977.

Lieberman, Nancy, and Myrna and Harvey Frommer. *Basketball My Way.* New York: Scribner, 1982.

Liquori, Marty, and Skip Myslenski. *On the Run: In Search of the Perfect Race.* New York: Morrow, 1978.

Littler, Gene, and Jack Tobin. *The Real Score.* Waco, Tex.: Word, 1976.

Lloyd, Chris Evert, and Neil Amdur. *Chrissie: My Own Story.* New York: Simon and Schuster, 1982.

Lloyd, Chris and John, and Carol Thatcher. *Lloyd on Lloyd.* New York: Beaufort, 1985.

Locke, Tates, and Bob Ibach. *Caught in the Net.* New York: Leisure Press, 1982.

Lomax, Neil, and David Miller. *Third and Long.* New York: Revell, 1986.

Lopez, Nancy, and Peter Schwed. *Nancy Lopez.* New York: Simon and Schuster, 1979.

Lyle, Sparky, and Peter Golenbock. *The Bronx Zoo.* New York: Crown, 1979.

Mandell, Arnold. *The Nightmare Season.* New York: Random House, 1979.

Madden, John and Dave Anderson. *Hey, Wait A Minute.* New York: Random House, 1984.

Mantle, Mickey, and Herb Gluck. *The Mick.* New York: Doubleday, 1985.

Markbreit, Jerry, and Alan Steinberg. *Born to Referee: My Life on the Grid-Iron.* New York: Morrow, 1988.

Martin, Billy, and Peter Golenbock. *Number One.* New York: Delacorte, 1980.

Martin, Billy, and Phil Pepe. *Billyball.* Garden City, N.Y.: Doubleday, 1987.

Mays, Willie. *Say Hey.* New York: Simon and Schuster, 1988.

McCarver, Tim, and Ray Robinson. *Oh Baby, I Love It.* New York: Villard, 1987.

McClain, Denny. *Nobody's Perfect.* New York: Dial, 1975.

McConkey, Phil, Phil Simms, and Dick Schaap. *Simms to McConkey: Blood, Sweat, and Gatorade.* New York: Crown, 1987.

McKeon, Jack, and Tom Friend. *Jack of All Trades.* New York: Contemporary Books, 1988.

McMahon, Jim, and Bob Verdi. *McMahon.* New York: Warner, 1986.

Miller, Johnny, and Dale Shankland. *Pure Golf.* Garden City, N.Y.: Doubleday, 1976.

Montana, Joe, and Bob Raissman. *Audibles: My Life in Football.* New York: William Morrow, 1986.

Morris, Eugene, and Steve Fiffer. *Against the Grain.* New York: McGraw-Hill, 1988.

Motta, Dick, and Jerry Jenkins. *Stuff It: The Story of Dick Motta, Toughest Little Coach in the NBA.* Radnor, Pa.: Chilton, 1975.

Munson, Thurman, and Martin Appel. *Thurman Munson: An Autobiography*. New York: Coward, McCann and Geoghegan, 1978.

Navratilova, Martina, and George Vecsey. *Martina*. New York: Knopf, 1985.

Nelsen, Lindsey. *Hello Everybody. I'm Lindsey Nelson*. New York: Beech Tree, 1985.

Nettles, Graig, and Peter Golenbock. *Balls*. New York: Putnam, 1984.

Nicklaus, Jack, and Ken Bowden. *On and Off the Fairway: A Pictorial Autobiography*. New York: Simon and Schuster, 1978.

Niekro, Phil, Joe Niekro, and Ken Pickering. *The Niekro Files: Uncensored Letters of Baseball's Most Notorious Brothers*. New York: Contemporary Books, 1988.

Oh, Sadaharu, and David Falkner. *Sadaharu Oh: A Zen Way of Baseball*. New York: New York Times Books, 1984.

Oriard, Michael. *The End of Autumn: Reflections on My Life in Football*. Garden City, N.Y.: Doubleday, 1982.

Pacheco, Ferdie. *Fight Doctor*. New York: Simon and Schuster, 1977.

Parcells, Bill, and Mike Lupica. *Parcells: Autobiography of the Biggest Giant of Them All*. New York: Bonus, 1987.

Pearson, Preston. *Hearing the Noise: My Life in the NFL*. New York: William Morrow, 1985.

Pepitone, Joe, and Barry Steinback. *Joe, You Coulda Made Us Proud*. Chicago: Playboy, 1975.

Petty, Richard. *King of the Road*. New York: Rutledge, Macmillan, 1977.

Pinella, Lou, and Maury Allen. *Sweet Lou*. New York: Putnam, 1986.

Plant, Mike. *Iron Will: The Heart and Soul of the Triathlon's Ultimate Challenge*. Chicago: Contemporary Books, 1987.

Player, Gary, and Tolhurst Desmond. *Golf Begins at 50: Playing the Lifetime Game Better than Ever*. New York: Simon and Schuster, 1988.

Plunkett, Jim, and David Newhouse. *The Jim Plunkett Story: A Saga about a Man Who Came Back*. New York: Arbor House, 1981.

Porter, Darrell, and William Deerfield. *Snap Me Perfect: The Darrel Porter Story*. Nashville: Nelson, 1984.

Powers, Ritchie, and Mark Mulvoy. *Overtime: An Uninhibited Account of a Referee's Life in the NBA*. New York: David McKay, 1975.

Rashad, Ahmad, and Peter Bodo. *Rashad: Vikes, Mikes, and Something on the Backside*. New York: Viking, 1988.

Reeves, Dan, and Dick Connor. *Reeves: An Autobiography*. New York: Bonus, 1988.

Retton, Mary Lou, and Bela Karolyi. *Mary Lou: Creating an Olympic Gymnast*. New York: McGraw-Hill, 1985.

Richards, Renee, and John Ames. *Second Serve*. New York: Stein and Day, 1983.

Richards, Barry. *The Barry Richards Story*. New York: Faber and Faber, 1978.

Riley, Pat. *Showtime: Inside the Lakers' Breakthrough Season*. Los Angeles: Warner, 1988.

Robinson, Frank, and Dave Anderson. *Frank: The First Year*. New York: Holt, Rinehart, and Winston, 1976.

Robinson, Frank, and Al Silverman. *My Life is Baseball*. Garden City, N.Y.: Doubleday, 1975.

Robinson, Frank, and Barry Steinback. *Extra Innings*. New York: McGraw-Hill, 1988.

Rodgers, Bill, and Joe Concannon. *Marathoning*. New York: Simon and Schuster, 1980.

Rose, Pete, and Bob Hertzel. *Charlie Hustle*. Englewood Cliffs, N.J.: Prentice-Hall, 1975.

Ryun, Jim, and Mike Phillips. *In Quest of Gold*. San Francisco: Harper and Row, 1984.

Roseboro, John, and Bill Libby. *Glory Days with the Dodgers*. New York: Atheneum, 1978.

Russell, Bill, and Taylor Branch. *Second Wind: The Memoirs of an Opinionated Man*. New York: Random House, 1979.

Rutigliano, Sam. *Pressure*. New York: Thomas Nelson, 1988.

Ryan, Nolan, and Bill Libby. *The Other Game*. Waco, Tex.: Word, 1977.

Salvino, Carmen, and Frederick Klein. *Fast Lanes*. New York: Bonus, 1988.

Sandberg, Ryne, and Fred Mitchell. *Ryno*. Chicago: Contemporary Books, 1985.

Semple, Jock, and John Kelly. *Just Call Me Jock: The Story of Jock Semple, Boston's Mr. Marathon*. Boston: Waterford, 1982.

Shero, Fred, and Vijay Kothare. *Shero: The Man behind the System*. Radnor, Pa.: Chilton, 1975.

Shoemaker, Willie, and Dan Smith. *The Shoe*. Chicago: Rand, 1976.

Shorter, Frank, and Marc Bloom. *Olympic Gold: A Runner's Life and Times*. Boston: Houghton Mifflin, 1984.

Shriver, Pam, and Frank Deford. *Passing Shots*. New York: McGraw-Hill, 1986.

Singletary, Mike, and Armen Keteyian. *Calling the Shots: Inside the Chicago Bears*. Chicago: Contemporary Books, 1986.

Skillman, Don, and Lolly Skillman. *Pedaling across America*. New York: Velo-News, 1988.

Slater, Joy, and Steven Price. *Riding's a Joy*. Garden City, N.Y.: Doubleday, 1982.

Sloan, Stephen. *A Whole New Ball Game*. Nashville: Broadman Press, 1975.

Smith, David, and Franklin Russell. *Healing Journey: The Odyssey of an Uncommon Athlete*. San Francisco: Sierra Club Books, 1983.

Smith, Ozzie, and Rob Rains. *Wizard*. Chicago: Contemporary Books, 1988.

Snead, Sam, and George Mendoza. *Slammin' Sam*. New York: David Fine, 1986.

Stabler, Ken, and Barry Steinback. *Snake*. Garden City, N.Y.: Doubleday, 1986.

Stargell, Willie, and Tom Bird. *Willie Stargell: An Autobiography*. New York: Harper and Row, 1984.

Stargell, Willie, and Susan Hall. *Out in Leftfield: Willie Stargell and the Pittsburg Pirates*. New York: Two Continents Publishing, 1975.

Staubach, Roger, and Frank Luksa. *Time Enough to Win*. Waco, Tex.: Word, 1980.

Stephens, Woody, and James Brough. *Guess I'm Lucky: My Life in Horse Racing*. New York: Doubleday, 1985.

Stieb, Dave, and Kevin Boland. *Tomorrow I'll Be Perfect*. New York: Doubleday, 1986.

Stingley, Darryl, and Mark Mulvoy. *Happy to Be Alive*. New York: Beaufort, 1983.

Stram, Hank, and Lou Sahadi. *They're Playing My Game*. New York: Morrow, 1986.

Tatum, Jack, and Bill Kushner. *They Call Me Assassin*. New York: Everest House, 1977.

Taylor, Lawrence, and David Falkner. *LT: Living on the Edge*. New York: New York Times Books, 1987.

Thompson, Danny, and Bob Fowler. *E-6: The Diary of a Major League Shortstop*. Minneapolis: Dillon, 1976.

Toomay, Pat. *The Crunch.* New York: Norton, 1975.

Torrez, Danielle Gagnon, and Ken Lizotte. *High Inside: Memoirs of a Baseball Wife.* New York: Putnam, 1983.

Torvill, Jayne, Christopher Dean, and John Hennessy. *Torvill and Dean.* New York: St. Martin's, 1983.

Trevino, Lee, and Sam Blair. *The Snake in the Sandtrap.* New York: Holt, Rinehart, and Winston, 1985.

Trevino, Lee, and Sam Blair. *They Call Me Supermex.* New York: Random House, 1982.

Trouppe, Quincy. *Twenty Years Too Soon.* Los Angeles: S and S Enterprises, 1977.

Wade, Virginia, and Mary Lou Mellace. *Courting Triumph.* New York: Mayflower, 1978.

Weaver, Earl, and Barry Steinback. *It's What You Learn after You Know It All that Counts.* New York: Doubleday, 1982.

Welch, Bob, and George Vecsey. *Five O'clock Comes Early.* New York: Morrow, 1982.

Winfield, Dave, and Tom Parker. *Winfield: A Player's Life.* New York: Norton, 1988.

Wolff, Rick, and Phil Pepe. *What's a Nice Boy Like You Doing in the Bushes.* Englewood Cliffs, N.J.: Prentice-Hall, 1975.

Wolf, Warner, and William Taffe. *Gimme a Break.* New York: McGraw-Hill, 1983.

Woolf, Robert, and Mickey Herskowitz. *Behind Closed Doors.* New York: Atheneum, 1976.

Woy, William, and Jack Patterson. *Sign 'em Up, Bucky: The Adventures of a Sports Agent.* New York: Hawthorn, 1975.

Youngblood, Jack, and Joel Engel. *Blood.* Chicago: Contemporary Books, 1988.

Sports History/Sport Literature: Some Future Directions and Challenges

MICHAEL ORIARD

Elliot Gorn's *The Manly Art* is the latest, and to my mind the best, of the many recent books by sports historians that are beginning to ground our understanding of sport in a rich sense of its intricate relations to American culture. Following the general surveys of the subject by John Rickards Betts, John A. Lucas and Ronald A. Smith, Betty Spears and Richard A. Swanson, and Benjamin Rader; as well as specialized studies of single sports or sporting figures or eras by Harold Seymour, David Voigt, Donald Mrozek, Steven Reiss, Jules Tygiel, Peter Levine, and others; Gorn is less a pathfinder than a pioneer, bringing in a rich harvest where others blazed a trail. While football awaits its historian, baseball has been served abundantly if unevenly by several writers. Now Gorn does for nineteenth-century prize fighting in America what only the best have done for other sports: he's given us a lively narrative about a lively subject in such a way as to illuminate a great deal about gender, race, and class, and their cultural values in America. Quite simply, *The Manly Art* is the best history of American sport I have read.

This review, however, appears in a journal of sport *literature,* not history; although Gorn would likely not presume to insist on this point, *The Manly Art* says a great deal to those of us primarily interested in the literature of sport. I will return to this subject shortly, but first, what about *The Manly Art* as history? The story of American prize fighting properly begins in England, as is true for nearly all American sports. A golden age of English boxing, from the last quarter of the eighteenth century through the first quarter of the nineteenth, rested on an alliance between the aristocracy and

---

Review of Elliott J. Gorn, *The Manly Art: Bare-Knuckle Prize Fighting in America* (Ithaca: Cornell University Press, 1986). First printed in *Aethlon* (formerly *Arete*): *The Journal of Sport Literature* © 1987. Reprinted by permission.

the lower classes against the emerging middle class. The lower classes provided the boxers, of course, the gentry only the patrons, but the two extremes of British society shared a set of values— "love of pageantry, bold risk taking, and martial courage" (27)—at odds with the bourgeois capitalist ethic. The dominance of the bourgeoisie after 1825 or so led to prize fighting's suppression. George IV had "an honor guard of twenty leading pugilists" at his coronation in 1821 (26); within a few years their profession was declared illegal and denounced from pulpit and editor's chair.

The early American prize ring knew no such golden era, only suppression. Lacking a traditional aristocracy to legitimize its values, prize fighting existed until the end of the nineteenth century as an illegal enterprise of the urban underclass. Only scattered references to boxing in the eighteenth and early nineteenth centuries suggest that the sport existed at all; the first full newspaper coverage of a fight in 1823 made the event's problematical moral and legal status clear. Prize fighting thrived in the oral culture of saloons and streets in the developing cities, rooted not in official approval but in the community ties, ethnic loyalties, and masculine ethos of laborers, gamblers, and others on the fringe of society— the "fancy," as they were first named in England. Given the scarcity of sources on such a subculture, Gorn does a splendid job of recreating the memorable bouts—Ned Hammond vs. George Kensett in the 1820s; "Deaf" Burke vs. Sam O'Rourke in the '30s; Chris Lilly vs. Tom McCoy in 1842 (the first fatal championship fight); Yankee Sullivan vs. Tom Hyer, Sullivan vs. John Morrissey, Morrissey vs. Tom Heenan, and Heenan vs. Tom Sayers in the 1840s and '50s; finally, John L. Sullivan vs. first Jake Kilrain and then Gentleman Jim Corbett in 1889 and 1891 at the end of the bare-knuckle era. From neighborhood loyalties to ethnic antagonisms, to immigrant vs. nativist and American vs. English partisanship, championship prize fights have always functioned as social dramas playing out fundamental conflicts in the culture. Fighters, too, as well as fights, come to life through Gorn's supple prose; the author is particularly good at establishing the ambiance of urban working-class life at midcentury and the curious partnership of prizefighters, gamblers, and politicians that dominated local governments for a time.

Gorn also very effectively places prize fighting at the center of nineteenth-century gender concerns: the anxieties of middle- and upper-class males over their emasculation in a feminized culture, resulting in a paradoxical glorification of ring heroes in the face of persisting moral, legal, class, and ethnic revulsions. Pugilism mocked liberal faith in triumphant rationality and moral progress. But while the antibourgeois values of the prize ring ("personal toughness, local honor, drunken conviviality, violent display" [66]) were deeply troubling to genteel America, the ring also represented those qualities of physical courage and force which genteel America felt it lacked. Parallel to the rise of prize fighting, then, the gentleman's sport of sparring had attracted enthusiasts from the 1820s on, eventually providing the platform from which the "respectable" classes embraced the barbarian pastime of their social inferiors. Gorn's story ends with the beginning of commercialized prize fighting: with the transformation of public ritual into spectator sport. Putting on gloves eliminated little of boxing's brutality (the reverse in fact was true), but it assured the prize ring's eventual acceptance by middle-class America.

Thus, through boxing Gorn writes not just sport history but gender history, social history, and labor history. He joins others in his field who seek to complement political and economic history with a portrait of America's voiceless citizens. Gorn's closest kin are not pure sport historians but such social and labor historians as Daniel T. Rodgers and Roy Rosenzweig, who approach sport obliquely as part of working-class leisure. Gorn, on the other hand, is a social historian who places a lower-class sport at the center of his narrative. The 1850s from this perspective—a decade known in other contexts as the "American Renaissance" or the "Feminine Fifties"—becomes the "Era of John Morrissey" in Gorn's telling, not to the exclusion of those other versions but in addition to them. A composite portrait of American culture at midcentury comes much more clearly into focus as the subculture surrounding pugilism emerges from Gorn's pages. About his main subject, prize fighting itself, Gorn is never simplistic. The sport was both brutal and meaningfully ritualistic, expressive of a varied lower class's deepest values, hopes, and fears. In his preface Gorn declares that he tends "to take the part of the lions over the Christians" (12), but this sympathy in no way interferes with the historian's responsibilities. He is merely forthright where others have been evasive. And he avoids altogether the simplistic extremes in accounting for boxing's cultural meaning, as in this typical passage: "Neither restraint nor untrammeled aggressiveness but razor-edged balance between rules of decorum and violence, a poetic tension between fair play and bloodletting, lay at the heart of boxing's aesthetic appeal" (65–66). Or again, "Boxing's appeal always rested on a creative dualism between violence and order, impulsiveness and self-control, brutality and restraint" (171). The reader feels confidence in the judgments of a historian who writes with such expansive clear-sightedness.

As history, then, *The Manly Art* seems impeccable; as a history of sport *literature*, it also speaks directly to readers of *Arete*. What seems potentially of especial interest to us is the fact that Gorn's subject is as much the "literature" of nineteenth-century boxing as the sport itself. His sources are primarily newspapers and popular pamphlets—the *Spirit of the Times*, the *National Police Gazette*, the *New York Herald* and other working-class newspapers; and such publications as *American Fistiana*, first published in 1849 and revised in 1860 and 1873. This is "literature" of a distinctly nonliterary sort, of course, but one of our failures to this point as historians of sport literature has been our insufficient attention to such materials. Gorn brings some fiction and "poetry" into the discussion: a story-paper sketch in 1838 of a country lad dying in the despised prize ring to save his mother's mortgage; popular ballads and other doggerel verse that celebrated famous fights. Such poetry will never displace Whitman or Dickinson from the canon (a sample: "Both men looked well, in excellent training,/ In capital order for cutting and maiming"), but it is nonetheless important as popular literary expression.

But more important is the journalism that provides the bulk of Gorn's sources. The *language* itself of sport, as it has developed over a century and a half, should be of particular interest to us literary folk, and we have explored it far too little. We have established a canon of major writers (Lardner, Malamud, Coover, DeLillo, Roth), and we have traced the subordinate treatment of sport through the fiction of Fitzgerald, Faulkner, Hemingway, and other mainstream figures. We have looked briefly at the popular tradition of Gilbert Patten and his successors but have kept such subliterature entirely separate from our core of masterpieces. Most telling, we have not yet mapped out the fuller literary history of sport that lies primarily in sporting journalism. Lardner was not influenced by Mark Twain after all but Hugh Fullerton, Hugh Keogh, George Ade, and other contemporary newspapermen. In writing about *The Natural*, we pay ample attention to the Fraser-Weston-Eliot sources but little to the sources of the colloquial language of sport that clash so interestingly with the mythic language. We note the influence of Joyce and Borges on Coover and DeLillo, but largely ignore the ideas and vernacular of sport they would have likely absorbed from the mass culture. From Lardner and Van Loan to Deford and Kahn, the bulk of sports fiction has been written by journalists, but we have little sense of the developing language of sport that those journalists, and their predecessors in the nineteenth century, chiefly created.

"Sport Literature," in other words, is found not just in novels and poems but in nineteenth-century story papers and dime novels, in the *Police Gazette* and *St. Nicholas,* in the *Chicago Tribune* and the *Saturday Evening Post.* As literary historians we have mapped out a topography with most of the mountain peaks and an occasional hillock below, but with little of the terrain from which these mounds and peaks rise. We have long been aware of a basic anomaly, that the literature about the most popular form of American mass culture has itself never been popular. But we have inadequately explored sport's truly popular expressions in newspapers and magazines. If we are to be interested in sport as a cultural expression, we need to widen our gaze to include the literature of the masses, but we have an obstacle to overcome in order to do so. In *The Manly Art,* Elliot Gorn writes a kind of social history that is currently fashionable (the book began as a Ph.D. dissertation in American Studies at Yale). Literary scholars interested in the ephemeral writing on sport have had no such model to follow. Most of us, I suspect, have feared straying too far from Hemingway and Faulkner or Coover and DeLillo; our place in the profession, we acknowledge uneasily, is on the margins already. A full-scale literary study of the *Police Gazette*—with all its difficulties in finding primary sources, assimilating masses of material, and coming to rewarding conclusions—even if successful might seem to settle our marginality for good. But the current interest in gender, class, canonicity, and other revisionist concerns can provide us a forum. Few publishers, I suspect, would welcome a close reading of *The Fairport Nine,* but many editors at presses and journals would undoubtedly welcome good, substantial historical/sociological work on nineteenth-century mass literature out of which would emerge a fuller understanding of the relations among gender, class, audience, and "literature" itself. Gorn's book is published by Cornell University Press; Chris Messenger's and Allen Guttman's have been brought out by Columbia. Oxford University Press and the University of Illinois Press have recently established monograph series on sport; *Modern Fiction Studies* has just published a special issue on sport literature. Devotees of sport literature have been invited into the mainstream; it is up to us to accept the invitation.

We need a history of the language of sport. We need a history of the culture's positive and negative images of the athlete and of the various sports as they have changed through the decades. We need studies of gender, race, and class in the writing on sport. In our age of television, we need not just studies of print journalism but studies of the language that comes from the broadcast booth (as Tom Dodge reminded us at the first meeting of the Sport Literature Association in his wonderfully evocative talk on Gordon McClendon). As first radio and then TV have appropriated the role of creating the language of sport for popular consumption, we need to appropriate some of the study of these media—not reflections on a season's viewing of "Monday Night Football," but historical studies based on thorough archival research. We also need studies of the popular iconography of sport from Currier & Ives to Norman Rockwell to Leroy Neiman—"language" only peripherally, in the Barthesian sense, but properly our concern. Such studies as these would not violate the basic delight in sport that has drawn us into the field, substituting pedantry for pleasure. Rather, they would direct that pleasure into the complementary intellectual pleasures of sound scholarship. Elliot Gorn's *The Manly Art* can provide a useful guide to many of the sources essential to our own studies of nineteenth-century sport literature. To discover others we will have to practice the historian's arts. Gorn's splendid book offers us an equally splendid challenge and invitation.

Bibliography

The following bibliography comprises noteworthy works that exemplify the wide range, diversity, and productivity of subject matter that have characterized American sport literature since the 1950s. While this list strives for completeness, some reputable works may have been inadvertently overlooked in the veritable deluge of sport-related publications that has appeared through 1989. However, those that are included are sufficiently representative of sport literature's current level of achievement in this country.

This bibliography is divided into two general categories: the creative literature, or primary sources—fiction, drama (film), and poetry—and the supplemental literature, an increasingly significant body of criticism, philosophy, biography, history, and special studies. (For autobiography, refer to the extensive bibliography that supplements Mary McElroy's essay on the subject.)

Inclusion in the supplemental category has been determined by either a work's direct impact on American sport literature as, for example, a critical study (e.g., *Laurel and Thorn: The Athlete in American Literature*), or by its overall humanistic, sociocultural import (e.g., *The Joy of Sports*) rather than by the research findings of the social sciences, another proliferating area of influential sport studies in recent years.

Helping to broaden the perspectives of creative literature, which has experienced an ongoing renaissance since the 1960s, are the human-interest explorations of such fields as biography and history, as well as the unique insights into human behavior uncovered by a seemingly endless stream of special studies. As a result, one finds fiction writers, for example, moved to incorporate actual figures and events of contemporary or historical relevance into their narratives in an apparent attempt to lend their imaginative postures more of a sociocultural ambiance in spite of any fantasylike intent they might be disposed to (see, e.g., Christian Messenger's analysis of this trend in his essay on baseball fiction in the 1980s).

In this regard, American sporting experience—the literature of which has always been polarized by elements of realism and fantasy—has become an ever-expanding source of inspiration for both the novelist/short-story writer and the biographer/historian, an unprecedented situation that sees both fiction and nonfiction enjoying a kind of symbiotic relationship—one that in both a creative and humanistic sense nourishes and replenishes the other in their ongoing quest to explore the widest possible range of the human condition. The bibliography that follows lends substantial testimony to this development.

(Editor's note: Because a number of classic studies such as Johan Huizinga's *Homo Ludens* and Roger Caillois's *Man, Play and Games* are common to the general field of sport/leisure studies and because such works are cited in a number of sources throughout this bibliography, they are not included here. For an extensive bibliography of juvenile sports fiction, the reader should consult Michael Oriard's critical study of American sports fiction, *Dreaming of Heroes.*)

The Creative (Primary) Literature

Fiction

Since fiction has inspired the greatest bulk of sport literature's creative output, the following novels have been arranged alphabetically by sport. (Short-story sources are identified where appropriate.) Only those sports which are the most common to American social experience are represented here. To qualify as sports fiction, the makeup of a work's major character(s) and/or its dominant atmosphere must be influenced or pervaded by the sociocultural values of American sporting experience. In most cases, subgenre works—detective fiction, e.g.—have not been included here.

(Editor's note: In addition to those mentioned below, other notable American writers prior to the 1950s who incorporated sporting experience into their fiction are Sherwood Anderson, Paul Annixter, Walter Van Tilburg Clark, Charles Einstein, Paul Gallico, John O'Hara, Frank O'Rourke, Damon Runyan, John R. Tunis, and Charles E. Van Loan.)

BASEBALL (AND SOFTBALL)

Ardizzone, Tony. *Heart of the Order.* New York: Henry Holt, 1986.

Asinof, Eliot. *Man on Spikes.* New York: McGraw-Hill, 1955.

Babitz, Eve. *Slow Days, Fast Company.* New York: Knopf, 1977.

Beckham, Barry. *Runner Mack.* New York: Morrow, 1972.

Bell, Marty. *Breaking Balls.* New York: New American Library, 1979.

Bowen, Michael. *Can't Miss.* New York: Harper and Row, 1987.

Brashler, William. *The Bingo Long Traveling All-Stars and Motor Kings.* New York: Harper and Row, 1973.

Carkeet, David. *The Greatest Slump of All Time.* New York: Harper and Row, 1984.

Charyn, Jerome. *The Seventh Babe*. New York: Arbor House, 1979.

Cooney, Ellen. *All the Way Home*. New York: Putnam, 1984.

Coover, Robert. *The Universal Baseball Association, J. Henry Waugh, Prop.* New York: Random House, 1968.

Craig, John. *Chappie and Me*. New York: Dodd, Mead, 1979.

Everett, Percival L. *Suder*. New York: Viking, 1984.

Foster, Alan S. *Goodbye, Bobby Thomson! Goodbye, John Wayne!* New York: Simon and Schuster, 1973.

Gethers, Peter. *Getting Blue*. New York: Delacorte, 1987.

Graham, John A. *Babe Ruth Caught in a Snowstorm*. Boston: Houghton Mifflin, 1973.

Green, Gerald. *To Brooklyn with Love*. New York: Trident, 1967.

Greenberg, Eric R. *The Celebrant*. New York: Everett House, 1982.

Gregorich, Barbara. *She's on First*. New York: Contemporary Books, 1987.

Harris, Mark. *Bang the Drum Slowly*. New York: Knopf, 1956.

————. *It Looked Like For Ever*. New York: McGraw-Hill, 1979.

————. *The Southpaw*. Indianapolis: Bobbs-Merrill, 1953.

————. *A Ticket for a Seamstitch*. New York: Knopf, 1956.

Hays, Donald. *The Dixie Association*. New York: Simon and Schuster, 1984.

Hemphill, Paul. *Long Gone*. New York: Viking, 1979.

Herrin, Lamar. *The Rio Loja Ringmaster*. New York: Viking, 1977.

Honig, Donald. *The Last Great Season*. New York: Simon and Schuster, 1979.

Hough, John. *The Conduct of the Game*. New York: Harcourt Brace Jovanovich, 1986.

Jordan, Pat. *The Cheat*. New York: Villard, 1984.

Kahn, Roger. *The Seventh Game*. New York: New American Library, 1982.

Kennedy, William. *Ironweed*. New York: Viking, 1983.

Kinsella, W. P. *The Iowa Baseball Confederacy*. Boston: Houghton Mifflin, 1986.

————. *Shoeless Joe*. Boston: Houghton Mifflin, 1982. Kinsella has also published two short-story collections: *The Thrill of the Grass* (New York: Penguin, 1984) and *The Further Adventures of Slugger McBatt* (Boston: Houghton Mifflin, 1988.)

Kluger, Steve. *Changing Pitches*. New York: St. Martin's, 1984.

Lorenz, Tom. *Guys Like Us*. New York: Viking, 1980.

Malamud, Bernard. *The Natural*. New York: Dell, 1952.

Mayer, Robert. *The Grace of Shortstops*. Garden City, N.Y.: Doubleday, 1984.

McManus, James. *Chin Music*. New York: Crown, 1985.

Morgenstein, Gary. *The Man Who Wanted to Play Centerfield for the New York Yankees*. New York: Atheneum, 1983.

————. *Take Me Out to the Ballgame*. New York: St. Martin's, 1980.

Neugeboren, Jay. *Sam's Legacy*. New York: Holt, Rinehart and Winston, 1974.

O'Connor, Philip F. *Stealing Home*. New York: Knopf, 1979.

Plimpton, George. *The Curious Case of Sidd Finch*. New York: Macmillan, 1987.

Pomeranz, Gary. *Out at Home*. Boston: Houghton Mifflin, 1985.

Quarrington, Paul. *Home Game*. New York: Doubleday, 1983.

Quigley, Martin. *Today's Game*. New York: Viking, 1965.

Ritz, David. *The Man Who Wanted to Bring the Dodgers Back to Brooklyn*. New York: Simon and Schuster, 1981.

✓ Roth, Philip. *The Great American Novel*. New York: Holt, 1973.

Rothweiler, Paul R. *The Sensuous Southpaw*. New York: Putnam, 1976.

Sayles, John. *Pride of the Bimbos*. Boston: Little, Brown, 1975.

Schiffer, Michael. *Ballpark*. New York: Simon and Schuster, 1982.

Shaw, Irwin. *Voices of a Summer Day*. New York: Delacorte, 1965.

Sheed, Wilfred. *The Boys of Winter*. New York: Knopf, 1987.

Small, David. *Almost Famous*. New York: Norton, 1982.

Snyder, Don J. *Veteran's Park*. New York: Franklin Watts, 1987.

Stein, Harry. *Hoopla*. New York: Knopf, 1983.

Tennenbaum, Silvia. *Rachel, the Rabbi's Wife*. New York: Morrow, 1978.

Vogan, Sara. *In Shelley's Leg*. St. Paul, Minn.: Graywolf Press, 1985.

Willard, Nancy. *Things Invisible to See*. New York: Knopf, 1984.

Wolff, Miles. *Season of the Owl*. New York: Stein and Day, 1980.

Zuckerman, George. *Farewell, Frank Merriwell*. New York: Dutton, 1973.

For a representative selection of short fiction, see Jerome Holtzman, ed., *Fielder's Choice: An Anthology of Baseball Fiction* (New York: Harcourt Brace Jovanovich, 1979). A well-received collection of short stories is Jerry Klinkowitz's *Short Season and Other Stories* (Baltimore: Johns Hopkins University Press, 1988).

(Editor's note: In earlier baseball fiction, the reader should also be aware of Ring Lardner, whose short fiction produced during the 1920s, particularly his epistolary collection, *You Know Me Al* (1925), has had an important, ongoing influence on the style and tone of numerous later writers of baseball fiction.)

BASKETBALL

Beckham, Barry. *Double Dunk*. New York: Holloway House, 1981.

Bower, George. *The Jordans*. New York: Arbor House, 1984.

Conroy, Pat. *The Lords of Discipline*. Boston: Houghton Mifflin, 1980.

Greenfield, Robert. *Haymon's Crowd*. New York: Simon and Schuster, 1978.

Kaylin, Walter. *The Power Forward*. New York: Atheneum, 1979.

Larner, Jeremy. *Drive, He Said*. New York: Dial, 1964.

Levin, Bob. *The Best Ride to New York*. New York: Harper and Row, 1978.

Levitt, Leonard. *The Long Way Round*. New York: Saturday Review, 1972.

Neugeboren, Jay. *Big Man*. Boston: Houghton Mifflin, 1966.

Olsen, Jack. *Massy's Game*. New York: Playboy, 1976.

Rosen, Charles. *Have Jump Shot, Will Travel*. New York: Arbor House, 1975.

———. *A Mile above the Rim*. New York: Arbor House, 1976.

✓ Roth, Philip. *Goodbye, Columbus*. Boston: Houghton Mifflin, 1959.

Rutman, Leo. *Five Good Boys*. New York: Viking, 1982.

Shainberg, Lawrence. *One on One*. New York: Holt, Rinehart and Winston, 1970.

Shields, David. *Heroes*. New York: Simon and Schuster, 1984.

✓ Updike, John. *Rabbit, Run*. New York: Crest, 1960. (Editor's note: The reader is also referred to the other works in the Rabbit Angstrom saga, *Rabbit Redux* and *Rabbit Is Rich*. While they are not strictly in the sports-fiction category, Updike's Rabbit novels are centered on a character who has been molded in large part by American sports experience, in his case, basketball.)

Walton, Todd. *Inside Moves*. Garden City, N.Y.: Doubleday, 1978.

Ward, Robert. *Red Baker*. New York: Dial, 1985.

Young, Al. *Ask Me Now*. New York: McGraw-Hill, 1980.

BOXING

(Editor's note: Prior to the 1950s, the reader should be aware of the fictional output of the following reputable American writers who drew on the boxing experience—Jack London, Ring Lardner, Ernest Hemingway, Nelson Algren, and Budd Schulberg.)

Apple, Max. *Zip: A Novel of the Left and Right*. New York: Viking, 1978.

Bishop, Leonard. *The Butchers*. New York: Dial, 1956.

Crews, Harry. *The Knockout Artist*. New York: Harper and Row, 1988.

Gardner, Leonard. *Fat City*. New York: Farrar, Strauss and Giroux, 1969.

Hamill, Pete. *Flesh & Blood*. New York: Random House, 1977.

Hoagland, Edward. *The Circle Home*. New York: Crowell, 1960.

Heinz, W. C. *The Professional*. New York: Harper, 1958.

Jones, James. *From Here to Eternity*. New York: Scribner's, 1951. (Editor's note: While not a boxing novel as such, this work has a central character whose makeup is compounded in large part of his experiences in boxing.)

Lowry, Robert J. *The Violent Wedding*. New York: Doubleday, 1953.

Milton, David S. *Skyline*. New York: Putnam, 1968.

Newman, Edwin. *Sunday Punch*. New York: Houghton Mifflin, 1979.

Oates, Joyce Carol. *You Must Remember This*. New York: Dutton, 1987.

Pellini, Francis. *The Crown*. New York: Putnam, 1968.

Robbins, Harold. *A Stone for Danny Fisher*. New York: Knopf, 1952.

Shaara, Michael. *The Broken Place*. New York: New American Library, 1968.

Shulman, Irving. *The Square Trap*. Boston: Little, Brown, 1953.

For a representative sampling of short fiction, see Martin H. Greenburg, ed., *In the Ring: A Treasury of Boxing Stories* (New York: Bonanza Books, 1986).

FISHING

(Editor's note: Before the 1950s, the reader should consult the influential works of Caroline Gordon and Ernest Hemingway that deal with the sport of fishing.)

Brooks, Winfield S. *The Shining Tides*. New York: Morrow, 1952.

Dexter, Bruce. *The Fishing Trip*. New York: New American Library, 1966.

Duncan, David James. *The River Why*. San Francisco: Sierra Club, 1983.

Fosburgh, Hugh. *The Sound of White Water.* New York: Scribner's, 1955.

Jones, Robert F. *Blood Sport.* New York: Simon and Schuster, 1974.

McGuane, Thomas. *Ninety-Two in the Shade.* New York: Farrar, Strauss, 1973.

An acclaimed collection of short fiction is Norman MacLean's *A River Runs through It and Other Stories* (Chicago: The University of Chicago Press, 1976).

FOOTBALL

(Editor's note: Earlier noteworthy sources of football as a fictional subject are F. Scott Fitzgerald, James T. Farrell, Irwin Shaw's short-story classic, "The Eighty-Yard Run" [1941], and Millard Lampell's novel *The Hero* [1949].)

Berry, Eliot. *Four Quarters Make a Season.* New York: Berkeley, 1973.

Bower, George. *Running.* New York: Playboy, 1982.

Brunner, Bernard. *Six Days to Sunday.* New York: McGraw-Hill, 1975.

Camerer, Dave. *Nine Saturdays Make a Year.* Garden City, N.Y.: Doubleday, 1962.

Cartwright, Gary. *The Hundred-Yard War.* Garden City, N.Y.: Doubleday, 1968.

Coover, Robert. *Whatever Happened to Gloomy Gus of the Chicago Bears?* New York: Simon and Schuster, 1987.

Cox, William, *The Running Back.* New York: Bantam, 1974.

Cronley, Jay. *Fall Guy.* Garden City, N.Y.: Doubleday, 1978.

Daley, Robert. *Only a Game.* New York: New American Library, 1967.

Deal, Babs H. *The Grail.* New York: McKay, 1963.

Deford, Frank. *Cut 'n' Run.* New York: Viking, 1973.

———. *Everybody's All-American.* New York: Viking, 1981.

DeLillo, Don. *End Zone.* Boston: Houghton Mifflin, 1972.

Exley, Frederick. *A Fan's Notes.* New York: Harper and Row, 1968.

Gent, Peter. *The Franchise.* New York: Random House, 1983.

———. *North Dallas after 40.* New York: Villard, 1989.

———. *North Dallas Forty.* New York: Morrow, 1973.

———. *Texas Celebrity Turkey Trot.* New York: Morrow, 1978.

Gerson, Noel B. *The Sunday Heroes.* New York: Morrow, 1972.

Guy, David. *Football Dreams.* New York: Playboy, 1980.

Jenkins, Dan. *Life Its Ownself.* New York: Simon and Schuster, 1984.

———. *Semi-Tough.* New York: Atheneum, 1972.

Jones, Jack. *The Animal.* New York: Morrow, 1975.

Kaifetz, Norman. *Welcome Sundays.* New York: Putnam, 1979.

Koperwas, Sam. *Westchester Bull.* New York: Simon and Schuster, 1976.

Loken, Chris. *Come Monday Mornin'.* New York: Evans, 1974.

Manchester, William. *The Long Gainer.* Boston: Little, Brown, 1961.

Maule, Hamilton (Tex). *Footsteps.* New York: Random House, 1961.

McCluskey, John. *Mr. America's Last Season Blues.* Baton Rouge: Louisiana State University Press, 1983.

McDowell, Edwin. *Three Cheers and a Tiger.* New York: Macmillan, 1966.

Milton, David Scott. *The Quarterback*. New York: Dell, 1970.

Monninger, Joseph. *Second Season*. New York: Atheneum, 1987.

Nemerov, Howard. *The Homecoming Game*. New York: Simon and Schuster, 1957.

Newcombe, Jack. *In Search of Billy Cole*. New York: Arbor House, 1984.

Olsen, Jack. *Alphabet Jackson*. New York: Playboy, 1974.

Pillitteri, Joseph. *Two Hours on Sunday*. New York: Dial, 1976.

Pye, Lloyd. *That Prosser Kid*. New York: Arbor House, 1977.

Segal, Fred. *The Broken-Field Runner*. New York: New American Library, 1967.

Steadman, Mark. *A Lion's Share*. New York: Holt, Rinehart and Winston, 1974.

Taylor, Casey. *Game Plan*. New York: Atheneum, 1975.

Taylor, Robert L. *Professor Fodorski*. Garden City, N.Y.: Doubleday, 1950.

Terry, Doug. *The Last Texas Hero*. Garden City, N.Y.: Doubleday, 1982.

Toomay, Pat. *On Any Given Sunday*. New York: Fine, 1984.

Wallop, Douglass. *So This Is What Happened to Charlie Moe*. New York: Norton, 1965.

Wells, Lawrence. *Let the Band Play Dixie*. Garden City, N.Y.: Doubleday, 1987.

Whitehead, James. *Joiner*. New York: Knopf, 1971.

Wilder, Robert. *Autumn Thunder*. Putnam, 1952.

Williams, John A. *The Junior Bachelor Society*. Garden City, N.Y.: Doubleday, 1976.

[Editor's note:] Before his untimely death, Herbert Wilner produced two short-story collections that contain football stories: *Dovisch in the Wilderness and Other Stories* (Indianapolis: Bobbs-Merrill, 1968) and *The Quarterback Speaks to His God* (Berkeley, Calif.: Cayuse Press, 1987).

GOLF

Fox, William Price. *Doctor Golf*. Philadelphia: Lippincott, 1963.

Hallberg, William. *The Rub of the Green*. Garden City, N.Y., Doubleday, 1988.

✓Jenkins, Dan. *Dead Solid Perfect*. New York: Atheneum, 1974.

Marquand, John P. *Life at Happy Knoll*. Boston: Little, Brown, 1957.

Murphy, Michael. *Golf in the Kingdom*. New York: Viking, 1972.

Olson, Toby. *Seaview*. New York: New Directions, 1983.

Packard, Bob. *The Pro*. New York: Leisure Books, 1979.

Pickens, Arthur E. *The Golf Bum*. New York: Crown, 1970.

Powers, J. F. *Morte D'Urban*. Garden City, N.Y.: Doubleday, 1962.

Tuttle, Anthony. *Drive for the Green*. Garden City, N.Y.: Doubleday, 1969.

(Editor's note: For a generous sampling of classic short fiction, see William Hallberg, ed. *Perfect Lies: A Century of Great Golf Stories* [Garden City, N.Y.: Doubleday, 1989].)

HUNTING

(Editor's note: Seminal works in this area published prior to the 1950s include William Faulkner's fiction, particularly "The Bear" (1942), Caroline Gordon's short

fiction as well as her novel *Aleck Maury, Sportsman* (1934), and Ernest Hemingway's short fiction.)

Eddings, David. *High Hunt*. New York: Putnam, 1973.
Erne, Richard B. *The Hunt*. New York: Crown, 1959.
Fosburgh, Hugh. *The Hunter*. New York: Scribner's, 1950.
Hassler, Jon. *The Love Hunter*. New York: Morrow, 1981.
Humphrey, William. *Home from the Hill*. New York: Knopf, 1957.
McGuane, Thomas. *The Sporting Club*. New York: Simon and Schuster, 1968.

SKIING

Hall, Oakley. *The Downhill Racers*. New York: Viking, 1963.
Shaw, Irwin. *The Top of the Hill*. New York: Delacorte, 1979.

SURFING

Nunn, Kem. *Tapping the Source*. New York: Delacorte, 1984.

SWIMMING

Levin, Jenifer. *Water Dancer*. New York: Poseidon, 1982.
West, Paul. *Out of My Depths*. Garden City, N.Y.: Doubleday, 1983.

TENNIS

Barker, Robert. *Love Forty*. Philadelphia: Lippincott, 1975.
Bradmer, Gary. *The Players*. New York: Pyramid, 1975.
Brennan, Peter. *Sudden Death*. New York: Rawson, 1978.
Brinkley, William. *Breakpoint*. New York: Morrow, 1978.
Brown, Rita Mae. *Sudden Death*. New York: Bantam, 1983.
Demers, Ralph M. *The Circuit*. New York: Viking, 1976.
Fadiman, Edwin. *The Professional*. New York: McKay, 1973.
Gustafson, Lars. *The Tennis Players*. New York: New Directions, 1983.
Hannah, Barry. *The Tennis Handsome*. New York: Knopf, 1983.
Oldham, Archie. *A Race through Summer*. New York: Dell, 1975.
Sklar, George. *The Promising Young Men*. New York: Crown, 1951.
Wallop, Douglas. *Mixed Singles*. New York: Norton, 1977.
See also Kent Nelson's *The Tennis Player and Other Stories* (Urbana: University
    of Illinois Press, 1974).

(Editor's note: An earlier influential short story is Irwin Shaw's 1947 work "Mixed
Doubles.")

TRACK (RUNNING)

Kram, Mark. *Miles to Go*. New York: Morrow, 1982.
Lear, Peter. *Goldengirl*. Garden City, N.Y.: Doubleday, 1978.
McNab, Tom. *The Fast Man*. New York: Simon and Schuster, 1988.
———. *Flanagan's Run*. New York: Morrow, 1982.

Prince, Victor. *The Other Kingdom*. Garden City, N.Y.: Doubleday, 1964.
Redgate, John. *The Last Decathlon*. New York: Delacorte, 1979.
Warren, Patricia N. *The Front Runner*. New York: Morrow, 1974.

(Editor's note: See also John Cleever's classic 1953 short story "O Youth and Beauty!")

WRESTLING

Davis, Terry. *Vision Quest*. New York: Viking, 1979.
Stark, Sharon S. *A Wrestling Season*. New York: Morrow, 1987.

MISCELLANEOUS

Butler, Jack. *Jujitsu for Christ*. New York: Penguin, 1988.
Ford, Richard. *The Sportswriter*. New York: Vintage, 1986.
Knowles, John. *A Separate Peace*. New York: Bantam, 1966.

Short-Fiction Anthologies and Collections

Camp, Raymond Russell, ed. *Hunting Trails: A Sportsman's Treasury*. New York: Appleton-Century-Crofts, 1966.
Gold, Robert S., ed. *The Roar of the Sneakers*. New York: Bantam, 1977.
Morris, Willie. *Always Stand in Against the Curve and Other Sports Stories*. Oxford, Miss.: Yoknapatawpha Press, 1983.
Schulman, L. M. *Winners and Losers: An Anthology of Great Sports Fiction*. New York: Collier, 1968.
Schwed, Peter, and Herbert H. Wind, eds. *Great Stories from the World of Sport*. 3 vols. New York: Simon and Schuster, 1958.

Drama (Film)

(Editor's note: Since the turn of the century, American drama has often portrayed characters with sports-oriented backgrounds, but the movies, due to their natural propensity for visualizing physical activity, have expanded considerably upon the dramatic possibilities in this area. Following are some sources that discuss sport in film, in addition to some sport-inspired stage productions that have appeared since the 1950s.)

Bergan, Ronald. *Sports in the Movies*. New York: Proteus Books, 1982.
Davis, Bill C. *Dancing in the End Zone*. New York: Samuel French, 1984.
Manchel, Frank. *Great Sports Movies*. New York: Franklin Watts, 1980.
La Russo, Louis. *Knockout*. New York: Samuel French, 1978.
Lindsay, Howard, and Russell Crouse. *Tall Story*. New York: Dramatists Play Service, 1959.
Miller, Jason. *That Championship Season*. New York: Atheneum, 1972.
Noonan John F. *The Year Boston Won the Pennant*. New York: Samuel French, 1968.

Reynolds, Jonathan. *Yanks 3 Detroit 0 Top of the Seventh.* New York: Dramatics Play Service, 1976.

Sackler, Howard. *The Great White Hope.* New York: Dial, 1968.

Serling, Rod. *Requiem for a Heavyweight.* New York: Samuel French, 1984. (Editor's note: This play was first produced for television in 1956 and made into a movie in 1963.)

Umphlett, Wiley Lee. *The Movies Go to College: Hollywood and the College-Life Film.* Madison, N.J.: Fairleigh Dickinson University Press, 1984.

Wallenfeldt, Jeffrey, ed. *Sports Movies.* Evanston, Ill.: Cine Books, 1989.

Editor's note: Some dramatic, fictional, and nonfictional sources have inspired musical plays, such as the following.

Abbott, George, and Douglass Wallop. *Damn Yankees.* (Music and lyrics by Richard Adler and Jerry Ross) New York: Dramatists Play Service, 1955.

Gibson, William, and Clifford Odets. *Golden Boy.* (Music by Charles Strouse and lyrics by Lee Adams) New York: Samuel French, 1964.

Siegel, Joel, and Martin Charmin. *The First.* (Music by Bob Brush and lyrics by Martin Charmin) New York: Samuel French, 1981.

Poetry

(Editor's note: In addition to the primary sources Don Johnson identifies in his essay and Brooke Horvath and Sharon Carson point out in theirs, the reader is referred to other sources and related material in the following works.)

Aethlon: The Journal of Sport Literature. Fall 1983–.

Buchwald, Emilie, and Ruth Roston, eds. *This Sporting Life.* Minneapolis: Milkweed Editions, 1987.

Evans, David. *Among Athletes.* New York: Folder Editions, 1971.

———, ed. *The Sport of Poetry/ The Poetry of Sport.* Brookings: South Dakota State University Foundation, 1981.

Kerrane, Kevin, and Richard Grossinger, eds. *Baseball, I Gave You All the Best Years of My Life.* Oakland, Calif.: North Atlantic, 1977.

Knudson, P. R., and P. K. Ebert, eds. *Sports Poems.* New York: Dell, 1976.

Morrison, Lillian, ed. *Sprints and Distances: Sports in Poetry and the Poetry of Sports.* New York: Crowell, 1965.

General Anthologies (various literary genres represented)

Brady, John, and James Hall, eds. *Sports Literature.* New York: McGraw-Hill, 1975.

Chapin, Henry B., ed. *Sports in Literature.* New York: McKay, 1976.

Dodge, Tom, ed. *A Literature of Sports.* Lexington, Mass.: D. C. Heath, 1980.

Einstein, Charles, ed. *The Baseball Reader.* New York: McGraw-Hill, 1983.

———. *The Fireside Book of Baseball.* 4th ed. New York: Simon and Schuster, 1987.

Higgs, Robert J., and Neil D. Isaacs, eds. *The Sporting Spirit: Athletes in Literature and Life*. New York: Harcourt, Brace, 1977.

Rudman, Daniel, ed. *Take It to the Hoop*. Richmond, Calif.: North Atlantic, 1980.

Siner, Howard, ed. *Sports Classics*. New York: Coward McCann, 1983.

See also *Aethlon: The Journal of Sport Literature* 6, no. 1 (Fall 1988)—"Special Creative Writing Issue."

Other Bibliographies

Burns, Grant. *The Sports Pages: A Critical Bibliography of Twentieth-Century American Novels and Stories Featuring Baseball, Basketball, Football and Other Athletic Pursuits*. Metuchen, N.J.: Scarecrow Press, 1987.

Wise, Suzanne. *Sports Fiction for Adults: An Annotated Bibliography of Novels, Plays, Short Stories, and Poetry with Sporting Settings*. New York: Garland, 1986.

The Supplemental Literature

Criticism and Philosophy

(Editor's note: For relevant essays and articles, consult the appropriate book-length works and specialized journals cited below.)

Aethlon: The Journal of Sport Literature (formerly *Arete*). Sport Literature Association/San Diego State University Press. Fall 1983–.

Baker, William J., and James A. Rog, eds. *Sports and the Humanities: A Symposium*. Orono: University of Maine Press, 1983.

Bandy, Susan J., ed. *Coroebus Triumphs: The Alliance of Sport and the Arts*. San Diego: San Diego State University Press, 1988.

Berman, Neil David. *Playful Fictions and Fictional Players: Game, Sport, and Survival in Contemporary American Fiction*. Port Washington, N.Y.: Kennikat, 1981.

Best, David. *Philosophy and Human Movement*. London: Allen and Unwin, 1978.

Coffin, Tristram Potter. *The Old Ball Game in Folklore and Fiction*. New York: Herder and Herder, 1971.

Costanzo, Angelo, ed. "The Sports Experience." *Proteus: A Journal of Ideas* 3 (1986).

Friedman, Melvin J., ed. "Focus on Academics in Sports." *Journal of American Culture* 4 (1981).

Gerber, Ellen, and William Morgan, eds. *Sport and the Body: A Philosophical Symposium*. 2d ed. Philadelphia: Lea and Febiger, 1979.

Hall, Donald. *Fathers Playing Catch with Sons: Essays on Sport*. San Francisco: North Point, 1985.

Higgs, Robert J. *Laurel and Thorn: The Athlete in American Literature*. Lexington: University Press of Kentucky, 1981.

Horvath, Brooke K., and William J. Palmer, eds. "Special Issue: Modern Sports Fiction." *Modern Fiction Studies* 33 (1987).

Jones, David A., and Leverett T. Smith, Jr. "Sports in America." *Journal of Popular Culture* 16 (1983).

Journal of the Philosophy of Sport. Philosophic Society for the Study of Sport, 1974–.

Journal of Sport History. North American Society for Sport, 1974–.

Lowe, Benjamin. *The Beauty of Sport: A Cross-Disciplinary Inquiry.* Englewood Cliffs, N.J.: Prentice-Hall, 1977.

McGuane, Thomas. *An Outside Chance: Essays on Sport.* New York: Farrar, Straus, and Giroux, 1980.

Messenger, Christian K. *Sport and the Spirit of Play in American Fiction: Hawthorne to Faulkner.* Columbia University Press, 1981. (Editor's note: At this time a companion volume on contemporary fiction is in the publication process.)

Mihalich, Joseph C. *Sports and Athletics: Philosophy in Action.* Totowa, N.J.: Rowman and Littlefield, 1982.

Miller, David. *Gods and Games: Toward a Theology of Play.* New York: World, 1970.

Mollow, John W., and Richard C. Adams, eds. *The Spirit of Sport: Essays about Sport and Values* Bristol, Ind.: Wyndham Hall, 1987.

Morgan, William J., ed. *Sport and the Humanities: A Collection of Original Essays.* Knoxville: University of Tennessee Press, 1979.

Morgan, William J. and Klaus V. Meier, eds. *Philosophic Inquiry in Sport.* Champaign, Ill.: Human Kinetics, 1988.

Oriard, Michael. *Dreaming of Heroes: American Sports Fiction, 1868–1980.* Chicago: Nelson-Hall, 1982.

Osterhoudt, Robert G., ed. *The Philosophy of Sport.* Springfield, Ill.: C. Thomas, 1973.

Smith, Leverett, Jr. *The American Dream and the National Game.* Bowling Green, Ohio: Popular Press, 1975.

Slusher, Howard S. *Man, Sport and Existence.* Philadelphia: Lea and Febiger, 1967.

Sojka, Gregory S. *Ernest Hemingway: The Angler as Artist.* New York: Peter Lang, 1985.

Umphlett, Wiley Lee, ed. *American Sport Culture: The Humanistic Dimensions.* Lewisburg, Pa.: Bucknell University Press, 1983.

———. *The Sporting Myth and the American Experience: Studies in Contemporary Fiction.* Lewisburg, Pa.: Bucknell University Press, 1975.

Vanderwerken, David, and Spencer K. Wertz, eds. *Sport Inside Out: Readings in Literature and Philosophy.* Fort Worth: Texas Christian University Press, 1985.

Vanderzwaag, Harold J. *Toward a Philosophy of Sport.* Reading, Mass.: Addison-Wesley, 1972.

Weiss, Paul. *Sport: A Philosophic Inquiry.* Carbondale: Southern Illinois University Press, 1969.

Whiting, H. T. A., and Don W. Masterson, eds. *Readings in the Aesthetics of Sport.* London: Lepus, 1974.

Biography, History, and Special Studies

(Editor's note: For autobiography, see the appendix to Mary McElroy's essay. Works included in this section are those published since the 1950s which have had a significant impact on the humanistic interpretation of American sport literature.)

Adelman, Melvin L. *A Sporting Time: New York City and the Rise of Modern Athletics, 1820–70.* Urbana: University of Illinois Press, 1986.

Alexander, Charles C. *John McGraw.* New York: Viking, 1988.

———. *Ty Cobb: Baseball's Fierce Immortal.* New York: Oxford University Press, 1984.

Allen, Maury. *Jackie Robinson: A Life Remembered.* New York: Franklin Watts, 1987.

Amdur, Neil. *The Fifth Down: Democracy and the Football Revolution.* New York: Delta, 1972.

Angell, Roger. *Five Seasons.* New York: Simon and Schuster, 1977.

———. *Late Innings.* New York: Simon and Schuster, 1982.

———. *Season Ticket.* New York: Houghton Mifflin, 1988.

———. *The Summer Game.* New York: Viking, 1972.

Ashe, Arthur R. Jr., *A Hard Road to Glory: A History of the African-American Athlete, 1619–1985.* 3 vols. New York: Warner, 1988.

Asinof, Eliot. *Eight Men Out.* New York: Holt, Rinehart and Winston, 1963.

Atyeo, Don. *Blood and Guts: Violence in Sports.* New York: Paddington, 1979.

Axthelm, Pete. *The City Game.* New York: Harper's, 1970.

Baker, William J. *Jesse Owens: An American Life.* New York: Free Press, 1986.

———. *Sports in the Western World.* Totowa, N.J.: Rowman and Littlefield, 1982.

Baker, William J., and John Carroll, eds. *Sports in Modern America.* St. Louis: River City, 1981.

Beezley, William H. *Locker Rumors: Folklore and Football.* Chicago: Nelson-Hall, 1986.

Bell, J. Bowyer. *To Play the Game: An Analysis of Sports.* New Brunswick, N.J.: Transaction, 1987.

Berkow, Ira. *Beyond the Dream: Occasional Heroes of Sports.* New York: Atheneum, 1975.

Betts, John. *America's Sporting Heritage.* Reading, Mass.: Addison-Wesley, 1974.

Boswell, Thomas. *The Heart of the Order.* Garden City, N.Y.: Doubleday, 1989.

———. *How Life Imitates the World Series: An Inquiry into the Game.* Garden City, N.Y.: Doubleday, 1982.

———. *Strokes of Genius.* Garden City, N.Y.: Doubleday, 1987.

———. *Why Time Begins on Opening Day.* Garden City, N.Y.: Doubleday, 1984.

Bowman, John and Joel Zoss. *Diamonds in the Rough: The Untold History of Baseball.* New York: Macmillan, 1989. (See, in particular, Chapter 9, "Baseball Lit.")

Boyle, Robert C. *Sport—Mirror of American Life.* Boston: Little, Brown, 1963.

———. *At the Top of Their Game.* Piscataway, N.J.: Winchester, 1983.

Brady, John T. *The Heisman: Symbol of Excellence.* New York: Atheneum, 1984.

Brashler, William. *Josh W. Gibson: A Life in the Negro Leagues.* New York: Harper and Row, 1978.

Bruce, Janet. *The Kansas City Monarchs: Champions of Black Baseball.* Lawrence: University Press of Kansas, 1985.

Bryan, Mike. *Baseball Lives.* New York: Pantheon, 1989.

Cady, Edwin H. *The Big Game: College Sports and American Life.* Knoxville: University of Tennessee Press, 1978.

Candelaria, Cordelia. *Seeking the Perfect Game: Baseball in American Literature.* Westport, Conn.: Greenwood, 1989.

Creamer, Robert W. *Babe: A Legend Comes to Life.* New York: Simon and Schuster, 1974.

———. *Stengel—His Life and Times.* New York: Simon and Schuster, 1984.

Chalk, Ocania. *Pioneers of Black Sport.* New York: Dodd, Mead, 1975.

Chandler, Joan. *Television and National Sport: The U.S. and Britain.* Champaign: University of Illinois Press, 1988.

Cohen, Stanley. *The Game They Played.* New York: Farrar, Strauss, and Giroux, 1977.

Crepeau, Richard C. *Baseball: America's Diamond Mind, 1918–1941.* Orlando: University Presses of Florida, 1980.

Cummings, Parke. *American Tennis: The Story of a Game and Its People.* Boston: Little, Brown, 1957.

Danzig, Allison. *Oh, How They Played the Game.* New York: Macmillan, 1976.

Deford, Frank. *Big Bill Tilden: The Triumph and the Tragedy.* New York: Simon and Schuster, 1976.

———. *The World's Tallest Midget: The Best of Frank Deford.* Boston: Little, Brown, 1987.

Dickey, Glenn. *The Jock Empire: Its Rise and Deserved Fall.* Radnor, Pa.: Chilton, 1974.

Dizikes, John. *Sportsmen and Gamesmen: From the Years that Shaped American Ideas about Winning and Losing and How to Play the Game.* Boston: Houghton Mifflin, 1981.

Dolson, Frank. *Beating the Bushes: Life in the Minor Leagues.* South Bend, Ind.: Icarus Press, 1982.

Durso, Joseph. *The Sports Factory: An Investigation into College Sports.* Boston, Houghton Mifflin, 1971.

Edwards, Harry. *The Revolt of the Black Athlete.* New York: Free Press, 1969.

Elder, Donald J. *Ring Lardner: A Biography.* Garden City, N.Y.: Doubleday, 1956.

Englemann, Larry. *The Goddess and the American Girl: The Story of Suzanne Lenglen and Helen Wills.* New York: Oxford University Press, 1988.

Espy, Richard. *The Politics of the Olympic Games.* Berkeley: University of California Press, 1979.

Feinstein, John. *A Season Inside: A Year in College Basketball.* New York: Simon and Schuster, 1988.

———. *A Season on the Brink: A Year with Bob Knight and the Indiana Hoosiers.* New York: Macmillan, 1986.

Figler, Stephen K. *Sport and Play in American Life.* Philadelphia: Saunders, 1981.

Fleming, G. H. *The Dizziest Season: The Gashouse Gang Chases the Pennant.* New York: Morrow, 1984.

———. *The Unforgettable Season.* New York: Holt, Rinehart, and Winston, 1981.

Frank, Lawrence. *Playing Hardball: The Dynamics of Baseball Folk Speech.* New York: Peter Lang, 1983.

Gerber, Ellen W., et al., eds. *The American Woman in Sport.* Reading, Mass.: Addison-Wesley, 1974.

Gerlach, Larry R. *The Men in Blue: Conversations with Umpires.* New York: Viking, 1980.

Gifford, Barry. *The Neighborhood of Baseball: A Personal History of the Chicago Cubs.* San Francisco: Creative Arts, 1981.

Gilmore, Al-Tony. *Bad Nigger: The National Impact of Jack Johnson.* Port Washington, N.Y.: Kennikat, 1974.

Goldstein, Richard. *Spartan Seasons: How Baseball Survived the Second World War.* New York: Macmillan, 1980.

Goldstein, Warren. *Playing for Keeps: A History of Early Baseball.* Ithaca: Cornell University Press, 1989.

Golenbock, Peter. *Bums: An Oral History of the Brooklyn Dodgers.* New York: Putnam, 1984.

———. *Dynasty: The New York Yankees, 1949–64.* Englewood Cliffs, N.J.: Prentice-Hall, 1975.

Goodman, Cary. *Choosing Sides: Playground and Street Life on the Lower East Side.* New York: Schocken, 1979.

Gorn, Elliott J. *The Manly Art: Bare-Knuckle Prize Fighting in America.* Ithaca: Cornell University Press, 1986.

Greenspan, Emily. *Little Winners: Inside the World of the Child Sports Star.* Boston: Little, Brown, 1983.

Gropman, Donald. *Say It Ain't So, Joe! The Story of Shoeless Joe Jackson.* Boston: Little, Brown, 1979.

Grossinger, Richard. *The Temple of Baseball.* Berkeley, Calif.: North Atlantic, 1985.

Guttmann, Allen. *A Whole New Ball Game: An Interpretation of American Sports.* Chapel Hill: University of North Carolina, 1988.

———. *From Ritual to Record: The Nature of Modern Sports.* New York: Columbia University Press, 1978.

———. *The Games Must Go On: Avery Brundage and the Olympic Movement.* New York: Columbia University Press, 1984.

———. *Sports Spectators.* New York: Columbia University Press, 1988.

Halberstam, David. *The Amateurs.* New York: Morrow, 1985.

———. *The Breaks of the Game.* New York: Knopf, 1981.

———. *Summer of '49.* New York: Morrow, 1989.

Hano, Arnold. *A Day in the Bleachers.* New York: DeCapo, 1982.

Hardy, Stephen. *How Boston Played: Sport, Recreation and Community, 1865–1915.* Boston: Northeastern University Press, 1982.

Harris, David. *The League: The Rise and Decline of the NFL.* New York: Bantam, 1986.

Hauser, Thomas. *The Black Lights: Inside the World of Professional Boxing.* New York: McGraw-Hill, 1985.

Hemery, David. *Sporting Excellence: A Study of Sport's Highest Achievers.* Champaign, Ill.: Human Kinetics, 1986.

Higgs, Robert J. *Sports: A Reference Guide.* Westport, Conn.: Greenwood, 1982.

Honig, Donald. *Baseball America.* New York: Macmillan, 1985. (Editor's note: Honig is the author of a number of other books on the cultural significance of baseball to which the reader is referred.)

Hoberman, John M. *Sport and Political Ideology.* Austin: University of Texas Press, 1985.

Hoch, Paul. *Rip Off the Big Game: The Exploitation of Sports by the Power Elite.* New York: Anchor, 1972.

Hoose, Phillip. M. *Racial Barriers in American Sports.* New York: Random House, 1989.

Howell, Reet, ed. *Her Story in Sport: A Historical Anthology of Women in Sports.* Champaign, Ill.: Human Kinetics, 1982.

Isaacs, Neil. *All the Moves: A History of U.S. College Basketball.* Philadelphia: Lippincott, 1975.

———. *Jock Culture, USA.* New York: Norton, 1978.

Isenberg, Michael T. *John L. Sullivan and His America.* Urbana: University of Illinois Press, 1988.

Johnson, William O. *Super Spectator and the Electric Lilliputians.* Boston: Little, Brown, 1971.

Jordan, Pat. *Black Coach.* New York: Dodd, Mead, 1971.

———. *Broken Patterns.* New York: Dodd, Mead, 1977.

Kahn, Roger. *The Boys of Summer.* New York: Harper and Row, 1972.

———. *Good Enough to Dream.* New York: Playboy, 1985.

Kaplan, Jim. *Pine-Tarred and Feathered: A Year on the Baseball Beat.* Chapel Hill, N.C.: Algonquin, 1984.

———. *Playing the Field.* Chapel Hill, N.C.: Algonquin Books, 1987.

Kaye, Ivan. *Good Clean Violence: A History of U.S. College Football.* Philadelphia, Lippincott, 1973.

Kerrane, Kevin. *Dollar Sign on the Muscle: The World of Baseball Scouting.* New York: Beaufort, 1984.

Kerrane, Kevin, and Richard Grossinger, eds. *Baseball Diamonds: Tales, Traces, Visions and Voodoo from a Native American Rite.* New York: Doubleday, 1980.

Kiesling, Stephen. *The Shell Game: Reflections on Rowing and the Pursuit of Excellence.* New York: Morrow, 1983.

King, Peter. *The Season After: Are Sports Dynasties Dead?* New York: Warner, 1989.

Kirsh, George B. *The Creation of American Team Sports: Baseball and Cricket, 1838–72.* Champaign: University of Illinois Press, 1989.

Klatell, David A., and Norman Marcus. *Sports for Sale: Television, Money, and the Fans.* New York: Oxford University Press, 1988.

Klein, Dave. *The Pro Football Mystique.* New York: New American Library, 1978.

Klein, Gene, and David Fisher. *First Down and a Billion: The Funny Business of Pro Football.* New York: Morrow, 1986.

Kohn, Alfie. *No Contest: The Case against Competition*. Boston: Houghton Mifflin, 1986.

Koppett, Leonard. *Sports Illusion, Sports Reality: A Reporter's View*. Boston: Houghton Mifflin, 1981.

Lapchick, Richard. *Broken Promises: Racism in American Sports*. New York: St. Martin's, 1984.

———, ed. *Fractured Focus: Sport as a Reflection of Society*. Lexington, Mass.: D. C. Heath, 1986.

———, and Robert Malekoff. *On the Mark: Putting the Student Back in Student-Athlete*. Lexington, Mass.: D. C. Heath, 1987.

———, and John B. Slaughter. *The Rules of the Game: Ethics in College Sport*. New York: Macmillan, 1989.

Lasch, Christopher. *The Culture of Narcissism*. New York: Norton, 1979. (Editor's note: This book's significance depends in the main on its chapter dealing with the corruption of modern sport.)

Lawrence, Paul R. *Unsportsmanlike Conduct: The NCAA and the Business of College Football*. New York: Praeger, 1987.

Leonard, George. *The Ultimate Athlete: Revisioning Sports, Physical Education and the Body*. New York: Viking, 1974.

Levine, Peter. *A. G. Spalding and the Rise of Baseball: The Promise of American Sport*. New York: Oxford University Press, 1985.

———. *American Sport: A Documentary History*. Englewood Cliffs, N.J.: Prentice-Hall, 1989.

Lipsky, Richard. *How We Play the Game: Why Sports Dominate American Life*. Boston: Beacon, 1981.

Lipsyte, Robert. *SportsWorld: An American Dreamland*. New York: Quadrangle, 1976.

Lowenfish, Lee, and Tony Lupien. *The Imperfect Diamond: The Story of Baseball's Reserve System and the Men Who fought to Change It*. New York: Stein and Day, 1980.

Lucas, John. *The Modern Olympic Games*. New York: A. S. Barnes, 1980.

Lucas, John A., and Ronald Smith. *Saga of American Sport*. Philadelphia: Lea and Febiger, 1978.

Mailer, Norman. *The Fight*. Boston: Little, Brown, 1975.

Mandell, Richard. *The First Modern Olympics*. Berkeley: University of California Press, 1976.

———. *The Nazi Olympics*. New York: Macmillan, 1971.

———. *Sport: A Cultural History*. New York: Columbia University Press, 1984.

McPhee, John. *Levels of the Game*. New York: Farrar, Straus, and Giroux, 1969.

———. *A Sense of Where You Are*. New York: Farrar, Straus, and Giroux, 1975.

Merchant, Larry. *The National Football Lottery*. New York: Holt, Rinehart and Winston, 1973.

Mewshaw, Michael. *Short Circuit*. New York: Atheneum, 1983.

Michener, James A. *Sports in America*. New York: Random House, 1976.

Moore, Jack B. *Joe DiMaggio: A Bio-Bibliography*. Westport, Conn.: Greenwood, 1986.

Morris, Willie. *The Courting of Marcus Dupree*. Garden City, N.Y.: Doubleday, 1983.

Mrozek, Donald J. *Sport and American Mentality, 1880–1910*. Knoxville: University of Tennessee Press, 1983.

Mungo, Raymond. *Confessions from Left Field: A Baseball Pilgrimage*. New York: Atheneum, 1981.

Murdock, Eugene C. *Ban Johnson: Czar of Baseball*. Westport, Conn.: Greenwood, 1982.

———. *Mighty Casey: All-American*. Westport, Conn.: Greenwood, 1984.

Murphy, Michael, and Rhea White. *The Psychic Side of Sports*. Reading, Mass.: Addison-Wesley, 1978.

Nixon, Howard L. *Sport and the American Dream*. New York: Leisure Press, 1984.

Novak, Michael. *The Joy of Sports*. New York: Basic Books, 1976.

Noverr, Douglas A., and Lawrence Ziewaez. *The Games They Played: Sports in American History, 1865–1980*. Chicago: Nelson-Hall, 1983.

Oates, Joyce Carol. *On Boxing*. Garden City, N.Y.: Doubleday, 1987.

———, and Daniel Halpern, eds. *Reading the Fights*. New York: Henry Holt, 1988.

Offen, Neil. *God Save the Players*. Chicago: Playboy, 1974.

Olsen, Jack. *The Black Athlete: A Shameful Story*. New York: Lions Press, 1969.

Oppenheimer, Joel. *The Wrong Season*. Indianapolis: Bobbs-Merrill, 1973.

Peper, George, ed. *Golf in America: The First One Hundred Years*. New York: Abrams, 1988.

Perrin, Tom. *Football: A College History*. Jefferson, N.C.: McFarland, 1987.

Peterson, Harold. *The Man Who Invented Baseball*. New York: Scribner's, 1969.

Peterson, Robert. *Only the Ball Was White*. Englewood Cliffs, N.J.: Prentice-Hall, 1970.

Quigley, Martin. *The Crooked Pitch: The Curveball in American Baseball History*. Chapel Hill, N.C.: Algonquin, 1984.

Rader, Benjamin G. *American Sports: From the Age of Folk Games to the Age of Spectators*. Englewood Cliffs, N.J.: Prentice-Hall, 1983.

———. *In Its Own Image: How Television Has Transformed Sports*. New York: Free Press, 1984.

Ralbovsky, Martin. *Lords of the Locker Room: The American Way of Coaching*. New York: Peter Wyden, 1974.

Reiss, Steven A. *The American Sporting Experience: A Historical Anthology of Sport in America*. New York: Leisure Press, 1984.

———. *City Games: The Evolution of American Urban Society and the Rise of Sports*. Champaign: University of Illinois Press, 1989.

———. *Touching Base: Professional Baseball and American Culture in the Progressive Era*. Westport, Conn.: Greenwood, 1980.

Ritter, Lawrence S. *The Glory of Their Times*. New York: Macmillan, 1966.

Roberts, Michael. *Fans! How We Go Crazy over Sports*. Washington, D.C.: New Republic, 1976.

Roberts, Randy. *Jack Dempsey, the Manassa Mauler.* Baton Rouge: Louisiana State University Press, 1979.

———. *Papa Jack: Jack Johnson and the Era of White Hopes.* New York: Free Press, 1983.

Roberts, Randy, and James Olson. *Winning Is the Only Thing: Sports in America since 1945.* Baltimore: Johns Hopkins University Press, 1989.

Rogosin, Donn. *Invisible Men: Life in Baseball's Negro Leagues.* New York: Atheneum, 1984.

Rosen, Charles. *The Scandals of 1951: How the Gamblers Almost Killed College Basketball.* New York: Holt, Rinehart, 1978.

Ruck, Rob. *Sandlot Seasons: Sport in Black Pittsburg.* Urbana: University of Illinois Press, 1987.

Russell, John. *Honey Russell: Between Games, between Halves.* Washington, D.C.: Dryad Press, 1986.

Sabo, Donald, and Ross Runfola, eds. *Jock: Sports and Male Identity.* Englewood Cliffs, N.J.: Prentice-Hall, 1980.

Salzsberg, Charles. *From Set Shot to Slam Dunk.* New York: Dutton, 1987.

Sammons, Jeffrey T. *Beyond the Ring: The Role of Boxing in American Society.* Urbana: University of Illinois Press, 1988.

Schecter, Leonard. *The Jocks.* Indianapolis: Bobbs-Merrill, 1969.

Schulien, John. *Writers' Fighters and Other Sweet Scientists.* New York: Andrews and McMeel, 1983.

Schultheis, Rob. *Bone Games: One Man's Search for the Ultimate Athletic High.* New York: Random House, 1984.

Scott, Jack. *The Athletic Revolution.* New York: Free Press, 1972.

Seidel, Michael. *Streak: Joe Dimaggio and the Summer of '41.* New York: McGraw-Hill, 1988.

Seymour, Harold. *Baseball,* 2 vols. New York: Oxford University Press, 1960.

Shaw, Gary. *Meat on the Hoof: The Hidden World of Texas Football.* New York: St. Martin's, 1972.

Simon, Robert L. *Sports and Social Values.* Englewood Cliffs, N.J.: Prentice-Hall, 1985.

Smelser, Marshall. *The Life That Ruth Built.* New York: Quadrangle, 1975.

Smith, Red. *The Red Smith Reader.* Ed. Dave Anderson. New York: Vintage, 1982.

Smith, Ronald A. *Sports & Freedom: The Rise of Big-Time College Athletics.* New York: Oxford University Press, 1988.

Somers, Dale A. *The Rise of Sports in New Orleans, 1850–1900.* Baton Rouge: Louisiana State University Press, 1972.

Spears, Betty and Richard Swanson. *A History of Sport and Physical Activity in the United States.* Dubuque: William C. Brown, 1978.

Spivey, Donald, ed. *Sport in America: New Historical Perspectives.* Westport, Conn.: Greenwood, 1985.

Steele, Michael R. *Knute Rockne.* Westport, Conn.: Greenwood, 1983.

Sullivan, Neil J. *The Dodgers Move West.* New York: Oxford University Press, 1987.

Telander, Rick. *Heaven Is a Playground.* New York: St. Martin's, 1976.

———. *The Hundred-Yard Lie*. New York: Simon and Schuster, 1989.

Toperoff, Sam. *Sugar Ray Leonard and Other Noble Warriors*. New York: McGraw-Hill, 1986.

Tunis, John R. *The American Way in Sport*. New York: Duell, Sloan and Pearce, 1958.

Tutko, Thomas, and William Bruns. *Winning Is Everything and Other American Myths*. New York: Macmillan, 1976.

Twombly, Wells. *200 Years of Sport in America: A Pageant of a Nation at Play*. New York: McGraw-Hill, 1976.

Tygiel, Jules. *Baseball's Great Experiment: Jackie Robinson and His Legacy*. New York: Oxford University Press, 1983.

Underwood, John. *Death of an American Game: The Crisis in Football*. Boston: Little, Brown, 1984.

———. *Spoiled Sport: The Troubles of Spectators*. Boston: Little, Brown, 1984.

Vincent, Ted. *Mudville's Revenge: The Rise and Fall of American Sport*. New York: Seaview, 1981.

Vinokur, Martin Barry. *More Than a Game: Sports and Politics*. Westport, Conn.: Greenwood, 1988.

David Q. Voigt. *American Baseball*. 3 vols. Norman: University of Oklahoma Press, 1966, 1970. (Volume 3 published by Pennsylvania State University Press, 1986.)

———. *American Basketball: From Gentlemen's Sport to the Commissioner System*. Norman: University of Oklahoma Press, 1966.

———. *America through Baseball*. Chicago: Nelson-Hall, 1976.

Webb, Bernice Larson. *The Basketball Man*. Lawrence: University Press of Kansas, 1973.

Williams, Joe, ed. *The Joe Williams Baseball Reader: Baseball from Ty Cobb to Satchel Paige as Chronicled by the Longtime Columnist of the New York World Telegram*. Chapel Hill, N.C.: Algonquin, 1989.

Wind, Herbert Warren. *Game, Set, and Match: The Tennis Boom of the 1960s and 70s*. New York: Dutton, 1979.

———. *The Gilded Age of Sport*. New York: Simon and Schuster, 1961.

Yardley, Jonathon. *Ring: A Biography of Ring Lardner*. New York: Random House, 1977.

Yeager, Robert C. *Season of Shame: The New Violence in Sports*. New York: McGraw-Hill, 1979.

Zingg, Paul J., ed. *The Sporting Image: Readings in American Sport History*. Lanham, Md.: University Press of America, 1988.

Contributors

SHARON G. CARSON is an associate professor of English at Kent State University. She is a frequent writer and speaker on women in fiction, film, and the popular media.

ROBERT W. COCHRAN, a professor of English at the University of Vermont, has published works in both the fiction and nonfiction areas of sport literature.

RONALD K. GILES, an associate professor of English at East Tennessee State University, has published essays on sport literature and poetry in the *English Journal, Poesis,* and *College Literature.*

DANIEL J. HERMAN is an associate professor of philosophy at the University of West Florida. His special areas of interest and publications are in continental philosophy and the philosophy of sport.

ROBERT J. HIGGS, professor of English at East Tennessee State University, is the author of *Laurel and Thorn: The Athlete in American Literature* (1982) and *Sports: A Reference Guide* (1982). With Neil D. Isaacs he coedited *The Sporting Spirit: Athletes in Literature and Life* (1977).

BROOKE K. HORVATH teaches at Kent State University. An associate editor of *The Review of Contemporary Fiction,* he coedited the sports fiction special issue of *Modern Fiction Studies* (Spring 1987). His work has appeared in a number of national literary journals.

DON JOHNSON, chairman of the English department at East Tennessee State University, is a poet who has also published a variety of articles on sport and literature. He is currently editing *Aethlon: The Journal of Sport Literature.*

MARY MCELROY is an associate professor and coordinator of graduate studies in Physical Education and Leisure Studies at Kansas

State University. Her publications deal with sporting topics in both classic and contemporary literature.

CHRISTIAN K. MESSENGER is associate professor of English at the University of Illinois at Chicago. He is currently completing the contemporary literature sequel to *Sport and the Spirit of Play in American Fiction: Hawthorne to Faulkner* (1981).

LYLE I. OLSEN conceived the idea for a journal of sport literature while teaching in the physical education department at San Diego State University. As managing editor, he saw his dream become reality in the form of *Aethlon: The Journal of Sport Literature* (formerly *Arete*).

MICHAEL ORIARD, who teaches English at Oregon State University, writes about sports from a background of high school, college, and professional football involvement. He is the author of *Dreaming of Heroes: American Sports Fiction* (1982) and *The End of Autumn: Reflections on My Life in Football* (1982).

LEVERETT T. SMITH, JR., is professor of English and associate dean at North Carolina Wesleyan College. He is the author of *The American Dream and the National Game* (1975) and various articles about twentieth-century American literature and culture.

WILEY LEE UMPHLETT produced the earliest literary study of sports and American literature in *The Sporting Myth and the American Experience* (1975). An administrator at the University of West Florida, he is the author of four other books that deal with topics related to American culture.

Index

Editor's note: The following authors, critics, philosophers, and educational leaders cited in the text of this collection have been influential in the development of sport literature's reputation in America. For other influences, the reader is referred to the bibliographical sources in this collection.